"A romp through the Jazz Age in the company of one of its liveliest figures."

—William Wright, *The New York Times*

"Intrinsically interesting . . . Rosenblum is a formidable researcher."

—Charlotte Hays, *The Washington Post*

"Rosenblum wisely recasts Joyce as a symbol of the explosion of celeb journalism and the prototype of fifteen-minute fame. . . . The book is a marvel."

—Bill Bell, *New York Daily News*

"With gusto and energy, humor and fabulous detail, the irrepressible Ms. Joyce is brought to life once again. A juicy, delicious biography."

—Phillip Lopate

"Beyond irony, *Gold Digger* does go down, wholesale, like cotton candy, seductively, irresistibly, sweet."

—Bill Ruehlmann, *The Virginian-Pilot*

"A lively and wonderfully intelligent tale about a woman famous for collecting furs, jewels, railroad cars, headlines—and men. Every page is a pleasure."

—Susan Isaacs

"Even years after she's been forgotten, Joyce makes for fabulous reading."

—Paige Smoron, *Chicago Sun-Times*

"A lively, intelligent tale about fame and fickle fortune."

—Doug Wyatt, *Savannah News*

"If Peggy Hopkins Joyce had not existed, America would have had to invent her, and maybe did. But Constance Rosenblum has captured her (and us) in *Gold Digger*. It's a rib-tickler and a heartbreaker and a wonderful read."

—Steven Bach

GOLD DIGGER

GOLD DIGGER

---

*The Outrageous Life
and Times of
Peggy Hopkins Joyce*

Constance
Rosenblum

AN OWL BOOK

HENRY HOLT AND COMPANY ✦ NEW YORK

Henry Holt and Company, LLC
Publishers since 1866
115 West 18th Street
New York, New York 10011

Henry Holt® is a registered trademark
of Henry Holt and Company, LLC.

Published in Canada by Fitzhenry & Whiteside Ltd.,
195 Allstate Parkway, Markham, Ontario L3R 4T8

Library of Congress Cataloging-in-Publication Data
Gold digger : the outrageous life and times of
Peggy Hopkins Joyce / Constance Rosenblum.
          p.   cm.
Includes bibliographical references and index.
ISBN 0-8050-6641-1
1. Joyce, Peggy Hopkins, 1893–1957. 2. Motion picture actors
and actresses—United States—Biography.
3. Entertainers—United States—Biography.   I. Title.
PN2287.J7R67 2000   99-047455
791.43'028'092—dc21   CIP

First published in hardcover in 2000 by Metropolitan Books

First Owl Books Edition 2001

Designed by Victoria Hartman

Printed in the United States of America

1   3   5   7   9   10   8   6   4   2

To my mother, Beatrice Rosenblum,
and to my late father, Martin Rosenblum

Contents

Introduction

She had wanted her funeral to be held at Saint Patrick's Cathedral, the Gothic shrine to Catholicism on Fifth Avenue in Manhattan. The setting would have suited her—a glamorous church for the woman who had been the quintessential glamour girl of her era. But arrangements with the church proved difficult, not surprisingly, given what a wild thing the deceased had been during her lifetime, and so on June 14, 1957, Peggy Hopkins Joyce's last performance took place at the far more modest Saint Catherine of Siena, a sedate redbrick building a few blocks away on East Sixty-eighth Street. The funeral was small, attended by only a handful of people, none of them particularly famous. No record remains of what was said in her memory. After the service, escorted by her sixth and final husband, a retired bank clerk named Andrew Meyer, Peggy's body was transported north to Gate of Heaven Cemetery in Mount Pleasant, New York. In the humidity of an early summer's day, Peggy Hopkins Joyce was laid to rest in a dignified marble mausoleum shaded by two dogwoods, one red, one white.

Mausoleum notwithstanding, the rites by which Peggy found her eternal repose were fairly modest, with good reason. By the time she died, the same day as bandleader Jimmy Dorsey, her legacy was fading fast. Her obituary in the *New York Times* was buried deep in the paper, and most galling of all for a woman who had once been the photographers' darling, a picture taken in her prime, all glowing and golden, was cruelly contrasted with one from the end of her life, when she had become fleshy and double-chinned. The show-business bible *Variety* gave her death just a few sentences, and the event merited only a brief item in *Time* magazine.

As the years passed, memories of Peggy Hopkins Joyce grew dimmer still. The twenties began to enjoy a renaissance as Will Rogers and habitués of the Algonquin Round Table found themselves immortalized on stage and screen. But hardly anyone remembered Peggy, despite the fact that she had been a Jazz Age diva who made international headlines for her extravagant lifestyle, her flamboyant ways, her frequent trips to the altar—not to mention the divorce court—and her torrid affairs with Charlie Chaplin, Walter Chrysler, all manner of European royalty, and dozens of other rich and celebrated men.

By the end of the century, only a few people—grizzled press agents who had toiled for Walter Winchell, veteran observers of the Broadway scene—had firsthand recollections, and even those were blurry. Just what had she been so famous for, anyway? For husbands, was that it? Six millionaire husbands, or so it was said; "the much-married Peggy Joyce," she was called. And for her long-running role as a lover, although some people used less flattering terms like *tramp*. And for diamonds. And for furs.

I had never heard of Peggy Hopkins Joyce, and I came to know of her through a most unlikely route. Some years ago, my mother, an antiques expert, was asked whether she had any interest in a large carton of mysterious documents—yellowed clippings from long-defunct newspapers, letters in faded ink, receipts from bankers and jewelers who had closed their doors decades ago—discovered in an attic in

Poughkeepsie, New York. How the box got there no one knew, but the contents had sat untouched for half a century.

The carton, it turned out, contained Peggy Joyce's personal papers, and Peggy, I subsequently learned, had been the real-life inspiration for Anita Loos's madcap heroine Lorelei Lee, the original blonde whom gentlemen preferred. Smart as a fox when it came to manipulating the opposite sex, Peggy had amassed the men, the furs, and especially the diamonds that were a girl's best friend. Still, her name initially meant nothing to me, so for several years the papers remained crumpled in their box, slowly gathering more dust.

On the day that I finally began looking through them, however, I couldn't stop. There were hundreds of newspaper articles from all over the world, tracing in minute detail the life of a woman who seemed constantly to be falling in and out of love. There were notes on stiff cream-colored vellum, hastily scribbled in foreign hands and begging for late-night assignations. There were ardent love letters, pages and pages long, pitiful in their passion and desperation. There were Christmas cards from movie stars, invitations to parties at the smartest nightclubs, dunning letters from the most exclusive jewelers and dress shops in New York City. There were scrawled notes from impoverished young women in the hinterlands begging for a cast-off dress or a discarded diamond. One envelope contained the scraps of a newspaper article; when I pieced them together, I read a lurid account of a scandal involving high-class call girls in which Peggy had been implicated. She had clearly been furious but could not bear to throw away the evidence; despite the scurrilous allegations, her fear of being ignored was more powerful than her desire for respectability.

There were descriptions of her star turn in Earl Carroll's *Vanities,* one of the lusty revues of the twenties, from which a picture emerged—Peggy descending a sweeping marble staircase, swathed in a flowing chinchilla gown worth tens of thousands of dollars, her throat and wrists aglitter with jewels, her hair a blonde cloud framing her exquisite face, her every glance and gesture sending charges of erotic energy toward a mostly male audience that all but salivated at the sight of her. Peggy was always a vision, it seemed, but never more so than when two thousand pairs of male eyes and a megawatt spotlight were riveted upon her, as they were the night she conquered Broadway.

In one small envelope I found a tiny golden horseshoe, a gift from an admirer. Another contained a lock of pale, peach-colored hair, slightly rough to the touch. Alone at my desk in the semidarkness, holding the little horseshoe and the faded curl, I had an eerie sense that the spirit of Peggy Joyce was not too far away.

This extraordinary cache of material, these tattered remains of a life, represented, it seemed, the achievement of a woman who had scaled the heights armed with nothing more than good looks, good luck, and sheer driving ambition. In this respect, the life of Peggy Hopkins Joyce represented a landmark in the evolution of American celebrity: she was hardly the first to flash into the public eye, but she was arguably the first to become famous in a certain way.

She made headlines not because she triumphed on the silver screen like Mary Pickford, or flew across the Atlantic alone like Amelia Earhart, or swam the English Channel like Gertrude Ederle, or helped precipitate a constitutional crisis like Wallis Warfield Simpson, or stood at the center of a sensational crime like Evelyn Nesbit, or nestled under the wing of a powerful media baron like Marion Davies, or was anointed debutante of the year like Brenda Frazier. She did nothing of significance except collect and discard rich husbands in rapid succession in an age when such behavior was severely frowned on. The husbands themselves were nothing special; what little fame they accrued came solely from having their names linked with hers.

In lieu of real accomplishments, however, Peggy had something far more important, the almost undivided attention of the newly powerful mass media, and over a remarkably long period. Her entrance onto the national stage was providential: she appeared just as the tabloid newspaper was poised to reshape American society, and the two had a perfect symbiotic relationship. She made a name for herself simply because they put her name in the papers; she was blasted into public prominence entirely by way of the screaming headline, the grainy tabloid photo, the frantic, dot-dot-dot item in the gossip column. She was a product of technology; she and Jazz Age journalism were born for each other, and they used each other shamelessly and with equal abandon. Much of what the newsmen wrote was pure fiction, not surprising given a subject who was so much a creature of her own invention. But no one ever complained, least of all the subject of their fabrications. Peggy was blessed with a profound understanding of the uses of publicity, not to mention an enormous hunger for its fruits, and she never met a reporter she was not delighted to accommodate, preferably in the privacy of her boudoir as she lounged about in a diaphanous negligee.

Peggy's every move—the acquisition of a new hairdo, a new pet, a new lover, or a new diamond, the flimsiest rumor of a possible engagement or a pending divorce—was front-page news. Her exploits made headlines on two continents, sometimes banner headlines and on a daily basis. The mere mention of her—in a Cole Porter song, in a Damon Runyon story, in an Irving Berlin musical, in a Will Rogers witticism—unleashed a flood of vivid associations. From the early twenties well into the thirties, the name Peggy Hopkins Joyce resonated mightily in the culture.

With her come-hither features and her candy-box coloring, her blonde marcelled bob, her complexion, flawless as alabaster—a cliché that in her case seems to have been true—her creamy shoulders, and the luminous ropes of pearls inevitably twisted provocatively in her fingers, Peggy Hopkins Joyce was a compelling creature, glamorous in a way that no longer exists. It is easy to see why the tabloid photographers adored her, and the gossip columnists too. She was so deliciously quotable, so prone to outrageous pronouncements, such as her observation about her ideal man: "He must be rich but have a very competent secretary so that he will not have to pay too much attention to business," she told a reporter. What's more, she added, "My ideal man must be willing to quarrel a little with me, just once in a while."

Officially, she was an actress, and she did have a career of sorts. She had a brief fling as a Ziegfeld girl, which meant an enormous amount in those days, and her name appeared atop W. C. Fields's in *International House,* one of the lighthearted romps Paramount churned out in the thirties to divert audiences wearied by the Depression. Capitalizing on her media fame, she dipped into vaudeville, and she was briefly a fixture on Broadway, not only as the star of *Vanities* but also in a handful of featherweight comedies. She wrote, or took credit for writing, two books, a breathless memoir and a thinly disguised autobiographical novel, along with a weekly advice-to-the-lovelorn column that ran in the pages of New York City's raciest tabloid.

The roster of her lovers read like a who's who of the era and included not only Chaplin, who was so taken with her life story he used it as the armature of one of his most memorable films, and Chrysler, who gave her a winking blue diamond worth $300,000, but also the producers Irving Thalberg and Lee Shubert and an impressive sampling of Continental nobility. She claimed she had been engaged fifty times, and while not all six of her husbands were millionaires, she certainly left people with that impression. When she split up with a lumber baron after a sensational divorce trial, she walked away with nearly a million dollars' worth of jewelry, an impressive sum back in 1921.

But Peggy Hopkins Joyce captured the public's attention not because of her career in show business, which was spotty, or her talent, which was nonexistent, or her accomplishments, which were dubious, or even her wealth—others were wealthy as well—but because of what her image signified. She strode to the forefront of the nation's consciousness because she was the perfect, complete embodiment of the glittery, gaudy period in which she lived—the hedonism, the speculative spirit, the rush of sexual freedom for women. In an age that required emblematic, larger-than-life characters, she seemed like a gift from heaven.

With her luxurious lifestyle, whose settings ranged from New York's elegant hotels to the playlands of the French Riviera; her passion for diamonds, ermine, and other symbols of opulence; her wild spending sprees; her steamy sex life; her indifference to the conservative moral standards of the day, Peggy Hopkins Joyce was the apotheosis of her era, the ultimate metaphor for the Jazz Age, its dreams and dramas, its desires and taboos. She seemed to have stepped from the pages of an F. Scott Fitzgerald novel, a minor character perhaps, but one who perfectly symbolized a look, an ethos, a moment.

As with all great celebrities, people could read into her story whatever they wished; her life spoke to theirs, often in ways they scarcely understood. She excited envy and admiration at the same instant and for much the same reasons. She could be worshiped for her gorgeous looks and her romantic escapades even as she was castigated for being a loose woman, a superficial and mercenary husband hunter. She was both role model and cautionary tale.

It seems incredible that someone celebrated so intensely for so many years could have sunk into such complete oblivion. But her decline reveals as much about the star-making machinery as does her ascent. The same forces that led to her creation brought about her fall. She and her age fell out of synch. The reporters and photographers moved on, as they always do, and Peggy grew old, a sin for a woman who made her name as she made hers. Although she navigated Zelig-like among the famous men and women of the day, brushing up against Will Rogers, Fanny Brice, Marion Davies, Eddie Cantor, Walter Winchell, Harpo Marx, James Montgomery Flagg, and countless other celebrated figures, the reasons for her fame were so paper-thin, there was little to keep the legend alive.

Asked in recent years if she had known Peggy Joyce, the actress Celeste Holm replied with a sniff: "No! She was a flamboyant, silly woman. I'm glad I didn't know her." In time, Peggy's name became the punch line to bad jokes, her behavior the subject of wicked parody, and the memory of her exploits as evanescent as a flickering image from a forgotten one-reeler.

Yet nearly half a century after her death, the life of Peggy Hopkins Joyce is a reminder of how very pinched a woman's options once were and how much drive and determination women needed to make their way in the world, even if that way might strike us as tawdry. Peggy Hopkins Joyce was the ultimate creature of ambition, a young woman from the provinces who took advantage of an increasingly fluid society and the benefits to be gained from marriage to rich men. She carved out for herself the best existence she could in the best way she knew how by making herself irresistible to the opposite sex and becoming a courtesan, a breed that had a distinguished history abroad but was scorned in her native land. She knew what she wanted, went after it with her whole heart, and lived the life she yearned to live. That is no small achievement, then or now.

1

"I Am Not Going to
Have a Dull & Dreary Life"

Peggy Hopkins Joyce, heartbreaker, gold digger, and international celebrity, was invariably described by reporters as a barber's daughter from Norfolk. Her audience took this sort of narrative to their hearts, for Peggy's story vindicated their belief in the possibility of limitless achievement and showed that even a person of humble origins could escape the confines of her class. As it happened, for once the description was true. She was born and primarily raised in Virginia, or more precisely Berkley, a community across the river from Norfolk that was later incorporated into its larger neighbor. And her father, Sam Upton, was indeed the local barber, although the village in which he plied his trade shifted over the years as he moved from one part of the South to another.

Peggy never objected to mentions of her roots, but her family was less enthusiastic about publicizing its ties to their loose-living progeny. Once the scandals started and Peggy began accumulating and shedding husbands, relatives on both her parents' sides were reluctant to acknowledge her as kin, especially in front of their children. When her movies came to town, even first cousins kept quiet about her being one of their own. In the conservative small towns of the South where her forebears lived, a person had little to gain by admitting a connection with a girl like Peggy Joyce.

Her father's people, the Uptons, were country folk who lived close to the land and tended to marry the girl or boy next door or at least down the road. Their roots were in the Albemarle, a cluster of communities in northeastern North Carolina that, like the people who inhabited them, possessed long histories. Its largest metropolis, bustling Elizabeth City, had been a seafaring town since the seventeenth century; residents boasted that the pirate Bluebeard once hid there. On the other side of the Pasquotank River lay the tiny crossroads of Camden, dominated by a traditional redbrick courthouse facing a tidy town green. It was in and around this speck of a village that generations of Uptons made their homes, raised their families, and tilled a living from the rich, loamy soil.

The family patriarch, Mark Upton, with his wife, Margaret Boushall, produced five children in the early years of the nineteenth century. Their son Samuel also married a local girl called Margaret, siring seven children in the space of a decade. His namesake, Samuel Boushall Upton Jr., Peggy's father, was born in 1864. Following family tradition, at the age of twenty-four he married a young neighbor named Maggie Sawyer.

The bodies of many of these early Uptons rest in a family burial ground just off Camden's main road, the weathered slabs of granite almost hidden in the thicket of honeysuckle, periwinkle, and wild grape. Even to a sharp eye, the names of the dead and the traditional Baptist inscriptions that comforted their loved ones are barely legible. "Sallie H. Upton, born April 14, 1858, died August 29, 1891. Weep not, she is not dead but sleepeth." "Samuel Upton, 1830–Feb. 27, 1896. Asleep in Jesus."

Little information survives beyond the dates on which these stolid Southerners entered and left the world. But the Uptons of Camden are remembered by their descendants as a pious, God-fearing lot, strict Southern Baptists who were dutiful worshipers at the local Shiloh Baptist Church and attended to their earthly duties by producing generous harvests of cabbage, potatoes, and soybeans on their small family farms. Though not particularly rich, they were industrious. And for country people with little time to fuss over their appearance, they were also remarkably attractive. Family photographs reveal that young Sam Upton was an especially fine-looking specimen, a tall, lanky fellow with regular features and thick brown hair parted neatly in the center. The women tended to be blonde and blue-eyed, blessed with fine skin, inviting smiles, and an unexpected air of glamour that would have turned more than a few heads in a quiet Southern town.

If Peggy's family on her father's side represented the enduring traditions of nineteenth-century rural America, her mother's people exemplified the life of the nation's burgeoning towns and cities. They were more adventurous, more restive, and more willing to move and marry outside the small circles in which they had been raised.

Peggy's grandmother Emma Jane Sykes, the rebel of the family, was born in 1850 in Princess Anne County, the part of Virginia later known as Virginia Beach. At the age of fifteen she shocked her little world by marrying Laderna Wood, a feisty Union soldier from Elmira, New York, who had come south during the Civil War and stayed after his discharge. It was bad enough for a Southern girl to marry a Yankee, and this particular Yankee had a reputation as a wild man. He had a celebrated temper, going after his enemies with a pair of brass knuckles, and his pugnacity was exacerbated by his taste for liquor. "Emma Jane used to say Laderna was fine until he started hitting the bottle," their grandson Francis Price recalled years later. "But then he'd be mean as the devil."

Emma Jane herself was a stern figure. In a formal photograph, she presides unmistakably as the family matriarch, a dour, unsmiling woman in a dark, high-necked dress, wedged into an ornately carved chair. With her pince-nez glasses hanging on a chain around her neck, her white gloves clenched tightly in her hand, and a grim ex-

pression in her beady eyes, she has the decided appearance of someone not to be trifled with.

After their marriage in 1865, the Woods settled in Berkley, then a
small town that was fast becoming a thriving center for shipbuilding
and lumber mills. It was there that Emma Jane bore sixteen children,
four of whom survived. Dora Selena, born in 1873, was the eldest.
Although she had a soft side, earning the family nickname Pattycake
for the hours she spent playing clapping games with her nieces and
nephews, she had inherited her mother's sturdy backbone, not to
mention a generous dose of Emma Jane's rebellious spirit.

Dora was a teenager when Sam Upton left his people for reasons
no one remembers exactly. Perhaps he wanted to escape ghosts of the
past; according to some accounts, a child born early in his marriage
did not survive infancy, and his wife may have died in childbirth. In
any event, by the early 1890s he had made his way north to Berkley.
A garrulous man, Sam found cutting hair more to his taste than farming and before long he was the chief attraction at the most popular
barbershop in town. He also found time to walk out with the dark-
haired, high-spirited Dora Wood, and in April 1892 the local paper
reported "a large crowd present at the Christian Church" for the
wedding of the twenty-eight-year-old Carolinian and his nineteen-
year-old bride.

The Uptons set up housekeeping in a buff-colored bungalow with
a peaked roof at 318 Lee Street, one of three identical houses on a
quiet residential street. Except for a rose arbor by the back porch,
both the house and its neighborhood were utterly nondescript, although they did offer the comforting advantage of proximity to family: Emma Jane lived next door, and Dora's sister Evelyn lived one
house down from Emma Jane. Census documents indicate that in
1893, thirteen months after her marriage, Dora gave birth to a
daughter. The infant was christened Marguerite, a prettified version
of the name that had been in the father's family for generations. Like
many of her Upton cousins, the baby had silky blonde hair and mem-

orable blue eyes. Although she would always celebrate May 26 as her birthday, no official certificate survives to mark the actual year—a lucky stroke of fate for a woman who would start fudging her exact age the moment she became famous.

Marguerite Upton's timing was excellent. She entered the world together with the modern age, her arrival happily coinciding with a series of profound social, cultural, and technological changes of which the most pertinent involved the transmission of information. The Graphic Revolution, as historian Daniel J. Boorstin calls it, was based on the rapid and inexpensive dissemination of both word and image by a number of common technologies. The invention of the telegraph helped give birth to the modern news service. The rotary press made it possible to print newspapers faster and more cheaply. Halftone engraving meant newspapers could publish pictures as well. The railroad and automobile enabled rapid distribution. Whether earthshaking or trivial, news would soon travel incredibly quickly and cheaply and be consumed voraciously by an increasingly urban and literate populace. Movies, too, would become an enormously powerful cultural force. Not long before Marguerite Upton's birth, Thomas Edison had demonstrated a device he called a Kinetoscope, a box in which a strip of film was moved past a light to create the illusion of moving images, and the first public showing of a motion picture had taken place two years later.

Taken as a whole, these developments would hasten the emergence of a "culture of personality" and affect the very nature of fame. The definition of what made a life worthy of note would begin to shift rapidly. The emphasis was less on achievement and increasingly on behavior, on the image one projected—on personality. Adorable Mary Pickford and sultry Theda Bara would be as well known and at least as interesting as the men who commanded armies and waged wars. A face, even a voice, from the worlds of politics, sports, and especially show business would be instantly recognizable to millions of people.

Across the country, Americans would soon have access to motion pictures, phonograph records, mass-circulation magazines, and many more newspapers. So significant would the newspaper be that by the 1920s up to a dozen would compete furiously in a single metropolis, with new editions spewing out every few hours.

Still other momentous changes were afoot in those waning years of the nineteenth century when Marguerite Upton was playing with her dolls under the cigar tree in her backyard and listening to carriage wheels clatter along the cobblestones of Lee Street. Henry Ford's contraption would make a vast nation smaller. The Wright brothers were fooling around with kites. Far to the north, a great bridge would help give birth to the metropolis of New York. The fresh-faced Gibson Girl was striding into public consciousness, tennis racquet in hand and a purposeful gleam in her eye. Women were still wearing voluminous long skirts and pounds of heavy cotton petticoats, but they would shed them, along with their stiff hats and even stiffer manners, in the century ahead. The music would change. The beat would quicken.

But Marguerite Upton was born in the deeply traditional South. It would be years before the modern age reached Berkley. In the meantime, life there was dull and constricting, with little to excite the soul or tempt the spirit. Marguerite Upton would seek to make her escape as fast and as completely as possible.

For a girl who dreamed of going places, nothing mattered more than a pretty face, and in that respect young Marguerite Upton was supremely blessed. "She was a smashingly beautiful child with flawless skin and enormous blue eyes," George Tucker, a local newspaper columnist, wrote nearly a century later in an article about Berkley's most famous daughter. Some dyspeptic naysayers claimed she had hair the texture of straw and the gait of a turkey, but a photograph taken when she was not yet in her teens reveals an angelic-looking creature with classically even features—a high forehead, straight brows, large, wide-set eyes, a shapely, slightly turned-up nose, and exquisitely sculpted lips. Her blonde hair is swept back from her face and held with a ribbon; around her neck is an ornate lace collar. She looks both innocent and knowing, a combustible mixture.

Though Margie, as she was called, had a willful streak, she also had a quick smile and pretty ways, and when in the mood she could be the most agreeable of children. "She learned early that smiling rather than bawling got her the candy suckers that she craved," George Tucker wrote, and classmates remembered her as bubbly and good-natured, an easygoing youngster who rarely took offense. "She had nice manners and people liked her," her father once told a reporter. "She would do anything in the world to please anybody, and she never cried unless she was sick." She charmed her crusty grandfather—Daddy Wood, as she called him—who bought her candy and took her walking, and she endeared herself to the imperious-looking Emma Jane. She also became a frequent visitor at her father's barbershop, bringing his dinner in a basket and receiving a nickel for her trouble. "The men getting haircuts talked to her, and they used to be carried away with her," her cousin Elizabeth Nixon recalls. "People said she was real cute when she was little."

As a child, she had scant interest in her studies at the local one-room schoolhouse, but she did adore an audience, and happily for such a youngster she could sing, dance, and recite better than most of her peers—at least that became the accepted wisdom. "Every Friday we had to speak a piece, and Margie would always speak the nicest piece of all," a classmate remembered. "When we had plays, Margie was always better than the rest of us. . . . We all used to say Margie will someday be an actress." Townspeople invariably uttered such comments after a local offspring made it big on the stage, but in this case, the people of Berkley recognized that, at the very least, the gangly extrovert with the unruly golden curls had a passionate appetite for the spotlight.

Early on, Marguerite realized that her appearance would be her passport. In a rare moment of candor she admitted years later in her memoirs that she knew her beauty could be an asset and was determined to use it, however shamelessly, to achieve her goals. "Deep inside me ever since I was a little girl I have always wanted nice things and luxuries and love," she wrote, "and I suppose once or twice I have said to myself, why be beautiful if you can't have what you want." The child had good looks, charm, ambition, and a taste for an audience, all attributes that could help a girl make her way in the world.

Around 1900, Sam Upton packed up his little family and moved back to Camden, North Carolina. He set up his shop next to the courthouse and established his wife and daughter in a modest house down the road, not far from his brothers and sisters. Maybe he was homesick; more likely his marriage was in trouble and a change of scene seemed advisable. But the shift in environment did nothing to improve relations in the Upton household; the tedium of life in turn-of-the-century rural North Carolina surely exacerbated the tensions, as did Dora's own personality, for she had always been the wildest and most rebellious of Emma Jane's children. After three years in her new home, Dora took off, leaving her husband and daughter, and headed north to Richmond, Virginia. She settled into a boardinghouse, where she met a young railroad worker named Arthur Hudson, and after a brief courtship, she divorced her first husband and remarried. Sam left Camden as well. With his ten-year-old in hand, he too went north, to the central Virginia hamlet of Farmville, where he promptly took a third wife, a straitlaced fellow Baptist named Josephine Bowman. Within a few years the household included a baby girl called Lucille.

Sam did the best he could with his elder daughter. He sent her to Sunday school and urged her to read the Bible, giving her a palm-sized New Testament with the words "Marguerite Upton, a preasant from Papa" written in a childish hand inside the back cover. He arranged for her to take piano lessons; she practiced her scales on an elaborate old upright decorated with gold scrollwork. And for a time, she found ways to amuse herself. She made something of a local reputation reciting poems at parties and other get-togethers, and at a charity benefit for the Baptist church she offered a memorable portrayal of a mechanical doll. Wearing a pink organdy frock and matching ribbons in her hair, her vivid features accented by dabs of red chalk and burnt cork, she held herself rigid as she was carried onto the jerry-built stage for her grand entrance. Despite the primitive setting and the harsh glow of the flickering kerosene lamps, her performance brought down the house.

But Farmville was a backwater, and an unpleasant one at that. Marguerite quarreled with her stepsister and fought even more bitterly with her strict stepmother, who was none too happy to be saddled with another woman's strong-willed child. By the time she entered her teens, Marguerite had persuaded her father that the best place for her was back with her grandmother in Berkley. It would be her fourth home in thirteen years.

There is no indication that Peggy was particularly troubled by the domestic upheavals of her early years. And despite the stigma attached to divorce in early-twentieth-century America, Sam and Dora's separation taught their daughter one crucial lesson: if a marriage was not working, there was an out. If a woman grew tired of her husband, for whatever reason, she could leave and make a new life for herself elsewhere; though shameful, such things were possible. Few girls knew that, at the dawn of a new century in the sleepy small towns of the South.

For Peggy, as she began calling herself back at her grandmother's house, the return to southern Virginia had come at the perfect moment. Norfolk in the early 1900s had much to offer a pretty, impressionable teenager, particularly in the way of men, entertainment, and a deliciously teasing mix of excitement and danger.

Unlike most Southern municipalities of the day, the city was a lively, cosmopolitan place. As part of the Port of Hampton Roads, one of the world's great naval and shipbuilding bases, it derived much of its energy from the endless waves of sailors who descended on the metropolis. With its heavy population of transients, Norfolk also had its predictable share of urban vices: bootlegging, drugs, prostitution, political corruption. A wide-open town, it didn't lack for the unsavory, and this, of course, was part of its charm.

The city was entering its boom years as Peggy was entering her teens. She had returned just in time for the Jamestown Exposition of 1907, a lavish world's fair that attracted an international crush of dignitaries and was capped by the star-studded departure of Theodore Roosevelt's Great White Fleet for its journey around the globe. The Ocean View Amusement Park offered so many diversions local people dubbed the resort "the Coney Island of the South." And most important there was vaudeville, which by the early twentieth century had established itself as the country's premier form of entertainment.

Norfolk had always had theatrics of a sort, primarily genteel, sedate versions of Shakespeare and other classics, but there was nothing genteel or sedate about the dazzling array of performers that paraded across the vaudeville stage—singers, dancers, musicians, ethnic comics, jugglers, acrobats, ventriloquists, animal acts, kid acts, novelty acts, and much else. Though the fare was relatively tame, especially in the hinterlands, where audiences included women and even children, vaudeville was richer, more urbane, more sophisticated, and certainly more amusing than anything Virginians had seen before. With its verve, impudence, and undeniable flash, it served a critical cultural function as well, doing much to destroy any lingering notions of Victorian propriety.

Norfolk was an important stop on the vaudeville circuit. As girls like Peggy strolled around the town, along thoroughfares bustling with pedestrians, trolleys, and that newfangled invention called the automobile, they could not have helped but be riveted by the temples to entertainment lining the streets. At the Majestic Theater, a Tudor Gothic building on East Main Street, nearly a thousand people could plunk down a dime or a quarter to watch not only the latest in vaudeville but also its seamier cousin, burlesque. Rising on Tazewell Street was the two-thousand-seat Wells Theater, its orange brick facade punctuated by accents of stained glass, grinning theatrical masks, bright copper lighting fixtures, and other Beaux Arts froufrou.

Also on Tazewell Street was the palatial Colonial, with its vaulted ceiling, gold wallpaper, and maroon velvet curtain that fell to the stage in huge scallops. After opening in 1907 with thirty-two performances of *Pocahontas,* the Colonial went on to present such vaudeville stars as Al Jolson, wearing blackface and down on one knee as he belted out his signature "Swanee"; Harry Houdini, dripping wet as he emerged victorious from the tank of water in which he had been bound and held captive; and, slightly later, Eddie Cantor and a blonde bombshell named Mae West, who always drew a standing ovation from the crowd.

Even more compelling were the stories about the women of the stage. The curvaceous singer and actress Lillian Russell was famed not only for her spectacular gowns but also for her four marriages and numerous love affairs. It was impossible not to have heard of her: her picture was in all the magazines, and toward the end of her career, when Peggy was a teenager, she even performed in Norfolk. Legendary, too, were the Florodora Girls, those six charmers in frilly pink skirts who twirled their parasols so saucily on the stage of the Casino Theatre up in New York and went on to marry millionaires, every last one of them.

Equally memorable, not to mention shocking, was the showgirl Evelyn Nesbit, the "Girl in the Red Velvet Swing" who flashed into the headlines in 1906 when her wealthy husband Harry K. Thaw murdered her celebrated lover, the architect Stanford White. Parents whispered about Nesbit in hushed tones: Was it true she wasn't wearing so much as a garter when she cavorted for Stanny White on that swing? And how extraordinary that the scandal actually helped her career, propelling her back onto the stage for a brief turn as a vaudeville star. Young girls, too, were enthralled by the men and women of the silent screen; by 1909 nine thousand theaters nationwide offered picture shows, and the Norfolk newspapers were filled with advertisements for coming attractions.

Photographs show that Peggy herself was growing up to be quite entrancing, if a bit gawky, with long legs and a slender figure, her hair tied back from her face in a style that accentuated her chiseled features. Shortly after her return to Norfolk around 1906, she had dropped out of school and shaken off her grandmother's authority by leaving home, freeing herself to explore the city's varied amusements, ponder her future, and experiment with various roles, if only in her imagination.

Peggy hungered for adventure, and her hunger was fueled by the rich lode of fantasy mined by the magazines and newspapers she consumed. Although Norfolk offered more than Berkley, a girl's options were limited in the traditional South. If she did not have to earn her living, which generally meant as a servant or factory worker, or care to settle down to a humdrum life of marriage and motherhood, what then? Getting a job, even as a respectable schoolteacher, was much frowned on, an admission that a father could not support his family.

The theater, by contrast, held an undeniable glamour. The stage was considered a wicked place, and the men and especially the women who peopled that world were considered more disreputable still, but the thrills it offered were considerable. The theater could take one to exotic cities like New York, where women wore glossy fur coats and the thinnest of silk underthings. It brought women adoring men in smart evening clothes who showed up at stage doors with diamond bracelets discreetly wrapped in romantic notes. The thunderclap of applause, the warmth of the amber spotlight, the lavish bouquets, the intoxicating compliments—all this the theater made possible. It was hardly surprising that vaudeville offered Peggy her ticket out of town.

My life really began yesterday when I met Mr. Huertin, and when a person runs Away From Home, she really hasn't the time to begin a Diary. So now I am on a train going Sixty Miles an Hour toward my Future."

The year was 1910. Peggy was sixteen and had just run away with a vaudeville cyclist—or so she told posterity. As she described her first great adventure in the opening chapter of *Men, Marriage and Me,* her 1930 memoirs written in the breathless style of a diary begun in childhood, events began unspooling the day she and a few friends were hanging around the lobby of the Lorraine Hotel, one of Norfolk's classier establishments, in search of a little excitement. They were approached by an older man—all of thirty-five—who introduced himself as the great cyclist Jack Huertin and said he was looking for a pretty girl to work in his vaudeville act, on its way to Utah after winding up an engagement at the Colonial. Peggy made an immediate decision. In less than twenty-four hours she informed Huertin that her parents were dead, packed her schoolbag with a few essentials, and boarded a train heading west with her new companion. "I am not going to have a Dull & Dreary life," she wrote in her memoirs. "I am going to have a thrilling and exciting life full of Ginger and Glory."

In her account, the journey to Salt Lake City, the site of their first performance, was punctuated by the appearance of a string of men much taken with the lively young Southerner. By the time they got to Chicago, the man selling newspapers aboard the train had told her she was a "knockout" and added, "I knew you was an actress." She found her latest admirer slightly déclassé—"I don't think an Actress should speak to news butchers after all, it is not dignified," she wrote—and turned her attention to a passenger wearing a diamond bracelet. She reacted indignantly when Huertin urged her to keep her mind on her career. "Well, I think a person can concentrate on her career and still think about diamond bracelets," she explained. "I would not mind my lover giving me a Diamond Bracelet but he could not buy me, no man will ever Buy me."

At Denver, the next stop, the good looks and vivacious manner that had attracted her fellow passengers during her journey made her an instant success onstage. By then she had been outfitted in a costume with tights that showed off her shapely legs, and as she recalled it in her memoirs, the local paper reported that "a winsome little Blonde girl thrilled the audience with a combination of Beauty and Talent." She had picked up a few more vaudeville routines, such as standing still on a wheel—apparently a staple of a vaudeville cyclist's act—and the natural charm and stage presence that had manifested themselves during amateur theatricals back in Virginia did much to enhance her performance on the Denver stage. Offstage, she was an even greater hit, especially with a tall, well-dressed young man—"like the scenery, big and handsome"—who introduced himself as Everett Archer, bought her a sarsaparilla, and showered her with compliments.

"I think Mr. Archer is grand," she wrote. "He is one of those Big Rugged strong men and he is very Rich because his father is the Borax King of America." Speculating further, she continued: "I wonder what it would be like to fall in love with Mr. Archer, he says call me Everett, but I told him I could not be so familiar because I really have not known him long enough, only since 9 a.m. this morning."

According to Peggy's account, Archer proposed the day after they met and the couple were married the same afternoon. "It is exciting being married but I am scared at this big house and Everett's parents who shook hands and pretended to smile," she recounted. "I suppose they wanted to talk over the marriage and decide what is to be done." To cheer herself up further, and with memories of the diamond bracelet she had seen on the train lingering in her mind, she began contemplating the purchase of the rings Everett planned to buy her, clearly a prime attraction of matrimony. "He is going to buy me an engagement ring and also a wedding ring tomorrow at the best jewelers in Denver," she wrote. "Isn't that wonderful?"

Within seventy-two hours, the romance was over, or so she claimed. "Oh God God God why wasn't I told marriage was like this?" she moaned. "My heart is broken I am bruised and sick and I hope I shall die soon so I shall never have to remember those three terrible days." Apparently the travails of her wedding night had simply been too much for her. "I feel like an old woman of Thirty, full of disillusion and despair," she went on. "Every time I see a man on the street I shudder & despair and remember my terrible experience with Mr. Archer, my husband. I am through with all men for I know what they are. I shall never speak to one again." Glossing over the exact details ("Certain experiences in a young girl's life cannot be written even in a diary," the alleged editor of her memoirs explained in an excruciatingly tactful parenthesis) but aware that she had transgressed badly ("Mother will kill me"), she headed back east, and the marriage was eventually annulled.

The chance meeting in the swanky Norfolk hotel, Peggy's daring deception, the breakneck courtship and three-day marriage—it made for a thrilling story, but it just wasn't true. In fact, the seeds of Peggy's theatrical career were sown when she was working as a manicurist in Richmond during a brief stay with her mother and happened to buff the nails of some small-time performers in a ragtag vaudeville troupe. She was much taken with their tales of barnstorming around the country, and after considerable nagging and pleading, she persuaded the players to take her along.

There was little to stop her. Sam Upton, involved with his new family in a distant corner of the state, had long since lost touch with his elder daughter. Dora was preoccupied with her second husband

and not particularly eager to resume responsibility for her. Nor was Dora herself any model of rectitude; having run off from one husband, and abandoned her child, she was hardly in a position to insist that Peggy remain within the family bosom. Emma Jane, despite her imposing appearance, had been unable to control her own eldest daughter and could only have wrung her hands at this latest manifestation of domestic rebellion; whatever her private thoughts about her headstrong granddaughter, she was relatively far away in Norfolk. And so at sixteen Peggy set off in pursuit of a career on the stage.

Amazingly, given her lack of experience, she pulled it off. "Sheer strength of determination for success, adoration, wealth may have projected Peggy so suddenly upon her meteoric career," concluded the team of Hearst reporters that dug around in her past a few years later. "Of course she couldn't act just then. But the fact remains that by the time her company reached Denver, Peggy was the one compelling individual in the cast." Another newspaper called her "the sensation of the mountain town that season." That much was true. And among those who caught her act, there was indeed a young Westerner named Everette Archibald Jr. Though he may have looked like a millionaire to the impressionable country girl from the South, Archibald was simply the twenty-two-year-old scion of a prominent Denver family, a rich man's son employed as a traveling salesman for a Utah wholesale grocery company. But he liked what he saw on stage, and on May 18, 1910, after an eight-month courtship, he and Peggy were married by an elder of the Mormon Church in Salt Lake City.

The trouble started shortly thereafter. Contrary to her professed horror of men, the bride, now seventeen, had already developed a healthy sexual appetite. Her days of roaming the streets of Norfolk, combined with her experiences on the road, had given her a decided taste for male companionship. Although there is no record of exactly what happened to Peggy as she made her way west with her fellow performers, her frequent references to men she met on her journey make it seem unlikely she spent many minutes alone. And given the freewheeling life enjoyed on the road in the early years of the twentieth century, not to mention the assumptions about women who took to the stage, an attractive and outgoing young woman traveling cross-country would have had plenty of encounters with the male sex. Nor did Peggy have any intention of forgoing these pleasures just because she happened to be married. Using as her base the handsomely furnished house her husband had established on the outskirts of town, she took advantage of his frequent absences to entertain a wide selection of the city's eligible bachelors.

Initially, Archibald heard only rumors about her indiscretions. "I had one or two discussions with her about keeping company with other men while I was away from home," he told a reporter a few years later. But, he added, "I walked into it one night." He had returned unexpectedly from a business trip to Pueblo, Colorado, to find his wife and a sweaty young companion savoring an intimate moment in his parlor. Restraining his anger, he headed back out on the road, only to be summoned home four days later by an urgent telegram from his father. Peggy had disappeared altogether, taking all her clothes and a few hundred dollars. Archibald heard nothing from her until he received a postcard the following year—just a line to inform him that she wanted a divorce. Although she offered no explanation for her behavior, the life of a salesman's wife in a rough-hewn city in the West was clearly not to her liking.

Despite Peggy's messy departure, Archibald admired her until the end. Two decades later, when he was in the process of divorcing a subsequent wife, court papers revealed that he persisted in extolling Peggy's virtues to his current spouse, telling the second Mrs. Archibald: "Peggy is the only woman I ever cared for."

After her adventures out West, Peggy returned east, not to her grandmother's place but to a gypsylike existence that took her from one spot to another, including her mother's house in Richmond. In her memoirs, she says that she remained at home convalescing from what she described as a nervous breakdown. In reality, she was pregnant. A son named Everette was born in Richmond in April 1911, less than a year after the wedding. But his time on earth proved short. When he was four months old and suffering from a cough, a relative accidentally gave him an overdose of a syrup laced with opium. He died on August 3. His small body was returned to Berkley, placed in a twenty-five-dollar pine coffin, and buried in Berkley's Magnolia Cemetery in an unmarked grave that is the only tangible evidence of his mother's first romance.

Predictably, the baby never figured in official or even unofficial accounts of Peggy's life. An infant born of a teenage elopement and accidentally poisoned hardly fit the polished image Peggy sought to fashion for herself. Even to her family, the baby became a secret, never mentioned to outsiders and seldom talked about among themselves. An air of mystery shrouded the father, too. "There were little snatches, but no conversation," Peggy's cousin Hudson Price recalls. "My mother would say, 'Well, she was very young to go off and leave home.' We knew nothing about Archibald."

Years later, in a slightly maudlin interview, Peggy bemoaned the fact that she had "no chick or child," and every so often, usually on the eve of a new love affair, she would reiterate her desire for offspring. "All I want is to marry and have babies," she told Charlie Chaplin during a quiet tête-à-tête. Her longing for motherhood was probably fleeting, however. The truth is, Peggy could never have become the woman she did had her child survived. A child would have almost certainly kept her from the glamorous existence she craved and from the rich men who could pay for it. Free of encumbrances, she was able to seize the opportunities that came her way. Whether she aborted any subsequent pregnancies or, given her energetic love life, knew how to prevent them in the first place, she never had another baby.

In many respects, Peggy's story was the typical cautionary Victorian tale of a willful young woman who leaves home in search of excitement, marries badly along the way, and returns with a swollen belly. But she represented another facet of turn-of-the-century womanhood as well: she recognized the limitations of her world, she wanted to escape, and she satisfied her desire. Though she ended up back at home, she did not remain there for long.

2

"I Would Do Anything
for a Real Silk Chemise"

Among finishing schools for elegant young ladies, few places had the cachet of Chevy Chase College and Seminary, situated in a fashionable new neighborhood springing up just north of the nation's capital. Its tasteful name befitted its surroundings, the "most exclusive and aristocratic suburb of the city," as an advertisement for the school boasted. A trolley line from downtown had been installed to attract "the better classes of Washington," and soon fine homes were rising along either side.

The institution itself occupied a handsome Georgian-style building, red brick flanked by thick white columns, that overlooked a broad expanse of lawn facing Connecticut Avenue. By the early teens Chevy Chase College had established a reputation as the ideal place to groom diplomats' girls and daughters of the South, teach them the art of gracious living, and prepare them for the career of matrimony, the only suitable occupation for a young lady from a well-born family.

"There are hundreds of girls, but I don't like any of them, and they do not like me," Peggy wrote in her memoirs in sketching a picture of that world. "The other girls are hateful to me because I have not nice things to wear like them. Betty Hyte who comes from

Charleston called me Miss Yokel the other day and they laughed and I was very unhappy and real mad but I did not let them see.

"Nancy Morrow has at least a dozen silk chemises," she continued. "I would do anything for a real silk chemise. That sounds terrible, but really a silk chemise means a lot."

How did Peggy make her way from a redneck backwater to an exclusive finishing school? She didn't. She probably never even set foot in the place. Early on, however, she realized that presenting herself as a product of an East Coast finishing school would do far more for her image than admitting the disreputable truth about her ill-fated romance in the rawboned West and the rough-and-tumble existence that followed it.

The version of her story somewhat closer to the truth is that after her brief marriage to Archibald, Peggy spent several years crisscrossing the country. She made her way first to New York, then headed west to Oklahoma City, where she hooked up with a man she described as "a live wire," and finally settled in Washington and proceeded to enjoy as wild a life as was possible in the nation's capital. Although she rarely spoke publicly about those years, a team of Hearst reporters who excavated her past a decade later concluded that "her taste for speed and the spectacular already had been well developed" by the time she reached Washington. "She never turned down an invitation to a party if she learned that it might get rough," a friend reported of those days, and for a time she passed herself off as the wife of an army lieutenant with whom she was living in an apartment house on N Street. When a particularly riotous mood struck, she worked off her excess energy by riding around town on the roofs of taxicabs, presumably after downing one too many champagne cocktails. When the pace slackened, she made occasional expeditions to the entertainment districts of New York in search of a few extra jolts of excitement.

During those years she came to know one of the capital's most popular women's tailors, a man named Pasternak, and in an agreement that was clearly mutually advantageous—both to the often penniless Peggy and to the merchant seeking a way to make a buck—she began wearing his clothes wherever possible, especially at the Monday evening vaudeville shows at Keith's, where women showed up simply to ascertain what elegant frock Peggy was sporting on a particular night. "She was so fashionable that it almost hurt," her friend Francis Daily, an editor of the *Washington Herald,* told the Hearst team. "She was forever playing her part—and attracting men." Pasternak's offerings were supplemented by a seemingly endless supply of dresses and silk stockings, courtesy of the wealthy if slightly dissolute young Washingtonians she ran around with.

During these years, Peggy's version of her past changed nearly as often as her outfits. After briefly adopting, then abandoning, a clipped British accent, she began boasting to friends of her "hot-blooded Southern father." Before long, she was waxing nostalgic about those "dear days spent at my finishing school" and suggesting that the dearest of those days had been spent at Chevy Chase College. The city was full of graduates of the institution, and an observant young woman like Peggy would have had ample opportunity to hear their stories, observe their refined and gentle ways, and drop broad hints that she was an alumna, albeit a reluctant one, of this very proper milieu.

As she so often did in her life, Peggy was making up her story as she went along. But even at a relatively early age she intuitively realized that social barriers in her native land had become so fluid that clothes did make the woman after all. She also grasped the notion that a slightly snobbish finishing school was just the sort of place where a girl from humble circumstances, a girl much like herself, might be thrust onto a larger stage, one that offered far more opportunities than the modest world of her childhood. In such an environment a girl might meet someone with whose help she could take a giant step up the social and economic ladder that loomed so appealingly in her dreams and sample the luxuries that might accompany such a climb. In her travels around the city Peggy had already come across such a person, a young law clerk from a distinguished Washington family. All she needed was a suitably romantic canvas on which to paint a tempestuous portrait of their meeting.

As Peggy describes her first encounter with Sherburne Philbrick Hopkins in her memoirs, she had been ready to leave a school dance for lack of appropriate partners when a tall young man in evening dress approached.

"You are Miss Upton, aren't you?" he asked politely. "Trust me to find out the name of the prettiest girl in the hall." With a rush of flowery compliments he introduced himself as Sherburne Hopkins, Sherby to his friends, and asked her to dance. Gratefully she accepted, and by evening's end they had made a date to meet the next day at the Willard Hotel. Peggy was delirious. "It is nearly midnight, and I have had the most wonderful experience," she wrote of that encounter. "I have met a Millionaire and I am going to lunch with him tomorrow!"

For a young woman eager to make a matrimonial splash, the blond, blue-eyed Sherburne Philbrick Hopkins seemed an ideal candidate. He came equipped with impeccable credentials, the most impressive being that he was an eighth- or ninth-generation Mayflower descendant, depending on how one computed the genealogy. He also came from unblemished professional stock. "Each generation of the line has sent forth members of high ideals, courage, and talent," a local historian wrote glowingly of the family.

Sherburne's grandfather, Thomas Snell Hopkins, had fought in the Civil War, been wounded at the battle of Fredericksburg, served as an officer of the General Society of Mayflower Descendants, and currently headed the family firm of Hopkins and Hopkins, which specialized in international law. Sherburne's father, Sherburne Gillette Hopkins, was one of the capital's best-known attorneys. For a quarter of a century, he served as confidant and adviser to the governments of Mexico and other countries in the region. When the state of Mexican–American relations was an important story, his name was a fixture in the newspapers, and only in the most complimentary fashion.

Unfortunately, these exemplary genes had begun to thin by the time they got to Sherburne Philbrick. Twenty-one when he met Peggy, he was studying law in the family firm or perhaps just hanging around the office trying with limited success to stay out of trouble. His track record was not impressive. While still in his teens, he had eloped with a young Washingtonian named Margaret Ordway Maury. The marriage was quickly annulled because both parties were so young, and when last heard from, the ex-bride was exposing her legs as a member of the Winter Garden chorus in New York. In subsequent years the junior Sherburne would find himself in repeated trouble with the law on charges of fraud, and at one point he was even jailed. So thoroughly was he the family black sheep that his father's obituary in the local paper made no mention of a son among the survivors.

But most of these transgressions were far in the future when Sherburne fell for Peggy. According to her breathless account of their whirlwind courtship—her second—the pair had known each other less than twenty-four hours when he marched into the Willard in his Savile Row suit, maneuvered her into a secluded alcove, and proposed marriage. Before she could catch her breath, he whisked her off to the fashionable Washington department store Woodward and Lothrop—"I had never even been *inside,*" she confessed—and bought her a selection of tea frocks and evening gowns, half a dozen pair of shoes, six sets of silk lingerie, and a vanity case outfitted with silver brushes. Loading their purchases into Sherburne's chauffeur-driven Packard, the couple headed north to Maryland in search of a minister willing to tie the knot on short notice.

In other, slightly more candid descriptions of her relationship with Sherburne Hopkins, Peggy admitted that the romance did not proceed in quite such thrilling fashion. In reality, reported one newspaper account, the courtship was a rocky and protracted affair. And although there is no record as to how the two met, given Peggy's footloose existence in Washington and Sherburne's taste for fast young women, one can surmise that they did not cross one another's paths through any socially correct channels. But however the meeting took place, whatever tales she told her future husband about her past, and however much she embellished the facts for posterity, there was no question that by the age of twenty she had collected her second well-to-do husband. On September 1, 1913, she and Sherburne were married at the home of A. Burtis Hallock, a Presbyterian minister, in the small Maryland town of Bel Air, just north of Baltimore.

As with her first marriage, the ceremony was a private, bare-bones affair. For Sherburne, a quick and discreet ceremony made sense; he had already eloped once with a woman whose behavior left a lot to be desired. And since an ex-vaudeville performer with a previous matrimonial entanglement was hardly the sort of daughter-in-law the Hopkins family envisioned clasping to their bosom, it is unlikely that he told his parents much, if anything, about his second wife's background. "Beyond telling their secret to Mr. Hopkins' father, the young couple had not intended to make any announcement for the present of their marriage," the *Washington Star* noted tactfully in its account of the elopement. Nor was it surprising, as the newspaper added, that the groom "did not take his friends into his confidence."

The match would have seemed similarly unlikely to the bride's mother and grandmother, living modestly in Virginia, but it would have struck them as highly advantageous, a fact Peggy was well aware of. "After all," she wrote in her memoirs with her usual indisputable logic, "Sherby is a millionaire and very prominent socially and a girl cannot marry a millionaire who is prominent socially every day."

* ★ ★

The newlyweds settled into the top floor of the Hopkins town house on Nineteenth Street in the chic and leafy Dupont Circle neighborhood northwest of the White House. It would not have been unusual for a young couple of the day to set up housekeeping under a parental roof, and there were additional reasons why such an arrangement might have suited the newest Sherburne Hopkinses. Sherburne's parents were living apart at the time, and his mother, Hester, who remained in the town house, might have been delighted to have her son function as the man of the family. For Sherburne, who was clearly the most junior member of the family firm, the opportunity to live in an established household with an existing fleet of servants would have seemed equally enticing, especially since his wife had absolutely no interest in domestic matters.

Peggy did, however, appreciate opulence, and though the couple's quarters were in the attic, she found them luxurious; her eyes widened especially at the sight of the gleaming antique furnishings. She was equally taken with the private bath—her first—and the gold- and ivory-flecked vanity table, on which she promptly arranged her silver brushes.

Just what the senior Hopkinses thought of their daughter-in-law can only be imagined. But whether or not she bothered to pass herself off as a finishing-school graduate, the reception they offered left little doubt as to their true feelings. "She is very charming to me but did not say anything I expected she would say, like how is my new daughter, or how do you like your new mother?" Peggy wrote in her memoirs of her mother-in-law. "She just took my arm and kissed my cheek just once." Her father-in-law, she freely admitted, regarded her as a "silly little brat."

There was initially some debate within the family as to whether Peggy should master the social pastimes of the day—golf, tennis, bridge—but she quickly made it clear that her main activity would be shopping. The finery available in the capital's luxury department stores struck her as the height of fashion, and she intended to take full advantage, especially now that she had a wealthy husband in tow. "When a girl is not riding or shopping or playing golf or dancing in Washington she is changing her clothes," Peggy observed in her memoirs. "It is queer how many clothes one has to have in Washington. I have two riding habits, two tailor-mades for shopping, some tea dresses and five evening gowns, only I think I shall buy some more evening gowns as really I cannot be seen in the same one twice in the same week and we go out almost every single night somewhere." Since Sherburne had opened charge accounts for her at all the better stores—Rizik Brothers and Garfinkle's were among the more important emporiums—she did not even have to inquire about prices.

She found much to acquire. Along with clothes, there was jewelry, to complement the diamond bracelet her husband had given her during the early days of their marriage. And there were other generous offerings. "It will be splendid to have a car of my own," she wrote of the day Sherburne promised her an automobile. "I always think a girl looks very smart if she is driving with a well-dressed man sitting beside her, but not too close." Before long, Washingtonians were being treated to the sight of the new Mrs. Hopkins cruising endlessly about the city, her uniformed chauffeur at the wheel and her fur-trimmed motoring coat draped about her delicate shoulders. Nestled snugly on her lap was her pedigreed Pomeranian, the first of a long string of dogs she would become deeply attached to over the years.

The one blight on the horizon was the war abroad, which had started in July 1914 and was proving an unexpected inconvenience. "Sherby says if it wasn't for the war we could go to Europe," Peggy complained in her memoirs. "He says that it would be the season there if they were not fighting, but nobody is going this year because they have no music or dancing in Paris, and as Sherby says, why go to Paris if you cannot dance or listen to the music? I do not understand much about wars but it seems to me very unreasonable of the politicians to have them at this time of the year when everyone wants to go to Paris."

Aside from interfering with her travel plans, the war also put a crimp in her blossoming social life. The French and the Germans were no fun around a dinner table, and, much to her disappointment, the embassies of nations caught up in the conflict were not giving receptions just at that moment. "It is very tense here in Washington because of the war," Peggy wrote, "and a lot of people who were great friends have become enemies and will not speak to each other, which makes it very difficult when you are giving a party. I am going to give a dinner party and Sherby says I may invite Englishmen and Americans but not Germans or Frenchmen, they take the war too seriously."

Although a city shadowed by war clouds was not the ideal setting in which an ambitious young woman might make a name for herself, Peggy did the best she could under the circumstances. She was as celebrated as anyone could be, not only for her appearance—"the prettiest and best-dressed woman in the nation's capital," one reporter insisted—but also for her increasingly hectic social life. Despite the fact that Woodrow Wilson, the onetime professor, hardly qualified as Washington's most popular social figure, the capital during the mid-teens did not lack for amusements. A Texas congressman's wife named Ellen Maury Slayden recalls in her gossipy memoir *Washington Wife* that practically every evening one donned fancy dress and trooped to a formal dinner, a reception, or a banquet, either at the elegant Willard or Shoreham hotel or at the headquarters of a foreign embassy or legation. At the private supper parties that were a fixture of Washington life, tables were dressed with silver bowls heaped with flowers and weighty with terrapin and canvasback duck; candles flickered on even the hottest nights. The etiquette for paying calls was as sharply prescribed as anything that took place in the halls of Congress, and one's afternoon schedule was rounded out by an endless series of teas and garden parties in which dozens and sometimes hundreds of guests chatted politely on damp lawns and shaded terraces while nibbling sandwiches and ice cream and downing quantities of champagne punch.

Given the links between Peggy's father-in-law and the Mexican government, much of Peggy's life revolved around diplomatic functions hosted by Central and South American countries. "Had a wonderful time at Chilean Embassy last night, did not get home until 3 a.m.," she wrote in her memoirs of one typical evening. "There is a very handsome man who is one of the Chief Secretaries, he is a wonderful dancer and very charming, but I cannot spell his name."

Sometimes her inexperience got the best of her, as it did the evening she brought festivities to a halt during an embassy ball at the Shoreham. The party marked her first outing in a dress with a train. As she stood at the head of a long staircase preparing to make a grand entrance, she tripped over the unfamiliar tail of satin snaking around her ankles and careened headlong toward a cluster of astonished guests. Yet even that humiliating episode did nothing to slow her progress. "In the brilliant social circles of Washington, at the White House receptions, the diplomatic entertainments and the general round of balls and teas, Mrs. Sherburne Hopkins Jr. has been one of the most notable figures of the younger set," the *Philadelphia Record* reported a few years later in describing her whirl through capital society. "Her youth and charm have helped to set her on a little pedestal envied by all women."

For more than a year, married life offered virtually everything Peggy could have desired. She had an attentive, well-to-do husband who showered her with pretty things. Everywhere she went, people made a fuss over her and paid her lavish compliments. Although she was not the only beautiful society matron in town, she had become an increasingly attractive and poised young woman, and her obvious delight in her role served merely to enhance her appeal. But fame in the capital could take even a very alluring person only so far. With its sheen of diplomatic entertainments, Washington represented an ideal setting in which to hone one's social skills, but at heart the city was deeply provincial, especially compared with the great metropolises of the North. Had Peggy stayed in Washington, she would have remained as anonymous as the countless other women who attended the same decorous teas and wandered through the same hushed department stores. Any reputation she made there would always have remained local. The city simply didn't offer enough opportunities to capture the public imagination or satisfy her own restless spirit. With her drive and her desires, she yearned to be someplace else, someplace like New York, where slender towers grazed the stars and the theater was exciting beyond words, where the wine flowed endlessly, small bands of Hungarian gypsies played soft music in dimly lit hideaways, and the crowds stayed out long after the last marquee turned dark. Her occasional visits to New York prior to her marriage had given her a brief taste of such a life. She wanted more.

Peggy's chafing against the constraints of Washington was paralleled by her growing disaffection with her marriage to the son of a sober diplomatic lawyer. Sherburne was turning out to be a lackluster character, not to mention something of a bore—at least that is the impression one gets from her description of this period in her memoirs. Her writings reveal an escalating level of frustration as well as a series of marital squabbles centering mostly on whether she was behaving like a properly affectionate wife and paying sufficient attention to her husband. "Sherby asked me today if I still love him," she wrote of one particularly nasty tiff. "Well, of course I still love him. I think he is wonderful, but really when a girl is in society and has so many things to do can she spend all her time in loving?"

Sherburne, however, felt neglected. One afternoon when he was home with a cold and feeling peevish, he complained irritably, "You never tell me you love me anymore."

"Well, I do not see any great evidence that you are still loving me," his wife reported replying in an injured tone.

When reminded that he had given her yet another diamond bracelet just the week before, she claimed to have shot back: "You know perfectly well I had no such thing in my mind. Besides, you forgot you promised me some earrings that day we were downtown, and you forgot also that it was not last week you gave me the bracelet it was two weeks ago. And besides that has nothing to do with it. I would love you without any presents and you know it."

The arrival of the earrings in question—"very pretty and are being worn just now by the best people here"—patched things over, but just temporarily. Another quarrel erupted when Sherburne discovered that one of his wife's admirers had presented her with a costly embroidered silk shawl. She in turn had been hearing persistent rumors that her husband was running around with another woman. "I think its a queer way to show love when a man objects to his wife getting a lovely present and then gets himself talked about with another woman," she wrote in her memoirs. "I can't stand having Sherby so indifferent."

Through her endless social rounds, Peggy had been exposed to a wider world, and she had become more and more impatient with Sherburne, whom she cast increasingly as a tiresome, nagging spouse. The first secretary of the Chilean embassy had told her she was the most beautiful woman he had ever seen and urged her to seek a career on the stage. His words gave her pause. "I wonder if a girl could go on the stage and still be in society?" she asked herself. "Of course I do not mean myself." Any sense of obligation toward her husband was fading fast. "Mother seems to think I should go down on my knees to Sherby and thank him for marrying me," she wrote. "Well, I felt like that once, but after all he has got *me*."

Tensions in the Hopkins household escalated, and the constant presence of an overprotective and disapproving mother-in-law did little to help matters. "His mother watched over me every minute," she told a reporter a few years later. "I never realized how much bitter truth there was behind those old mother-in-law jokes. Oh, girls, if the man you marry cannot give you a home by yourself, never marry him. He put me there and had his mother watch me like a prisoner, while he could go here and there at all times of day or night and it was all right. That might have been all right in the Dark Ages or in the Orient, where standards are not what they are here, but we are becoming too intelligent to stand for that sort of thing, for a husband to say, there, you stick around at home, mother will watch you."

Then came the end. "I cannot stand this any longer," she concluded after one particularly heated argument. "Unless he is much, much nicer to me tonight I am going to leave him." The next day: "I have left Sherburne Hopkins forever."

As mournfully described in her memoirs, Peggy's decision to leave her husband was the impetuous gesture of an unhappy wife. In her version of events, she marched out of the house with just a few dollars in her purse, announced she was heading south to visit her mother, and instead boarded a train going north. While it is unlikely she slammed the door of the Dupont Circle town house as dramatically as she suggested, and still less likely that she went anywhere without a thick wad of bills, her description of the frustrations of life in the Hopkins household and the broader constraints that limited the options of women contained germs of truth. Both economically and socially, an early-twentieth-century wife was her husband's property, and even an enterprising and strong-willed woman could rarely do as she pleased. Although Peggy had no particular education or talents beyond an ability to be a delightfully decorative dinner-party companion, what she now claimed would please her was to earn her own living.

And so one late-winter day in 1915, chafing under her mother-in-law's iron hand, tired of having her every flirtation scrutinized while her husband was free to take his pleasure where he wished, bored and at loose ends, she simply took French leave of a marriage that had become increasingly suffocating and humdrum and headed to New York with the vague notion of becoming an actress. The stagestruck teenager who had run away with a vaudeville troupe and later strutted about the capital in borrowed finery was alive in her still.

As always, her timing was flawless, for a series of far-reaching changes were taking place as Peggy set off to conquer New York. Although Queen Victoria cast a cold eye on the world from her grave and the glorious twenties were a few years away, seeds of emancipation were sprouting everywhere. Women were marching in support of women's suffrage, which would become a reality at the dawn of the next decade. People had not yet stopped buzzing about the Armory Show of 1913, which had introduced Americans to such radical artistic concepts as Cubism. Poets were writing free verse, and couples were doing the fox-trot and the more daring tango. Ragtime had arrived, with its unsettling, syncopated beat. The corset was a recent memory. Freud's shocking theories about sex and the subconscious had begun permeating the works of writers like Eugene O'Neill. Across the land mores were loosening, especially among the young; F. Scott Fitzgerald was already keeping meticulous notes about the petting parties and other sexual experimentations of the college set that would find their way into his Jazz Age classic *This Side of Paradise*.

A seismic shift in the nation's moral, social, and cultural weather, urged along by sweeping technological change, was under way the very moment Peggy was preparing to make a name for herself. The stage was being set for her entrance onto the national scene, and she was doing all she could to be ready. With astonishing speed she was accumulating a biography that the tabloids, and much of America, would soon find irresistible. Already she had experienced a brief fling on the stage and run through two wealthy husbands. And she was only twenty-two. Her years in Washington had facilitated her transformation from a slightly gawky blonde with a melting Southern accent into a sophisticated, if somewhat hardened, young woman. By 1915, Peggy had pretty much settled on the things she wanted out of life—money, excitement, and an endless stream of admirers, preferably uttering honeyed words and bearing small velvet boxes from the best jewelers in town.

3

"I Am a Celebrety"

In her memoirs Peggy described her transition from society wife to Broadway showgirl as the ultimate Cinderella story. As she told it, she left home in March of 1915 with a single suitcase full of clothes and headed by train to New York, where she ensconced herself in the Hopkins family suite in the St. Regis Hotel off Fifth Avenue. "I have been at the St. Regis a week and have no more money," she wrote of her first days in the city. "I spend all my time looking in the shop windows and walking up and down Fifth Avenue, which I love, but I cannot buy anything and I have to take all my meals in my room."

A few weeks later, her rags-to-riches tale continued, having been forced into more déclassé surroundings on Manhattan's seedier West Side and dependent on the kindness of strangers even for meals, she resolved to knock on the door of every theater along Broadway until she found work. Wearing torn stockings, her last pair of fresh underwear, and a plaid suit that badly needed cleaning, she headed south toward Times Square pondering the ways of the world. "Hunger certainly makes you think about things," she wrote. "When I was a kid I used to think that it was Love that was the most important thing in Life, then after that experience in Denver I thought it was money, but now I know it was food."

Door after door slammed in her face. Finally, half dead from exhaustion, she wandered into a dress shop and collapsed onto a chair. The owner emerged from the back room. "Did you wish to order anything?" she inquired politely. Overwhelmed by the sympathy in her voice, Peggy promptly burst into tears. "You poor kid," the woman said gently. "Come inside and tell me all about it."

The owner turned out to be Madame Frances, proprietor of one of the most fashionable dress salons in town. It was not uncommon for dressmakers at the time to take a deeply personal interest in the affairs of their customers, and while the word *procurer* would have been too harsh, many of these women went to great lengths to introduce attractive clients to prosperous men who in turn footed the bill for the creations whipped up in the back rooms of the shops. Anita Loos labeled Madame Frances "a sort of female Robin Hood" and described her premises as "a rendezvous for the most expensively kept gold diggers in town." Although the rumpled young blonde who had stumbled into her salon hardly looked her best, to an experienced eye she had potential.

"You are a beautiful little thing," Madame Frances told Peggy firmly. "I am going to take you in charge and fix you up with everything you need." Outfitting her in a new suit and stuffing a ten-dollar bill in her purse, the dressmaker deposited Peggy back at her hotel with the instructions "Now you rest and wait here until I telephone." The very next morning, or so Peggy claimed, she found herself in Florenz Ziegfeld's fabled New Amsterdam Theatre, displaying her shapely legs to the great showman himself.

It was the classic tale of show business, the trajectory of the understudy who steps onto the boards a nobody and steps off a star, the unknown perched on a drugstore stool who catches the famous director's eye. The Cinderella story also provided the stuff of innumerable plays and movies. Ziegfeld's own musical *Sally,* starring his adored Marilyn Miller, told of a scullery maid who metamorphoses overnight into a *Follies* star; the show proved one of Broadway's biggest hits of the twenties. Peggy's version of her ascent to showbiz heaven struck a similarly resonant chord, so much so that the gossip mill frequently embellished her account further. Sometimes W. C. Fields was the savior who rescued her from poverty and the streets and transported her to *Follies* heaven; other times her benefactor was Fanny Brice.

Only a hard-core romantic could picture the future Peggy Hopkins Joyce as a starving waif down to her last pair of clean underwear. Nor did she ascend to Ziegfeld's celebrated *Follies* as quickly or effortlessly as she liked to suggest; her rise involved several detours to less glamorous venues. But her recital was essentially true. She did move from the drawing rooms of the capital to the glittering world of the stage with unusual speed.

Vaudeville, the world that had enchanted her as a child, seemed the logical place for her to begin her climb. By the midteens both big-time and small-time versions were flourishing throughout the country, with the finest acts passing through New York's Palace Theatre at Broadway and Forty-seventh Street. The Palace had opened in 1913, just two years earlier, and showcased such internationally famous names as Sarah Bernhardt, the first lady of the theater, along with Evelyn Nesbit, who had taken to the vaudeville stage after her brush with scandal. For some performers vaudeville represented the pinnacle of a career, but it also offered a route by which even the rankest beginner could get started in legitimate show business, largely because it accommodated such a vast array of talents. A world that had room for tin-whistle virtuosos, trained pigs, armless men who wrote with their feet, and daredevils who swallowed live frogs could probably find a place for a charming blonde like Mrs. Sherburne Hopkins Jr., particularly given her intriguing pedigree.

By April 1915, newspapers were reporting that the fashionable Mrs. Hopkins had left her husband and would open shortly at the

Palace. "I knew I could find something when I got ready," Peggy told the *New York Times* reporter who tracked her down at the Hotel Belleclaire on Manhattan's West Side, the modest establishment she had mentioned in her memoirs. "I made up my mind about a month ago that I wanted to be independent, that I didn't want to be beholden to any man for anything, so I told Mr. Hopkins I was going home to visit my mother and came here instead. I had to fib or he would not have let me go, for he was mad about me." The reporter found his subject quite as enchanting as her narrative; he described her as "chic and pretty" and so youthful-looking she "might easily be taken for a member of last year's debutante class."

While there is no record of exactly how Peggy made her way to the Palace, she was ideally poised to break into show business thanks to contacts she had made over the past two years. According to her memoirs, several men she had known in Washington had offered to help her if she ever came to New York. And though she had arrived in the city only a month before, Madame Frances's salon would have been a logical early stop for a woman interested in fine clothes. There, amid the silk and lace and ruffles, a customer invariably met a great many men who could make the necessary introductions to bookers and agents on the lookout for fresh talent.

The act that showcased Peggy's charms represented one of the more decorative attractions on the vaudeville stage. "The Palace gave vaudeville something new in 1915 when it presented a 'Style Show,'" *Variety* editor Abel Green and his coauthor Joe Laurie Jr. recall in their history of Broadway, "complete with the latest fashions from abroad and from the salons of the leading dressmakers at home." Uniquely designed to build on Peggy's brief experience as a fashion model for Pasternak, the Washington tailor, the act, which opened the week of April 12, was an instant hit. It was so successful, in fact, that upon completing their New York engagement the cast immediately embarked on an extensive tour on the prestigious Keith and

Orpheum circuits, the two main routes by which vaudeville acts traveled around the country.

A program from the Orpheum Theatre in Los Angeles for the week of July 12, when the bill also included an appearance by Mercedes, "the psychic eighth wonder of the world," and Little Nip, "the most wonderful chimpanzee in the world," described the act as featuring "Mrs. Sherburne (Peggy) Hopkins Jr. of Washington, D.C., Supported by the Twenty Most Beautiful Models in the World, Displaying the Latest Models Milady Wears from Rising to Retiring." The star made three appearances—in sleeping attire, in a smart checkered suit and wing-tipped hat appropriate for strolling down Fifth Avenue, and in a "silver foam evening dress," an exquisite concoction of "chiffon, silver-threaded net, and roses."

Beyond a pleasing appearance and a dash of stage presence, the assignment demanded little. Peggy simply paraded before an audience in time to music. She did not have to sing, dance, or open her mouth; in fact, she was not allowed to. She just had to model stylish apparel, something Peggy could do brilliantly. Predictably, the critics were smitten, not only with her looks but also with her wonderfully unusual past.

"Someone has said that Peggy Hopkins wears a gown the way some prima donnas sing a song, that with her dressing is an art and an achievement," the *Philadelphia Record* wrote when she came to town. "And her decision to turn that art to account and earn her living by it has made a national social sensation." Her performance, the newspaper added, "is enough to make every woman in the audience sigh with envy and determine to copy her carriage. She brings into her acting too the ease of the woman accustomed to society and the charm that has made her the belle of diplomatic and social circles in Washington."

The *Grand Rapids Press* offered a sensational new wrinkle, one that had no apparent basis in fact but titillated readers nonetheless, when it described Peggy as the "wife of two millionaires and now the prospective bride of a third." Lest anyone miss the import of her actions, the newly minted actress never failed to remind her public of the world she had just left. "Of course, Washington feels dreadfully hurt about my doing this," Peggy told one reporter. "The society folks are just agasp. But then I will remain exclusive even in the theater. I will not mingle with the other actors and actresses."

That a woman who had married into an aristocratic household had taken to modeling smart clothes on the vaudeville stage, and had run away from home to do so, was enough to cause a sensation and guarantee endless coverage. Wherever Peggy went, the press latched on to the story and readers gobbled up every morsel. For in a small but potent way her actions lay directly on the fault lines of a society in flux. A key issue involved the profession she had chosen to pursue. Being an actress no longer represented the moral equivalent of prostitution. But "life upon the wicked stage," with its overtones of loose living and easy love, was hardly the most appropriate place for a woman, especially one from a respectable family. And though divorce had lost a little of its stigma, society women simply did not walk out on their husbands, even if the husbands in question were crashing bores. The sheer audacity of her gesture made Mrs. Sherburne Hopkins extremely good copy, and she cooperated with reporters most obligingly. The mythologizing of Peggy Hopkins had begun.

Having conquered vaudeville, or at least as much of vaudeville as interested her, the next step was film. By 1916, the year Peggy made her screen debut, movies had become the most exciting development in the world of entertainment, not to mention the fastest-growing. Cinema had exploded into a multimillion-dollar business, by some accounts the fifth-largest industry in the United States. With a weekly attendance of ten million people, film also represented an increasingly powerful cultural force, and the newly emerging star system, in which

names were attached to heretofore anonymous faces, gave birth to a
public consumed by those stars and the works that displayed them.

With the growing popularity of fan magazines, names like
Pickford, Chaplin, Theda Bara, and Douglas Fairbanks bubbled on
everyone's lips, and the American public found that it was spending
its most electrifying moments in the dark, staring in rapturous silence
at seductive, alluring images. While the production base of the fledgling industry was rapidly shifting to Hollywood, New York remained
its headquarters, and many films continued to be made on the East
Coast. For a young woman casting about for a foothold in show
business, becoming a star of the silent screen would have seemed
tempting indeed. Although there is no record of the route by which
Peggy entered the movies, as an attractive featured performer at the
Palace she would have invariably come to the attention of the talent
scouts who regularly attended its shows.

The first time the name Peggy Hopkins appeared in a movie credit
was in a forgotten film called *The Turmoil,* released in January 1916
by Metro Pictures Corporation, a New York distributor. The melodramatic story, based on a Booth Tarkington novel, revolved around
the misadventures of the members of a nouveau riche family struggling to better their social standing by marrying into a poor but aristocratic household. In a throwaway subplot, Peggy plays an unhappily
married wife who spends most of her time cheating on her husband.
Reviews were mixed, and her role was so minor, or her performance
so lackluster, that the definitive cast list published decades later by the
American Film Institute does not mention her, although audiences
familiar with her past would have appreciated the irony of a plot that
turned on the notion of marrying for money and came down firmly
against the idea.

Despite the fact that Peggy made no waves with her first movie
venture, the following month Metro gave her a small part in a film
called *Dimples,* about a young woman whose complicated machina-
tions bring happiness to the man she loves. *Dimples,* too, was an in-

consequential work, remembered only because the star, a young actress named Mary Miles Minter, went on to figure in one of the biggest scandals of the day, the 1922 murder of the Hollywood director William Desmond Taylor.

Metro then announced that Peggy would appear in *The Kiss of Hate,* a picture about anti-Semitism in Russia starring Ethel Barrymore. Sharing the screen with such a theatrical heavyweight might have done the beginner's career some good, but, like so many other casting decisions announced in cinema's early days, the opportunity for Peggy to appear with the great Barrymore never came to pass. The distributor, eventually to become part of the powerful MGM studio, seemed to have realized that its new acquisition was a bust as an actress, and Peggy herself may well have concluded that being part of the Metro forces was not helping her much either: she was getting only small parts in mediocre films, and people were not paying attention to her. Whatever the reason, it was time to move on.

Of all the people Peggy brushed up against professionally during her lifetime, none towered over his world as mightily as Florenz Ziegfeld Jr. The very name conjured an enchanted universe inhabited by females of indescribable loveliness, creatures whose intrinsic appeal was further enhanced by ravishing costumes of silks, feathers, imported lace, and bugle beads, not to mention hats that perched on their heads like preposterous sculptures. The girls' radiant faces, their appealing figures, the graceful way they paraded across the stage, leaning back slightly on their heels, chins up, in a manner that made them seem alluring yet reserved—the sight was enough to make a man slightly woozy with desire.

"Rome had its Vestal Virgins, and Japan its geisha girls; India flowered forth the soft-eyed temple dancers, and there were witches in Salem," *Vanity Fair* declared in evoking the aura that surrounded these beauties. Without going quite so far as to compare "Ziegfeld's houris with the Vestal Virgins," the magazine concluded that "in the anthropological sense" they had given rise to "the phrase historic: a Follies Girl. . . . So much of America is implicit in the phrase: the lavish display, the mushroom leap to fame and fortune, the quick oblivion." The near nudity that Ziegfeld made respectable was an especially potent draw, not only in the theater proper but also at the popular rooftop nightclub where his *Midnight Frolic* featured elaborately costumed chorus girls parading along an elevated glass walkway so patrons could glimpse—well, they couldn't glimpse much, but the titillating possibilities acted as a powerful aphrodisiac.

A Ziegfeld production offered much else—raconteurs such as Will Rogers, hilarious comics such as W. C. Fields, clowning songstresses such as Fanny Brice, memorable music from brilliant composers such as Victor Herbert and Jerome Kern, and magnificent costumes by Lady Duff-Gordon, a London fashion designer known professionally as Lucille who had survived the sinking of the *Titanic* and gone on to become one of the premier designers of her day. And starting in 1913, when the *Follies* established a beachhead in the New Amsterdam Theatre on West Forty-second Street, the performances were housed in a setting as exquisite as the girls themselves, an Art Nouveau jewel box regarded as the most lavish playhouse in New York. But the girls were Ziegfeld's most inspired invention, created solely so a man might let his gaze linger and his fantasies roam. The *Follies* were ground zero in show business, and to be a Ziegfeld girl represented the ultimate in glamour, charm, and of course sex appeal. Ziegfeld himself was the Great Glorifier, and for an ambitious woman with a taste for luxury and an audience, nothing compared to his attentions.

The mystique stayed with a woman for life, certifying that she had once been among the anointed. And anointed they were, which explained the nightly crush of reporters and photographers outside the New Amsterdam, along with the crowds of men in evening dress who hurried in and took their seats. These men, especially the sleek young bloods with the vast inherited fortunes, defined this world as much as the beauties on stage. They were the ones who wrote imploring notes tucked around diamond baubles that ushers delivered during intermission. They were the ones who waited at the stage door in their chauffeured Rolls-Royces bearing armfuls of long-stemmed roses, ready to whisk their quarry off to a sumptuous supper after the show.

The price a girl paid for such attention was the price a girl always paid. But if she was lucky, a man might one day propose, the capstone that made the whole effort worthwhile. For what was the point of being a Ziegfeld girl if you could not snag a prosperous mate? Over four decades, whenever the press mentioned Peggy and her millionaire spouses, it would remind readers that she had once been a *Follies* girl. Rich husbands came with the territory.

Exactly when and how Peggy came to Ziegfeld's attention is unclear. It is entirely possible that Madame Frances, who went on to become one of her close friends, made the necessary introductions. More likely, word of her appearances at the Palace had drifted back to Ziegfeld, who, like many other producers, found much to admire, and to snatch away, in the vaudeville house's offerings. "Broadway producers or their scouts got into the habit of coming to see which acts were good and who might be worth tempting away from vaudeville for the greater prestige of the legitimate theater," reports theater historian Marian Spitzer of the Monday matinees, when the new weekly lineup appeared. She goes on to suggest that it was Walter Kingsley, onetime press agent and a frequent spotter of talent for Ziegfeld, who early on singled Peggy out and suggested that Ziegfeld take a look at her.

But as Peggy later retold the tale in her memoirs, her meeting with Ziegfeld occurred shortly after her arrival in New York and had all the earmarks of one of her breathless courtships. As she described her first encounter with the great man, she was hardly alone the spring day she arrived at the tower of the New Amsterdam to meet Florenz Ziegfeld. The waiting room was packed with gorgeous, expensively turned-out women, one of whom glared at the anxious newcomer. After what seemed like hours, Ziegfeld's associate Sam Kingston finally summoned her to the inner sanctum. "He won't eat you," Kingston promised as he led the way.

There in his office, surrounded by pictures of the numerous show-girls he had favored on stage and off, the hawk-faced producer stared at Peggy in imperious silence. "I felt very bashful," she wrote in her memoirs, "because I had never been looked at like that before." Finally he spoke. "So you're the little lady from Washington who wants to go on the stage, are you? Well, you certainly are a knockout for looks, I will hand you that. Let us look at your legs." He and Kingston duly examined her legs, "not insultingly or anything like that but just like he was looking at a picture he was buying." The legendary connoisseur of feminine beauty apparently liked what he saw. "Well, if you can do *anything* at all on stage you will do," he concluded.

"A knockout," Kingston agreed.

Next, Ziegfeld escorted her to the playhouse of the New Amsterdam and introduced her to his associate Abe Erlanger. "Let's see you walk across the stage," Ziegfeld commanded. "Just naturally." Peggy dutifully complied, whereupon both men pronounced themselves satisfied.

"She's got the looks, all right," said Erlanger.

"She knows how to walk, too," Ziegfeld added.

He marched over to her. "Little one," he allegedly said. "If you listen to me I will make you the most famous girl in New York." After reciting the usual platitudes about the glories that awaited her in his employ, he added sternly: "I am going to pay you a hundred dollars a week but of course this is a great deal of money so you must work hard and try to justify my faith in you. I think you are a nice little girl and Mr. Erlanger does too, but you cannot get anywhere on the stage unless you work hard."

Peggy floated out of the theater on a cloud of joy. "I am the happiest girl in New York," she wrote of that moment. "I just love Madame Frances she is so wonderful and so are Mr. Ziegfeld and Mr. Erlanger wonderful too." Whether or not there was any reality to her description of events, clearly a young woman poised to take her place in Ziegfeld's *Follies* would have felt a considerable degree of gratitude to her benefactors.

Peggy was not a member of the chorus, not surprisingly, since she could neither sing nor dance. But as a showgirl, one of the fetching young things whose primary function was to parade around the stage wearing Lady Duff-Gordon's stunning costumes, she ranked higher on the *Follies* food chain, just below the headliners and stars. A place was found for her in scenes in which she simply had to move about draped in one elaborate costume after another, follow the instructions of director and choreographer Ned Wayburn, and avoid stepping on anyone else's lines or feet. "I really have not very much to do, only walk across the stage and so forth," Peggy acknowledged in her memoirs, "but I am to have glorious costumes and the spot."

Just traipsing about in elaborate outfits, she exhibited a certain quality anyone with an eye for stage presence would have recognized, a magnetism that glowed especially brightly when the spotlight was trained on her. "It was hard to put your finger on what was special about her," recalls Muriel Merrill, a Ziegfeld girl who performed with her. "But you couldn't help but take a second look and wonder who she was. Some of the women were much more beautiful, but there was something striking about her. It was just there."

She got along poorly with the other girls, though, and at one point the management threatened to fire her if she did not stop quarreling with Lilyan Tashman, another featured performer. But Peggy understood why rival beauties might be jealous, for in her eyes she was clearly a pet. "Mr. Ziegfeld said publicly that I was the most beautiful girl in the show and the other girls are very cruel and nasty to me," she wrote in her memoirs. "I am beginning to hate them."

Relations deteriorated further when she was assigned a scene requiring a few words of dialogue, assuming she could tame her lingering Southern accent. "It is only one line," she bragged, "but that is more than most of the other girls have. Because I have a line with Bert Williams, of course all the other girls are furious. They say I have a swelled head." In the interest of peace, she was ordered out of the general dressing area and told to share a room with Fanny Brice, the female star, and as Peggy carried her makeup box into Brice's quarters, she felt a flutter of excitement at the thought of rubbing shoulders with the great comedienne. But she had no intention of changing her ways. "A girl should always be a little superior," she reminded herself, "especially when she has a speaking part."

Little in the American theater compared with the exhilaration of opening night at the *Follies* during the show's glory years, a dazzling social event as much as a major theatrical one. Ticket scalpers hawked their wares along Forty-second Street, and luminaries from the worlds of culture, society, politics, and finance filled every corner of the seventeen-hundred-seat theater. A *Follies* opening was a not-to-be-missed evening for virtually everyone in society, both new money and old. Vanderbilts and Rockefellers were typically part of the opening-night audience, and on June 12, the first night of the 1917 edition, not only Mayor and Mrs. John Purroy Mitchel but also banker Otto Kahn joined the hordes in top hats and flowing dresses who swept through the New Amsterdam's vaulted foyer. One could sense a greater rush of anticipation than usual, for the *Follies* had been growing more impressive with each new season.

The House Beautiful, as the theater was known, enchanted audiences almost as much as the show itself. Above the stage soared a vast proscenium arch on which perched sixteen plaster peacocks; flanking them were murals in which slender nudes portrayed such allegorical figures as Poetry, Truth, and Chivalry. A dozen cantilevered boxes, each named for a different flower—heliotrope, buttercup, water lily—swung out from either side of the stage. A vast ceiling dome surrounded by garlands of berries, hydrangea wreaths, more peacocks, and giant angels floated high in the air. The color scheme of spring-like pastels—mother-of-pearl, lavender, orchid, rose, celadon—suggested a garden of the imagination, "a glance into fairyland," in one critic's words.

By 1917, all the famous Ziegfeld names were in place, an astonishing array of talent rarely equaled in show-business history: Will Rogers, W. C. Fields, Fanny Brice, the beloved comic Bert Williams, the first black to share the spotlight with Broadway's theatrical elite, and a goggle-eyed rookie named Eddie Cantor. Behind the scenes toiled an equally impressive roster that included Herbert, Kern, and Joseph Urban, creator of the translucent sets whose tiny dots of color conveyed an illusion of idyllic worlds.

When the curtain rose that warm summer evening, the audience was greeted by an image of Arabian splendor, or at least Arabian splendor as it might have been glimpsed had the audience been ensconced on a New York rooftop looking out into the distance. Against a purple sky bathed in theatrical moonlight, a bevy of women in various states of seminudity lounged seductively on plump gold pillows. The gathering included a newcomer in purple chiffon, her blonde curls peeping out from beneath a hat trimmed with gold lace and blue feathers. She mostly just stood there while dancers in gold-encrusted black chiffon slithered wantonly about the stage. But audience members scanning their programs to see who was playing the character of Dinozad would surely have deemed her a satisfactory addition to any sultan's harem.

Peggy made an appearance in five other numbers. She strolled across the stage during a skit involving a tennis match in which Fields sent the audience into hysterics juggling balls, racquets, and the occasional banana peel. Wearing a green and white costume and a white felt hat, she popped in during a sketch that featured Williams as a befuddled railway porter and Cantor in blackface as his supercilious son, and she made an even briefer appearance in a piece set in the New York subway. In a mini–fashion show called "Episode of Chiffon," Peggy modeled a Lucille gown with the beguiling name "Terrible Temptation." This segment was especially notable in that it starred Dolores, who, like Peggy, was making her *Follies* debut and who would go on to become one of Ziegfeld's quintessential showgirls, renowned especially for her tall, statuesque figure. Dolores, who had started life as an English farmer's daughter called Kathleen Mary Rose, had been a clerk in Lady Duff-Gordon's London shop when the proprietess took notice of her, trained her as a fashion model, and outfitted her with a more exotic name. When Ziegfeld discovered Dolores in Lady Duff-Gordon's New York salon, he was so impressed with her appearance and her bearing that he promptly hired her.

Most memorably, Peggy took part in the first-act finale, an extravagant patriotic number scored by Herbert with the rousing title "Can't You Hear Your Country Calling?" The subject matched the nation's current mood; the United States had entered the war only two months before, and as the playbill reminded audiences with an advertisement for the Our Boys in France Tobacco Fund ("Gunsmoke everywhere, but not a whiff of tobacco smoke to cheer a soldier up"), Americans were already gearing up for battle. Set designer Joseph Urban proved equal to the occasion; among the star-spangled images he created were a gold American eagle with a wingspread as wide as the stage, a giant American flag that unfurled above the heads of the audience, Paul Revere astride a white horse that galloped by means of a treadmill, and the unsettling tableau of three dreadnoughts that grew larger and more menacing as they neared the footlights.

Peggy, who was one of a bevy of women chosen to represent the Allied nations, America's friends across the sea, offered a far more agreeable sight. After military maneuvers executed by four dozen dancers snappily dressed as soldiers, she and her fellow "Allies" paraded out and arranged themselves in a graceful line across the length of the stage. Portraying the character of England, she wore a sleeveless gown of beaded chiffon that flowed nearly to her ankles and was set off by smart elbow-length gauntlets. On her head she carefully balanced a gleaming helmet topped by an enormous plume. With her slight figure, her china-blue eyes, her translucent skin, and the halo of feathery curls that framed her lovely face, she brought to mind, in one reporter's opinion, a perfect "English type of beauty."

All in all, Ziegfeld had outdone himself. Critics hailed the 1917 *Follies* as the best ever, praising the show especially for its splendid spectacle. The *Morning Telegraph* described the production as "so overwhelmingly glittering as to be positively staggering." The *New York Herald* added, "Not since Florenz Ziegfeld Jr. began his 'Follies' eleven years ago has he provided [such] a rainbow of fun, color and feminine beauty." Audiences agreed. The 1917 edition turned a healthy profit and remained at the New Amsterdam for the entire summer.

For Peggy, that summer brought exactly the sort of attention she had been fantasizing about for years. A delicate drawing of her had accompanied the review in the *New York World,* and critics who singled her out took pains to note how scrumptious-looking she was. Although soon after her stint in vaudeville she had begun identifying herself simply as Miss Peggy Hopkins rather than as Mrs. Sherburne Hopkins—she was still officially married, but with Sherburne out of the picture and her career under way, there seemed no need to remind her audience of his existence—everyone appeared familiar with her past. To her immense satisfaction, she was fast becoming a fixture on the New York social scene and reaping the very tangible rewards of being a *Follies* girl.

"Spent a hundred dollars today on a dress," she wrote in her account of those days. "It is the latest thing in the new straight-line models and makes me look very tall and slender." A short time later: "My pictures are in the papers every day nearly. I am a celebrety." Once, she and her new friend Fanny Brice drove to Belmont Park racetrack on Long Island in hopes of meeting some "society men"; although they got caught in traffic, were late for the races, and had a breakdown as they headed back to the city, the day was salvaged when a few presentable strangers stopped and offered them a lift. "They were not society men, only bookmakers or something like that," Peggy reported. But "one was quite nice," she consoled herself, "and we had refreshments on the way home at some roadhouse." Several days after that: "I have met a marvelous man, very good-looking, from Chili. His name is Billy. His sister is having trouble in New York on account of having shot her husband for being untrue to her and he is here on her account." Thanks to the diplomatic connections of the Hopkins family and Peggy's social life in the capital, she had come to know many Latin Americans during her time in Washington, and she had developed a decided taste for their company. The suitor in question this time, a well-connected young diplomat named William Errazuriz, was an undeniable catch; newspapers described him as a scion of the richest family in Chile and a person of exceptional charm—well-traveled, a linguist, and an elegant dancer. He had rushed to New York on learning that his sister, Blanca De Saulles, had been arrested for murdering her Yale-educated ex-husband in a child-custody dispute, but he made time to pursue his own romantic interests. "Billy and I are good friends," Peggy wrote in her memoirs, "but of course we could never be anything else because he has a wife."

Another evening: "A boy named Stewart, really very nice, sent me some flowers in a pot of earth called tulips. I could not imagine who had sent them until I read the card, William Rhinelander Stewart."

The generous admirer, William Rhinelander Stewart Jr., also boasted a distinguished pedigree. He was a descendant of one of New

York's most aristocratic families, and as an item in one of New York's society scandal sheets had noted, he had entered the picture several months before Peggy's *Follies* debut. "Have you seen Peggy Hopkins's new sparkler, a combination of sapphires and diamonds large enough to put your eye out?" *Town Topics* had asked back in March. "Although Peggy's friends have put her through the third degree, she will not disclose the source of the acquisition, nor will she even admit that the inquisitive are warm when they mention the initials W. R. S. Jr. as the likely donor."

When the floral offering arrived, Fanny was present, and though a pot of tulips hardly equaled a diamond, she was duly impressed, not so much by the gift as by the illustrious giver. "My God, child," she demanded, "who sent you those gorgeous tulips?" Inspecting the card, she exclaimed, "Why, he is one of the richest kids in New York." Then she noticed that her friend had removed the flowers from their container and had snipped off the clumps of dirt clinging to the stems. "Good heavens," she sighed in dismay, "the girl has cut off the flowers and thrown away the bulbs."

Peggy was annoyed. "Well, how can a girl know everything?" she sniffed.

Stewart was hardly the only rich man showering her with impressive gifts, which explained why in certain circles Peggy was coming to be regarded as nothing more than a high-class call girl. "The era [abounded] with millionaires who kept their sweethearts in love nests that dotted Manhattan all the way from Murray Hill to Riverside Drive," Anita Loos reminds her readers, and in her opinion Peggy ranked as the most shameless of such kept women. The acid-tongued Loos liked to point out that Peggy enjoyed a brief stint as the mistress of Hollywood producer Joe Schenck before he settled down with the actress Norma Talmadge and began his climb to the top of Twentieth Century–Fox. Much as Loos disapproved of Peggy's morals, she could understand her attraction to Schenck. The rotund, crass-looking producer was a notorious womanizer, and though no one would have mistaken him for a matinee idol, Loos observes trenchantly, "He was an outstanding example of the fascination that comes from power," not to mention the fascination that comes from a well-stuffed wallet.

However questionable her reputation, Peggy was briskly establishing a name for herself around town, and it was hardly surprising that Ziegfeld kept her on for his next show, a revue called *Miss 1917* that he and his coproducer, Charles Dillingham, were presenting at the Century Theatre, just off Columbus Circle. The production featured the usual array of Ziegfeld stars: Herbert and Kern composing the songs, P. G. Wodehouse and Guy Bolton writing the book and lyrics, and Joseph Urban designing the sets, plus such performers as dancer Irene Castle, funnyman Lew Fields, and, in the title role, an aspiring young actress named Marion Davies, who had recently caught the eye of publishing giant William Randolph Hearst.

Initially, Peggy had the impression she was one of the headliners, but she learned otherwise when she arrived at the theater for rehearsals and found Irene Castle occupying what she regarded as the star's dressing room. The discovery irked her greatly. In Peggy's opinion, a show had but a single star, and in *Miss 1917,* as she quickly discovered, she clearly was not that person. "I am sorry I had the fight over the star's dressing room," she wrote in her memoirs, "but really a girl is either a star or she isn't a star and I thought I was the star. It was just a misunderstanding. Anyway, I like Miss Castle."

Opening night on November 5 was dominated by the appearance of the veteran *Follies* performer Bessie McCoy Davis, who had laid aside her career as a singer upon her marriage to the dashing war correspondent Richard Harding Davis. Her return to the stage after his death, an event punctuated with a series of cartwheels, brought the audience to its feet for a four-minute ovation. The dizzyingly eclectic program also featured chorus girls dressed as mosquitoes and a "poem-choreographic" called "Falling Leaves" in which a nymph imprisoned in a golden birch tree was liberated by the wind. Peggy appeared in only three scenes: a lightweight sketch called "The Beauty Shop in the Hotel Blitz" starring Lew Fields, a segment called "Sammy" that took place in front of a backdrop picturesquely described as the "Swan Curtains," and "Who's Zoo in Girl Land," an elaborate production number in which she swooped around the stage trailing an enormous peacock's tail while one of Kern's creamy melodies drifted up from the orchestra.

The sheer size and scope of the production was noted by most critics—"not one cheap moment anywhere," the *New York Tribune* concluded—and indeed no expense had been spared, despite an enormous company of three hundred members. The $300,000 price tag included $35,000 for Urban's sets, tens of thousands of dollars for costumes, and $100 a week for Peggy and other Ziegfeld showgirls "noted for their pictorial effectiveness." In a season in which the average musical cost about $25,000 to produce, these figures represented a daunting undertaking. But despite its hefty price tag, *Miss 1917* turned out to be a bomb, one of Ziegfeld's most spectacular and embarrassing ever—a "historic floperoo," as Wodehouse and Bolton put it succinctly. Few people ventured uptown to witness the debacle, and *Miss 1917* was yanked after several dozen performances, leaving a blizzard of lawsuits in its wake. Had the show played nightly to full houses, its backers would still have lost thousands of dollars a week, so astronomical were the costs. The only noteworthy aspect of the whole affair, other than Bessie McCoy Davis's cartwheels, the antics of Bertie the performing seal, and the sight of Herbert and Kern screaming at each other backstage over some arcane musical dispute, was the rehearsal pianist, an obscure but talented teenager named George Gershwin.

While none of the reviews singled out Peggy for special mention, the swarm of men seeking her favors was, if anything, greater than before. "When I came to the theater tonight," she wrote in her memoirs, "my dressing room was full of flowers. They came from six different men." Although nearly all the donors were strangers, the bouquets arrived with the usual notes asking to meet her after the show, and she wondered, or claimed she did, just what sort of a name she was making for herself. But only fleetingly. "Believe me," she wrote, "if it was not for some of the men I know who at least take me to dinner and supper sometimes I would have a hard time because I wear nice clothes, I have to keep my job, and furs and silk stockings all the time, and sometimes getting a pair of silk stockings is almost as big a problem as a meal. . . . A girl cannot always afford to buy herself steaks when she needs silk lingerie."

Not that Peggy ever paid for a steak or much of anything else during her life; the idea was laughable. But even as she painted herself in her memoirs as an innocent when it came to exchanges involving money and sex, she made it clear that like any tough-minded woman in her position she fully understood the nature of the transaction. "Sometimes I have had to leave a man in the middle of the evening because he thought it was time for him to begin collecting something he thought I owed him," she wrote. "Of course I don't go out with men I don't know as a rule but after all how would you make any new friends if you sat around waiting until you'd known a man all your life before you would go out alone with him."

Will Hogg, a wealthy oilman whose father had been governor of Texas, stood out in her mind as one of the few who didn't expect a girl "to fall on his neck because he gives you a meal." He "never expects anything but a girl's friendship," Peggy added. But then, he was "more interested in oil than girls anyway."

James Montgomery Flagg was deeply interested in girls. A celebrated New York illustrator, Flagg had been a member of the opening-night audience of *Miss 1917*, and although he presumably felt as relieved as everyone else when the final curtain fell, the image of the glamorous blonde in the iridescent tail feathers lingered in his mind, especially since her picture had been picked up by magazines like *Vanity Fair,* which announced to the world that the incorrigible Peggy Hopkins had "gone and made a peacock feather her personal emblem."

Like Charles Dana Gibson, father of the Gibson Girl, and John Held Jr., creator of the archetypical flapper, Flagg drew the quintessential women of his age, and his pen-and-ink images of elegant urbanites at play defined an era. Though he was best known for his memorable "I Want You" poster of Uncle Sam, his portfolio included depictions of all the important society women of his day (a decade later he would draw a soignée Peggy Hopkins Joyce), along with virtually every notable actor and actress of Broadway and Hollywood. He also wrote plays and movies, and between 1917 and 1920 he created two dozen short satirical films, including twelve one-reelers grouped under the title *Girls You Know* that sketched recognizable feminine types. Peggy had not yet entered the orbit of women with whom Flagg typically traveled; in his autobiography, he described her only as a "beautiful young blonde, from Dixie, the Land of Man-Traps." But her name buzzed in the air, and as a result, she was cast in starring roles in two of his movies.

One was a forgotten effort called *Hick Manhattan*. The other, part of the *Girls You Know* series, was called *The Bride*. Given Peggy's past, not to mention her future, the casting represented a small stroke of inspiration. A gentle spoof of conventional weddings that included a nod to the star's already noticeable penchant for collecting spouses, the ten-minute black-and-white silent follows a young woman whose plans to elope go comically awry when her father intervenes and insists on a proper wedding. Peggy is first seen in bed, her hair adorably mussed and one strap of her lacy nightgown falling suggestively off her shoulder. "Will you be our bride?" a title asks. "You only promise to love, honor, and obey us for a thousand feet or one reel." She smiles. "Oh yes, one is never too busy to get married—charming habit." Before long Peggy makes her appearance in a bridal gown, a minister delivers a stream of blather—"If at first you don't succeed, wed, wed again"—and the film ends with the bride perched cozily on her husband's knees, her corkscrew curls brushing his shoulder as they struggle to drink from the same coffee cup. The concluding title, "Be it ever so humble, there's no husband like the first," was a nice touch that could not have helped but make audiences smile in knowing appreciation.

The film was an inconsequential bit of fluff—its plot thin, its style wooden, its merits negligible. On-screen, Peggy does little more than parade about in fussy costumes, and her only gesture involves gazing up soulfully from beneath deeply lowered lids. But the provocative mixture of innocence and savvy that was fast becoming her trademark was much in evidence. And though most of the women associated with these early Flagg films were quickly forgotten, Peggy's role provided yet another reason for the news media to pay attention to her, suggesting the potential power of even a minor one-reeler.

Suddenly newspapers and magazines all around town began running glamorous publicity stills from *The Bride,* especially an image that featured Peggy in a feathery black dress cut daringly low in back to reveal an alluring expanse of white skin. It had become accepted wisdom that she was one of the world's great beauties, perhaps right up there with Cleopatra, or, as the *New York Star* put it, one of the "most widely famed beauties of the century." James Montgomery Flagg had "selected eight of New York's most beautiful girls with a view to starring each in a production," gushed the *Morning Telegraph,* "and Miss Hopkins was chosen by Mr. Flagg as the most beautiful of the number." Around the time *The Bride* was released came the announcement that she would soon star in a musical extravaganza called *Peggy of the Follies* or in something with the dead-on title *Peggy Behave.* Like so many other projects her name was linked with, nothing more was heard of either idea, but the

mere mentions suggested that the comely Miss Hopkins was in demand on numerous fronts.

Although Peggy maintained a hint of innocence in *The Bride,* there
was nothing innocent about her next movie role, as the showgirl mistress of a South American playboy in *The Woman and the Law.* The
Fox film, written and directed by Raoul Walsh, a protégé of the legendary D. W. Griffith, was a thinly disguised account of the trial of
Blanca De Saulles, whose murder of her ex-husband had made headlines the previous summer and whose brother, Billy Errazuriz, had,
by a remarkable coincidence, been Peggy's suitor during her early
Ziegfeld days.

Lurid details of the proceedings had filled the papers, and in promoting the movie, Fox went all out to remind audiences of the true-
life incident that inspired it, the "internationally sensational De
Saulles domestic tragedy, which shocked not only the United States
but South America as well." The studio suggested that theaters install
in their lobbies a cardboard model of a blind figure of Justice, her
scales operated by a clock-type mechanism so as to swing ominously
between the words *life* and *death.* The opening-night program posed
the question: "Are there provocations which justify a woman to kill?"

Although not the star, Peggy had landed one of the juicier roles.
An overheated title describes the husband's mistress, Josie Sabel, as
"that type of woman which infests hotels—her professional smiles
drawing men into her web of destruction." Worse, she smokes; ads for
the film featured an image of Josie in sexily curved French heels and
a dangerously short skirt accepting a light from her lover.

In view of Josie's wanton ways, the casting struck movie insiders as
pure genius. Peggy was "a high-class tramp," wrote Miriam Cooper,
the director's wife, who was starring in her husband's movie. "She
wasn't very smart, either, and it was easy to keep the real meaning of
the role from her."

In fact, not until the premiere at Broadway's Lyric Theatre on March 3, 1918, when Peggy was sitting in the front of the house admiring her image on the screen, did she realize just how nasty a trick Walsh had played on her. As a title flashed noting that Josie lives "in a luxurious apartment where she entertains nobility and taxi drivers with equal adroitness," Peggy leaped from her seat with a howl and raced up the aisle through the darkened theater in search of the director. "Where's that son of a bitch?" she shouted. "I'll kill him!" Walsh ducked into the ticket booth until his pursuer calmed down, but even the critics seemed to be in on the joke. As *Variety* wrote with a broad nudge, "Peggy Hopkins as the adventuress who weaned [the husband] away from his family cleverly simulated a young lady of loose morals."

In two years Peggy had moved from vaudeville to the *Follies* to the movies. The next logical step was a Broadway play, which in those days meant the brothers Shubert, the most influential theater operators in America. The pair controlled the lion's share of playhouses in New York and throughout the country—at one point nine hundred theaters in the United States acquired their shows through the Shubert organization—and the words *Shubert* and *theater* had become virtually synonymous. For anyone who wanted to make a career on the stage, the immaculately tailored Lee and the perennially rumpled J. J. were the men to know.

As described in Peggy's memoirs, their overtures had all the earmarks of her typical courtships, surprising her and making her briefly ecstatic. "The Shuberts called up today, that is Lee did," Peggy wrote. "He wants me to come and see him about a play, he said. I am quite thrilled because of course that shows that I have been a success, but I am very nervous because I have heard Mr. Shubert is very severe although a wonderful producer."

Whether events moved as rapidly as she suggested, there was no question that the offer arrived at an opportune moment. Despite her dazzling appearance, Ziegfeld would not have been unhappy to let Peggy go; although she considered herself one of his pets, she never ranked among his favorites and any early glimmers of promise had failed to materialize, as he tacitly acknowledged by giving her a diminished part in *Miss 1917.* The Shuberts, in turn, were always delighted to steal performers from their most formidable rival, and Peggy's was a name audiences were becoming increasingly familiar with, if not always for professional reasons. Lee in particular might have been eager to take Peggy under his wing, for although the producer was a chronic workaholic, he made time for beautiful showgirls. It was not long before his newest ingenue was seen clinging to his arm as he escorted her to openings around town, and Broadway gossips were soon claiming she owed her career, not to mention her Russian sable coat, to the short, dapper producer with the jet-black hair. Whether or not Lee had presented her with the coat in question was never clear; Lee was not the sort of man known for making expensive gifts to his myriad female companions. But Peggy better than most women of her age understood the benefits to be gained from intimacy with powerful figures, and it would have been easy to overlook any stinginess in the face of his other considerable attributes.

Peggy's first outing with the Shubert organization, in April 1918, was a slight comedy called *It Pays to Flirt,* starring Clifton Webb. The production proved so dreadful it was hissed during its tryout in New Haven and closed out of town before it could inflict further harm. She fared little better with her next effort, an English trifle called *A Place in the Sun* that opened on Broadway later that year. Peggy, who received top billing with the actor Norman Trevor and the playwright Cyril Harcourt, portrayed the sister of a wastrel baronet who makes peace between two warring households and, as befits such a piece of froth, ends up lucky in love herself.

But in a season that included George S. Kaufman's first Broadway play, George Gershwin's first Broadway musical, Sergeant Irving

Berlin singing "Oh, How I Hate to Get Up in the Morning" in *Yip! Yip! Yaphank,* and a pair of O'Neill works staged by the Provincetown Players, *A Place in the Sun* could hardly have expected to shine brightly in the theatrical firmament. Matters were not helped by the opening-night gaffe in which Peggy made her entrance and began reciting her lines a good ten seconds before the hoofbeats of the horse she had allegedly galloped in on.

Although the critics were kind enough not to dwell on that embarrassing incident, most of them loathed the play, and they hated the star even more. "At least two shockingly bad performances were disclosed last night," wrote Heywood Broun in the *New York Tribune*. "Miss Peggy Hopkins, the leading woman, was hugely inadequate. She also played the piano badly." (He did concede that he liked her ermine coat.) Another critic concluded, "'A Place in the Sun' is about the worst play it would be possible to witness—and live," and as for the female star, "as a comedian she does not exist." Charles Darnton of the *Evening World* chimed in, "She is about as convincing as a doll hanging from the limb of a Christmas tree."

That one stung. "One of the papers says I am only a dressed-up doll and cannot act and I have been crying terribly because when a girl tries as hard as I do the critics could at least be kind," Peggy lamented in her memoirs. "A girl ought not to mind what the critics say, but I do somehow. I feel very blue and dispirited." At that moment, or so she claimed, a doorman bearing an armful of bouquets appeared at her dressing-room door. "I wish the critic who said I was only a dressed-up doll could see them," she wrote. "After all flowers mean a lot to a girl when the critics pan her."

She was also receiving consolation from another quarter, millionaire playboy Cornelius Vanderbilt Whitney, descendant of two of America's richest families. Though Sonny Whitney had been barred from joining a senior society at Yale because of an unfortunate breach-of-promise suit by an ex-*Follies* dancer, he was apparently unrepentant and provided considerable comfort to Peggy during her time of need. "Sonny, who comes to matinees and sends me flowers, has been wonderful, really too sweet, and he says I am great in the part and all the rest of the cast is terrible," she wrote. "I do think Sonny is the sweetest boy and the most perfect gentlemen I have ever met."

Dressed-up doll or not, the Shuberts found another production for Peggy, a bedroom farce called *A Sleepless Night,* about the misadventures of four young people at a house party. In it she portrayed a willful young woman who wants to be known as a Greenwich Village radical and pays what is delicately described as a "negligee call" to a gentleman's bedroom. "It is a great success," Peggy wrote of the opening at the Bijou in February 1919. "For once the critics are very kind." As she remembered it, Alan Dale of the *New York American* noted that "Shubert has a star who will make him money," the *New York Journal* described her as "the loveliest creature that ever bestrode the bright lights," and the man from the *World* said, "Peggy Hopkins is her own beautiful self in 'Sleepless Night' and developed unsuspected histrionic powers." She was not quite sure what histrionic powers were, but they sounded enchanting.

In her eyes, she was always the critics' darling, unless they were simply being horrible for some inexplicable reason having little to do with her talents. On this occasion, however, it was her elaborately constructed lilac satin pajamas that came in for most of the attention, along with the canopy bed draped with rose silk in which she disported herself, along with a cast that included Eugene O'Neill's future wife, Carlotta Monterey. Nor did the critics respond to her performance quite as she remembered it. Alan Dale suggested that at one point during the performance Peggy appeared to have fallen asleep. The man from the *Journal of Commerce*—the only *Journal* the Shuberts saw fit to cite in their roster of quotable reviews—while describing her as "charming," could not help acknowledging the crucial role of her attire in her performance. And the critic from the *World,* observing that the ingenue had been well supported, noted acidly, "To this extent she is fortunate, for surely no other young actress in the process of being forced into prominence for which she is not fitted by ability or experience is so desperately in need of support."

Theater critics, however, were secondary to Peggy's real public, her expanding stable of beaux and those reporters who covered society. She was living on Fifth Avenue and had started subscribing to a clipping service that diligently tracked news of her comings and goings. Anyone following the activities of the smart set during those years would have noticed how frequently the name Peggy Hopkins was appearing in the newspapers, not just on the theater pages but in the society columns as well.

Although actual gossip columns would not emerge until the 1920s, an embryonic gossip press had developed several decades earlier. These publications—there were really just two—were known as society journals, and they took considerable malicious delight in reporting on the doings of the rich and famous and blowing the whistle on their peccadilloes. The first such journal, *Town Topics,* was founded in the 1880s by a New York patent attorney named Louis Keller, who went on to start the *Social Register*. Although *Town Topics*'s infamous editor, Colonel William D'Alton Mann, was a person of "highly suspect reputation where blackmail was concerned," according to social chronicler Cleveland Amory, the publication was great fun to read. "When someone tells us a long story about mice in China, culled from the Encyclopedia Britannica, we are bored," *Town Topics* once boasted in an advertisement. "When we hear of Mrs. Brown's latest indiscretion, we are thrilled." The identities of culprits were sometimes artfully concealed, but readers got the point. Some years later came *Broadway Brevities,* whose editor, Stephen Clow, also found that blackmail—forcing his subjects to pay up sizable amounts of money to keep unpleasant personal tidbits out of the paper—was an efficient way to raise funds.

Given her lively lifestyle, Peggy was an irresistible subject for these publications, and *Town Topics* especially delighted in tracking her activities during those years. But even the more mainstream press found her endlessly fascinating. Seemingly no event, regardless of how trivial, failed to merit a paragraph or two. When she bobbed her hair, the news burned up the telegraph wires. When she acquired a pet goat, newspapers as far away as Toledo featured photographs of the little creature nestled in the arms of its new mistress, both of them wearing cheerful expressions. Entire articles were devoted to the lilac pajamas she had worn while cavorting about the stage of the Bijou, although critical opinion was divided as to whether the pajamas in question were lilac, lavender, or perhaps mauve. The New York *Evening Mail* ran a contest—"Can you design an Easter bonnet for Peggy?"—with the promise that the subject of the competition would wear the winning design on stage. "For your guidance," the entry form noted, "Miss Hopkins is a peach blonde."

There were even reports that the spurned Sherburne Hopkins had reentered the picture. "What a blow to the Broadway brethren when pretty Peggy Hopkins decided to go back to her husband from whom she had been separated for a couple of years," *Town Topics* had written some months earlier. "When he was an unromantic civilian, Peggy left the Washington dovecote and hit the high spots in the metropolis. Now that hubby has enlisted and started his service to his country by catching pneumonia in a Texas camp, his fair spouse turned out to be no more hero-proof than the rest of her sex, and she rushed off to join her liege lord."

In fact, the two did meet briefly, and Sherburne, at least, nursed hopes of a reconciliation. "Dearest sweetheart," he wrote from his army camp in Texas after her visit. "Have sneaked away a few moments to write you a little note. . . . I don't suppose you have given stupid old me much thought since you left here. But I am going to hope differently, and if I hope in vain, why I am simply 'out of luck.' I am just really and truly realizing what a wonderful difference your coming here has made to me. You know, dear, since a certain time in

February 1915 I have not much cared what became of me, or where I was, or who with, because there was only just me, and there will only be just one sweetheart for me. But things look different now, and it still seems that we may go down life's path together after all, if you will hold to what you told me, and if my prayers and work and thoughts can help at all. I have dreamed some wonderful daydreams of what maybe we shall do in the day to come. Won't you, too, do a little wishing that they come true?"

A separation of several years had apparently transformed Sherburne from something of a dullard into an ardent wooer, at least on paper. But however impassioned his pleas, Peggy was never the type to look back. Though she didn't bother with an actual divorce just at that moment, she made no further effort to pursue a rapprochement, and speculation about old romances quickly gave way to even more intense speculation about new flames. "Although it came about quite by chance, Angy Duke enjoyed his meeting with Peggy Hopkins at the Beaux Arts on Saturday evening, and he tripped the light fantastic with her for about an hour," a *Town Topics* writer babbled in a typical item, describing her encounter with tobacco heir Angier Buchanan Duke at a chic New York nightspot. "Peggy, needless to say, was enthusiastic about Angy's attentions. Later I again ran across Peggy at a midnight rendezvous farther uptown, and she confined her hoofing to a solitary dapper young fellow, who appeared to resent any intrusion from her numerous footlight or society acquaintances."

After the show ended, such nights on the town were common, and the winter of 1918–19 was an especially exhilarating time to be out and about in New York. The war had just ended, the great flu epidemic was abating, and despite ratification of the Eighteenth Amendment in January, Prohibition would not go into effect for another year. Getting home exhausted and disheveled at four in the morning after a riotous night made more riotous by the amount of champagne consumed was pretty much routine in Peggy's busy calendar.

The intensity of life around Times Square, where much of this carousing took place, felt almost tangible, not only inside the theaters, the clubs, and the restaurants but on the streets themselves, so ablaze with electric lights they appeared brighter after dark than during the day. As dusk fell, the crowds thickened to include an endlessly shifting parade of humanity—"Wall Street financiers, industrial magnates, gilded fractions of the Four Hundred, gaudy playboys, journalists, celebrities from the Bohemia of the arts, the greatest stars of the theater, gamblers, jockeys, pugilists, professional beauties, chorus girls, kept women," as one social historian describes the throng. The phrase *crossroads of the world* hardly did the district justice.

"Take me to Rectors," Eddie Cantor had warbled in his *Follies* number "The Modern Maiden's Prayer," and the famous lobster palace reigned as the undisputed capital of Times Square. "The supreme shrine of the cult of pleasure," the same historian calls the restaurant, "the American cathedral of froth and frivolity, the terminus of the primrose path, the tabernacle of that small hot bird and large cold bottle." Typically, the small hot bird was not of the culinary variety, but the food was first-rate, too. Diamond Jim Brady had been a famous regular, slurping down four dozen oysters, half a dozen lobsters, and much more at a single sitting. One could linger and mingle until the wee hours, at which point everyone headed over to Jack's on Sixth Avenue for an early breakfast, after which it really was time to call it a night.

For a woman who loved attention, such places offered the ideal environment for seeing and being seen, and Peggy was definitely acquiring a reputation as someone who adored being seen. Her picture was appearing regularly in all the glossy magazines—*Vanity Fair, Vogue, Harper's Bazaar*—whose copywriters waxed as rapturous about her clothes as about the lady herself. "Miss Peggy Hopkins is wearing a three-fourth length sable coat and two new frocks from Joseph," reported *Town and Country*. "The cloak speaks for itself. The effect achieved in the chiffon at the right is called 'the wild rose dress,' the chiffon taking the shades of the leaves and the roses the tints of the natural blossoms. The dinner gown is of lightweight black chiffon embroidered in a spiderweb design with jet sphinxes and steel beads. A rose ostrich tip is perched on the shoulders."

In between carousing and being photographed, Peggy was putting in her hours on the stage. *A Sleepless Night* lasted only a couple of months on Broadway, but by the late spring of 1919 the production had packed up and begun traveling west toward Chicago. Peggy had learned by now that each bounce in her public life led to a corresponding lift in her personal life, that each new role brought a new army of admirers, a new rush of gifts and social engagements, and made her fresh fodder for the journalists who delighted in recording the whole giddy scene. Heading out with the cast, Peggy was on her way. The next bounce would be the big one.

4

"It Is Marvelous to Be Rich"

James Stanley Joyce, whose greatest claim to fame consisted of bestowing his name on Peggy Hopkins Joyce, was an extremely wealthy man from an extremely wealthy place. His hometown, Clinton, Iowa, was the lumber capital of the Mississippi Valley in the late nineteenth century, and there were said to be more millionaires in a single block—"home of thirteen millionaires, all at one time," a local history crowed—than in any other comparably sized spot in the world.

The Clinton rich "breathed a different air" from other men. They threw lavish parties for which food, wine, and flowers were shipped in by rail, and they amused themselves by taking leisurely pleasure cruises up and down the Mississippi. To house themselves and their families, they erected splendid mansions on a bluff just outside the city that offered breathtaking views of the water. William Joyce, James Stanley's father, had built a particularly magnificent specimen, a cream-colored outpouring of Victoriana bristling with turrets, gables, and the decorative gingerbread carvings one might expect from a man who had made his money in wood.

Like many other affluent sons of the Midwest, James Stanley was shipped east as a teenager. He spent a year prepping at Andover and then headed for Yale, or more precisely to the university's Sheffield

Scientific School. Since Sheffield specialized in practical matters like engineering and a man could be admitted without knowing Greek or Latin, the institution lacked the social panache of Yale proper. But Stanley, as he was called, was not blessed with much social panache either, despite his family's fortune. A slight, unprepossessing figure, he had been something of a mama's boy, and one could see traces of his personality in his yearbook picture: he gazes out at the world from behind steel-rimmed glasses, his pale, serious face set off by a high forehead and delicate features that give him a sensitive, almost poetic air.

After an unremarkable academic career, he graduated with the class of 1910 and made his home in Chicago, where the family business was by then based. When the alumnus was asked for an update on his activities a decade later, he sent back a brief note reporting that he voted Republican, had joined the usual clubs, and "had been engaged in the manufacturing business in Chicago ever since graduation." He did not mention that starting in May of 1919 he was spending nearly all his evenings in a box of the city's Wood's Theater, smiling shyly at an alluring blonde in lilac pajamas.

Stanley Joyce was not the only Chicago male enjoying the sight of Peggy that first spring after the war. "Eight telephone calls in my box when I got home from the theater tonight, and I did not know one of the men," she complained in her memoirs. "Will they never let me alone?" In truth, she had little to grumble about, for the year 1919 was an ideal time for a high-spirited young woman to be passing through the city. New Orleans jazz bands had arrived not long before, and audiences quickly decided that dancing to the catchy new music was even more fun than simply listening. At the College Inn, a lively late-night hangout popular with Peggy and her friends, Isham Jones, the city's favorite band leader, was about to introduce Chicagoans to such instant classics as "It Had to Be You." In theater, Chicago ranked second only to New York in terms of lavish playhouses and productions. With the Eighteenth Amendment already a reality and the enforcement of Prohibition on the horizon, liquor flowed more plentifully than ever.

Peggy adored the fast pace of Chicago life and lapped her up new experiences hungrily. "The Chicago men are splendid," she wrote. "I have met a lot of them, they are not so smooth as New York men, they laugh and joke more, and I think they drink more too, but they certainly know how to spend money." By day she was comfortably installed at the glamorous Blackstone Hotel, whose lobby gleamed with gilt sconces and mahogany paneling. By night, after the curtain fell on *A Sleepless Night,* she was brushing up against everyone from alleged gangsters to a rakish young newspaperman named Charles MacArthur, who dreamed of writing plays. But the owlish-looking creature in the box remained a mystery. "Really, he is making me nervous," Peggy admitted. "I hope he is not an anarchist or something."

It was her friend Francine Larrimore, a young actress who was also performing in Chicago that season, who introduced the two, pointing him out one June evening right before showtime as the two women peeked from behind the curtain.

"Who's the boob?" Peggy reportedly demanded, according to a subsequent newspaper account of her first encounter with Joyce.

"He's a man who is crazy to meet you," Francine answered. "He has all sorts of money."

Peggy was unimpressed. "He can stay where he is," she replied, throwing her friend a look.

The final night of the run, Francine invited Stanley and a companion to dine at the Blackstone grill. "Personally," Peggy confessed in her memoirs, "I would rather I had got the other man who was tall and blond and not Mr. Joyce who was small and quite uninteresting, or rather unpresuming." His vast fortune did not interest her: "Lumber does not sound very romantic, and anyway I have no use for lumber." Her date, however, was smitten. Although he said very little over supper, he urged Peggy to postpone her departure, and to whet her appetite he showed her his car, a Mercedes Simplex. That did not do much for her, either, but he persisted. "Well," he announced amiably, "I will get you any car you want."

Peggy was in a slightly more receptive mood the following morning when Stanley appeared at her hotel bearing a large emerald. "Really it was very nice of him," she admitted in her account of their courtship. "Of course I would rather have had a diamond but anyway I suppose Emeralds are worth a little money to. So I have agreed to stay over one more day and here I am." Her stay stretched from one day to several weeks. Over that period she must have warmed to him slightly, because when he asked her to marry him during a romantic dinner at the Blackstone, she did not immediately turn him down. Although she demurred at first—"I said that was ridiculous I did not know him very well and besides I was married already"—her ears perked up when he promised to help her get a divorce. Then he did something even smarter; he gave her the diamond she had wanted in the first place.

Stanley continued pressing his case after Peggy returned to New York, telephoning several times a day and sending great bouquets of orchids and roses to her suite at the Gotham Hotel. Wisely, she had taken the emerald to a jeweler and had been gratified to learn the stone was worth an impressive $20,000. Very soon Stanley himself appeared on her doorstep, promising all the things a rich man in love promised in those days. He offered to put a railroad car at her disposal, and as a token of his good intentions he presented her with a platinum watch. He also set her up in an expensively appointed apartment on Park Avenue above a florist.

Finally in August, when the two met by prearrangement for a vacation in Colorado Springs and it was clear that Stanley's generosity showed no signs of abating, Peggy agreed to marry him. "After all, I have to get a divorce and divorces cost money and Stanley loves me and has the money," she wrote of his entreaties, "so maybe I had better do what he says." She did not delude herself into thinking she loved him, and while she recognized that her behavior had little to recommend it morally, any qualms she might have suffered were quickly dispelled. "I am wondering if I am really mercenary," she wrote. "Perhaps I am, but it is better to be mercenary than miserable."

The very month Peggy was being wooed in Chicago, a development was taking place a thousand miles away that would alter her life even more than marriage to a lumber king. On June 26, 1919, the *Illustrated Daily News* hit the streets of New York. Papers had traded in sensationalism in the past—there was nothing restrained about the penny press of the 1830s or the yellow journalism that helped plunge the country into the Spanish-American War—but this gritty upstart, the brainchild of Chicago publisher Joseph Medill Patterson, was unlike anything seen before. Though only half the size of a regular broadsheet, it fairly screamed its tidings via enormous headlines set in bold black type. Its language, drawn from the newly emerging slang of the day, was tough and brisk; the vigorous, grab-'em-by-the-lapels tone caught and echoed the strident rhythms of the city itself. And although earlier newspapers had included photographs, the new tabloid was positively brimming with images that depicted everyone from heiresses and tycoons to gangsters and murderers.

The newcomer, soon to be rechristened simply the *Daily News,* was the first modern American tabloid, the harbinger of a generation of newspapers that would reshape the country's journalism and provide the means by which Peggy and countless others like her would make a name for themselves. These papers helped create a new breed of celebrity, figures whose fame sprang not from real achievement but from the clarity of their images and the amount of ink and newsprint they commanded.

The *Daily News,* whose boast that it offered the "best fiction in New York" was not far off the mark, quickly established itself as the most popular paper in town. By 1924 two more tabloids began publishing in New York, William Randolph Hearst's *Daily Mirror* and

Bernarr Macfadden's *New York Evening Graphic,* and nearly a dozen more were flourishing in cities across the country. That same year the *News* became the nation's largest-circulation daily, with 750,000 readers; its circulation would soon top one million.

The swelling audiences for these new papers included both Americans who had not gone past grade school and millions of immigrants struggling with the complexities of English; in recognition, the papers offered news that was simple, dramatic, and most of all fun to read. They did not dwell on the subtleties of foreign policy or the intricacies of political debate. Instead, they concentrated on the verities of human existence—love, hate, life, and death, the gorier the better. They cared not about abstractions but about the grit and glitter of real life—the sexy blonde, the pool of blood, the staccato of the gunman's bullets.

The emphasis was on personalities, on heroes, villains, and the women who loved and loathed them. Which sharp-suited mobster had gunned down his rival? Which Broadway biggie had set up his latest chorine in a love nest? Which slimy pol had been caught yet again with his hand in the municipal till? What was the wily Dillinger up to, and the irrepressible Mayor Jimmy Walker, and sizzling Clara Bow? These were the people the tabs cared about, the larger-than-life figures whose escapades made good yarns, who stayed in character long enough for readers to learn to recognize them, but added new twists to their stories to hold the public's attention. Nor was it just the news pages that brimmed with their exploits but also the quickly proliferating gossip columns by such virtuoso tattlers as Walter Winchell, whose punchy reports for the *Evening Graphic* and later the *Daily Mirror* epitomized the spirit of the new publications.

These papers, so fresh, so racy, so snappy, were the truest expression of a country on the verge of sweeping change. The twenties were, of course, far more than the images that came to symbolize the era— the speakeasies and bathtub gin, the flappers with shingled hair and rouged knees, the upward jag of the stock tables, all set to the bouncy rhythms of jazz, the era's ubiquitous soundtrack. But these images vividly embodied many of the values and most of the myths of this extraordinary, incandescent period: its cynicism, its voracious appetites, its heedlessness, and especially its preoccupation with sex, money, and glamour, the decade's holy trinity. And few worshiped at the altar of these deities more passionately than the woman shortly to become Peggy Hopkins Joyce.

Tailor-made for the tabs, Peggy was the "city editor's dream girl," as one chronicler of Jazz Age journalism describes her. The scrappy little papers needed stories; they needed new types of heroes and villains. Peggy was ideally poised to take advantage of this new medium, and she did so with her usual aplomb. The tabloids would forge her image, and that image would sell newspapers: it was like the alignment of the planets.

Having left the cast of *A Sleepless Night* after the play ended its Chicago engagement, Peggy more or less severed her ties with the Shubert organization. Next on her agenda was obtaining the divorce from Sherburne Hopkins that would make possible her marriage to Stanley Joyce. Although a man as desperately in love as Stanley would presumably have been happy to help her, as he had promised, it was her own lawyers who actually handled the matter; and for various complicated legal reasons, it proved no easy task. "You have no idea how hard it was," William Klein, her attorney, wrote her. But by the end of 1919, after months of wrangling, the divorce appeared to be going through. Peggy counted down the days in fashionable Palm Beach, where despite her status as an engaged woman she found more than enough men eager to escort her to teas and dances, take her on moonlight cruises aboard their yachts, and squire her to Bradley's Beach Club, the smartest gambling establishment this side of Monte Carlo.

As usual she had another attentive audience. "The photographers are always snapping me here, especially on the Breakers beach, where a girl must wear stockings if she bathes," she wrote in her memoirs. "I think this is a ridiculous custom because a girl has to wear a garter belt and the salt water spoils it and also ruins expensive silk stockings. I suppose a lot of old rich ladies with hair on their legs got together and made that rule. However I have some wonderful bathing costumes and beautiful bathing wraps and it is really not necessary to bathe actually, just sit on the beach."

Finally, on January 21, 1920, Peggy received word that her divorce had been granted. Two days later, on January 23, she and Stanley were married before Dade County judge W. Frank Blanton in a Miami courthouse. As with her previous marriages, the ceremony was quick and quiet; despite her frequent trips to the altar, Peggy never went in for fancy weddings. The ceremony, however, was not the point. The point was the bridegroom's fortune and how it would change her life.

Years later, when regaling Charlie Chaplin with tales about her marriage to Stanley, Peggy often described how she locked herself in her bedroom on her wedding night and refused to let her new husband enter until he shoved a $500,000 check under the door. What was more, she added, "I cashed it the first thing in the morning before he was awake," because in her mercenary little heart she trusted no one, not even a worshipful spouse. The story, though apocryphal, spoke volumes about her priorities.

Those priorities had been on display since Peggy's Ziegfeld days, when the phrase *gold digger* first attached itself to her. Some people even claimed the term had been coined by a Hearst newspaperman to describe Peggy and her behavior, although in reality, the expression had made an appearance around 1915, and a few years later playwright Avery Hopwood selected it as the title of a comedy that began a long Broadway run during the 1919–20 season.

Whatever the origins of the phrase, the gold digger was a type peculiar to her century. With her peroxide curls, her full-length mink, and her grating nasal accent, it was no wonder she became one of the stock comic figures of the day, for the type was a familiar one on the landscape. The twenties offered particularly fertile soil for the cultivation of the breed: a great many people were terrifically rich, and an enormous amount of money seemed to be floating around, available not only to men who scored a killing in the stock market but also to women who played their cards right. It was an age of speculation, and Peggy proved as adept as any stockbroker in making something out of nothing. Starting out with little more than good looks, brazen charm, and a fierce desire to improve her lot in life, she soon found herself married to one of the richer men of her day. And she did so during a period that gave high marks to such shows of enterprise. The twenties were a time of sweeping changes that were reshaping virtually every aspect of life. Boundaries between classes were crumbling, bringing a new social fluidity. Growing sexual freedom for women was transforming relationships. Popular culture was exploding. On all fronts, it was an exhilarating era, one that prized adventurousness, scams, and daring, and promised the possibility of huge rewards. In such a climate, Peggy came across as a joyous figure, pursuing her ambitions with an air of happy abandon.

Though the gold digger is a comic, not a tragic figure, she is not totally uncomplicated. While men adored these creatures, they were also made slightly uneasy by them. It was appealing to have a glamorous plaything whose favors could be bought for no more than the price of a fashionable apartment, a generous allowance, and a regular supply of steak dinners and expensive jewelry. But in making such a hard-nosed exchange, these women exhibited not only a deep cynicism but also a degree of power, which is one reason men felt a certain anxiety in their presence. Men were also made uncomfortable by females who so flagrantly flouted the social rules designed to keep people in their place. Unlike the courtesans of Europe, who occupied an established and respected niche, the American gold digger was a renegade; there was nothing subtle, or admirable, about her methods or her goals.

Even if the phrase was not invented for Peggy, all agreed that she was the perfect embodiment of the type. And having married a man for his assets, she intended to lose no time tearing into them.

Her first order of business was housing. The gingerbread mansion in Clinton was clearly out of the question; local legend had it that Peggy stayed there one night and immediately boarded a train back to Chicago in disgust. Even more absurd was the tract of land Stanley had bought in the Minnesota north woods in the pathetic hope that his bride might enjoy occasionally roughing it. She wanted something flashy, or as she announced to her husband, "I think a home in Miami out in Coconut Grove would be nice to start with."

The real estate boom that would turn Miami into paradise lay a few years in the future. But by 1920 Coconut Grove was rapidly becoming the last word in elegant semitropical living, so much so that the strip of Brickell Avenue along Biscayne Bay had already earned the name Millionaire's Row. Most famously, Brickell Avenue was the address of Villa Vizcaya, a sumptuous pile that served as the winter quarters of International Harvester tycoon James Deering. His faux Renaissance palace, five years in the making, sat on a 160-acre estate, and estimates of its cost reached $22 million, not all that much, considering that Deering's taste ran to French tapestries and antique marble statuary.

Down the road stood Villa Serena, the slightly less palatial home of the area's most famous winter guest, former presidential candidate William Jennings Bryan. Next door to Villa Serena was a sprawling white Mission-style structure that had originally been built for New York businessman Clarence M. Busch. The house was set in a grove of palms and perched on a cliff overlooking the water. While less grand than Bryan's place, the fourteen-room mansion was grand enough, and on January 31 the *Miami Metropolis* reported that "Mr. and Mrs. Stanley Joyce of Chicago have bought the beautiful

Clarence M. Busch home and furnishings on Brickell Avenue and the bay adjoining the William Jennings Bryan estate for a consideration believed to have been close to $200,000." The furnishings, added the newspaper, included "a large number of costly antiques gathered by Mr. Busch from the four corners of the globe."

Even in Miami, no stranger to conspicuous consumption, the purchase itself and the woman who would serve as chatelaine raised eyebrows. "Florida [has] long been accustomed to dazzling displays of affluence, but even at that, Miami is rubbing its eyes over the extravagance of Peggy Hopkins, who recently married James Stanley Joyce," *Town Topics* wrote a month after the wedding. "Peggy, in the most sumptuous attire and the most magnificent jewels, is very much in evidence."

"It is marvelous to be rich," Peggy wrote in her memoirs of her latest acquisition. As for the house itself: "It is full of the most wonderful furniture. Some of the chairs are not very comfortable but they are valuable antiques and of course I can always buy new chairs." She herself would sleep in a bed that had belonged to a maharajah, or so she was informed.

Her infatuation with her precious furniture lasted for two weeks, until the evening a slightly overweight visitor from Chicago sat down hard on one of her priceless chairs and ended up sprawled on the floor. "The antiques are going out tomorrow or as soon as I can get a decorator and some new comfortable furniture," the mortified hostess concluded. "I don't care how much they cost and antiques may be antiques, but when a chair breaks and lets fall on the floor your most prominent guest, what does it matter if it costs a million?"

Taking a cue from Deering, Peggy decided it would be charming to keep pet monkeys, but they proved troublesome too; a neighbor complained about the smell emanating from her monkey house. She found his behavior in shockingly bad taste, and in any event she had no intention of accommodating him. "There is no other place to put my monkey house," she argued, "and I cannot keep my monkeys in the house very well, can I?" Besides, she added: "They do not smell half as bad as all that. . . . Anyone who doesn't like it can move away. And anyway some people are more objectionable than any monkey."

Still another problem involved Stanley's yacht. He wanted a new one, but Peggy thought it more prudent to invest the money in a $300,000 string of pearls. Although the necklace would cost even more than her house, at least it would not require any expensive upkeep, as she reminded her husband the evening she curled up in his lap and drew on her considerable arsenal of charm in an effort to help him see reason. "Really I think I am doing the right thing," she insisted in her memoirs. "Besides, I am always seasick on yachts and a pearl necklace will be wonderful."

Without a new yacht, they had no use for the dock, so Peggy replaced it with an $80,000 marble swimming pool fringed by coconut palms, a decorative outpouring even Deering admired when he strolled down from his seventy-room palace to pay a visit. She had acquired ten additional monkeys to play in the trees; she only hoped they would not spoil the orchids she had had grafted onto the branches. "The monkeys smell a little bit of course," she admitted, "but really one can't have everything and they are so cute." As a final flourish she added a few white leghorn chickens "because eggs are so expensive and anyway they are the smartest kind of chickens, everybody has them."

Although the marriage clearly offered Peggy immediate advantages, discord set in almost from the start. While Stanley was often on the road tending to business, when he was at home even the most trivial incidents caused tempers to flare. He bought his wife a set of golf clubs mounted with her initials in silver, but the time she moved her ball to an easier lie after it careened into the rocks he muttered darkly, "So that's the way you win, is it?" Peggy was so incensed she nearly lunged at him with one of her beautiful new irons. "I cried and quit and I think golf is a stupid game anyway," she concluded. "My maid can have my clubs."

A far nastier explosion around the same period occurred the day Stanley discovered his wife posing for a society photographer taking pictures of attractive women on the beach. Enraged, he knocked the camera out of the startled man's hands and shoved him unceremoniously into the water.

"You are making an exhibition of yourself!" Stanley hissed as he dragged his wife back to the house.

"Well, what do you think you are doing?" she shot back.

Peggy was livid, especially now that she had finally gotten a toehold in Coconut Grove society, and she was terrified that her wealthy Palm Beach neighbor Mrs. Horace Dodge, the automaker's wife, had witnessed the whole humiliating episode. "I wish you could have heard what I told Stanley when we got home," she wrote. "He will not do it again in a hurry."

That might have been the night she cracked a champagne bottle over his head so hard he had to be rushed to the hospital, an incident she shared with Chaplin a few years later. Or perhaps it was one of the times she scratched her husband's face so viciously she drew blood. In any case, the evening ended with a violent fight, the first of countless outbursts that punctuated the Joyces' time together. And as always, Peggy emerged the victor. After she threatened to march out of the house and board the first train back to New York, Stanley apologized profusely and swore he would never make her unhappy again. He also promised to take her on a belated honeymoon to Europe, with a stop in New York so she could pick up a few items for the trip.

It was hard for Stanley not to indulge her. Not only was she a stunning beauty, but she could be sweet and endearing when she wanted to be, like the time she posed for him on the beach during the early days of their marriage, kicking up her heels and playfully mugging for the camera as her husband happily snapped away. To Stanley, having such a wife must have seemed like incredible good fortune, even if he understood all too well why Peggy had singled him out. His shortcomings were painfully obvious, both to him and to everyone who knew him. He wasn't especially handsome, and his employees back in Chicago found him taciturn, uncomfortable around people, and standoffish to the point of rudeness. Hardly a ladies' man, he had few friends of either sex, and he suffered especially by comparison with his gregarious older brother, David. As one of his employees said bluntly, "Stanley was a man you had to know and had to know awful well to like a damn bit in the world." Yet despite his limitations this enchanting woman was his, at least when she wasn't trying to scratch his eyes out.

For Peggy, the arrangement was more complicated. In her opinion, Stanley's attraction lay solely in his immense fortune and his willingness to share it. She realized from the beginning that the marriage would be a sham. But twice before she had chosen husbands on the basis of money and had never regretted her decisions. This time around even the pretense of affection was absent, but she also knew there were means of escape if the arrangement failed. The price of the deal was steep; she had to put up with the attentions and often the raging jealousy of a man she did not particularly care for, and she had to look elsewhere for excitement and sexual thrills, two elements of life that were almost as important to her as riches. Fortunately for her, she was able to balance these needs for a while.

In her memoirs, Peggy described her New York shopping spree in the spring of 1920 as a fantastic adventure in which she raced through nearly a million dollars of her husband's money in the space of a single week. Like so many other of the stories she concocted, this one, too, contained a large dose of high drama. In the early twenties, when the average worker earned just over a thousand dollars a year, it was nearly impossible to drop a million dollars, the current equivalent of upward of eight million dollars, in a matter of days. But her version of the episode, in which she enumerated a few of her more important purchases, suggests that she was clearly spending at an impressive rate.

Her account of her pilgrimage through Manhattan's posh emporiums, detailed in the chapter of her memoirs entitled "How to Spend a Million a Week," began at Black, Starr and Frost, the venerable New York jewelers whose customers included Guggenheims, Vanderbilts, and the Prince of Wales. There, she chose a $200,000 diamond necklace, "not so much after all," she rationalized, "as I can always sell it for more in a few years." Briefly, she fantasized about what it would be like to be married to Witherbee Black, the firm's distinguished senior partner. "I should think it would be wonderful," she mused, "because then a person could wear all the jewels she wanted and they would not cost her anything."

At the equally exclusive Joseph, which had provided her with such flattering outfits during her Ziegfeld days, her choices included a Russian sable coat. She could hardly pass on it, she wrote, because Lee Shubert's brother-in-law worked there, and Lee had been so good to her. Besides, the coat cost only $65,000, quite cheap considering how durable and versatile a fur sable was. A $30,000 chinchilla from her old friend Madame Frances struck her as even more reasonable, especially since the dressmaker gave her a discount because she selected some suits at the same time. And these were just the highlights.

The gold digger was in full battle mode. This time she really had married a millionaire—the first two husbands were simply warmups—and she was savoring the moment, shopping wildly, almost desperately, and for once acquiring everything her heart desired. Although the press was not yet tracking her every move, and it would be nearly a year before reporters provided a blow-by-blow account of her purchases, the totals were truly astounding.

There is no way to determine exactly how much money Peggy

spent in the days before she sailed to Europe. But the detailed records the finicky Stanley kept so methodically show that between the time he started showering Peggy with gifts in the summer of 1919 until the last bill trickled in two years later, he spent almost one and a half million dollars on his beautiful blonde wife. Though that figure included nearly $100,000 for clothes and $200,000 for odds and ends, it was in the area of jewelry that she really went to town, dropping close to a million dollars on precious gems and the adornments made from them. Typical expenditures included the pearl necklace she had wangled out of Stanley during the early days of their marriage; two more ropes of pearls at $78,000 and $24,000 apiece; an emerald ring from Tiffany's for $26,000; a $17,000 diamond ring; a $35,000 emerald and diamond bracelet—she had come to love emeralds, which so thrillingly complemented her fair skin—and in the weeks before the couple departed for Europe, one whopping purchase after another at Black, Starr and Frost: a $32,000 diamond bracelet, a $20,000 emerald bracelet, and for nearly $200,000, a trio of diamond rings, a girl's best friend indeed. While she hadn't quite spent a million dollars in a single week, as she boasted in her memoirs, she had done very well for herself.

Stanley was a generous man and a weak one where Peggy was concerned, but even he seems to have been astounded by her capacity for shopping. "My God, have you been buying out a fur store?" he reportedly exploded when she finally mustered the courage to tell him about the coats she had purchased for the trip.

Immediately Peggy leaped to the defensive. "Well, you told me to get what I needed," she fired back, "and you are a millionaire, aren't you?"

Yes, he replied dryly, but he would not be one for long if she kept on at this rate. There ensued the usual battle, the usual recriminations—and the usual reconciliation.

"Stanley is not a bad husband," she wrote in her memoirs, "only a little funny about financial matters and he is a dear even if he is jealous."

★   ★   ★

By May 1920, when the Stanley Joyces set sail for Paris, Europe had evolved into one of the great playgrounds for the American rich. Changing their location from season to season—Paris in June for the races at Longchamps, the Channel resorts in August, the baths at Marienbad for a vigorous cleansing in the fall—these visitors found in the Continent's fabled capitals and watering places all the comforts of home filtered through a delightfully exotic scrim.

Americans found something else as well. However much standards of behavior had relaxed in cosmopolitan cities like New York, they could not compare to the moral flexibility to be found abroad. Europe was, after all, the land of courtesans, those "grand horizontals" who were as intrinsic a part of society as the army and the aristocracy and far more picturesque. Especially in France, "the land where dalliance is so passionately understood," as Arnold Bennett wrote, being married posed absolutely no obstacle for a woman eager to partake of the pleasures the country had to offer, pleasures that invariably led to the bedroom and the delights experienced therein. For Peggy, embarking on her first major journey and eager to have her pleasure despite her possessive husband, the Continent beckoned as an ideal destination.

Her adventures, as recounted in her memoirs, began shortly after their ship, the *France,* slipped its moorings with the Joyces lavishly ensconced in the bridal suite. Everyone admired the black lace gown she wore to the masquerade ball, and in between champagne toasts and introductions to the captain she was besieged by men eager to make her acquaintance and sweep her around the dance floor.

"I wonder which one they think is your husband," Stanley reportedly groused at one point during the evening. "Certainly they don't think it is me because you only danced with me once."

"Well," she replied tartly, "you dance so badly, and anyway a girl can dance with her husband any time."

"I hope Stanley is not going to be impossible in Paris," she wrote.

"Life won't be worth living if he is. After all because a girl is married does not mean she must never talk or dance with another man as he seems to think." She toyed with the idea of turning right around and boarding the next boat for home or, better yet, getting a divorce the moment she landed on French soil. "I wonder how much they cost?" she speculated. "A girl told me that all you have to do is ask for a divorce and smile at the judge and he gives it to you."

The city that greeted the newlyweds upon their arrival was experiencing a legendary moment in its history, having become the chosen gathering place of many of the world's most creative and iconoclastic minds. But the Stanley Joyces had little interest in the cultural ferment around them; they could not have cared less which geniuses were passionately debating the roots of modernism in Gertrude Stein's drawing room at 27 rue de Fleurus or what literary giants were gathering nightly at Natalie Barney's equally glittering salon on rue Jacob. For them, the charms of Paris lay elsewhere.

They settled into a lavishly decorated suite at the Meurice, a pied-à-terre so sought after by visiting monarchs from Denmark to Zanzibar it had come to be known as the Hotel of Kings. After a quick glance out the window at their sweeping view of the Tuileries, they set off for the races, where Stanley obligingly placed a series of five-thousand-franc bets on the horses that appealed to his wife. "I like betting on the races if I don't have to use my own money," Peggy wrote of that afternoon. "People here do not go to the races to watch the races, they stand about behind the stands and talk about one another and watch each other's clothes." Stanley told her she was the smartest-looking woman in the place, and though he had refused to buy her the tiara with two hundred tiny diamonds she had seen earlier that day at Cartier's, the one the salesman said would look "magnifique" on her, he did give her a diamond ring to make up for being cranky on the boat.

Their days and nights quickly assumed a desultory rhythm. They generally slept until well into the afternoon, rising only to chase away their pounding headaches with pints of champagne, although Peggy preferred to take nothing except aspirin until cocktail time. On the rare occasions Stanley rose before his wife, he slipped out while she was still asleep, or pretended to be. For this small act she felt profoundly grateful. "If husbands were clever they would never let us see them in the morning because that is the time a woman thinks," she reflected. "I lie awake sometimes in the morning or early afternoon, because we do not rise generally before two and I look at Stanley in the other bed and 'My God,' I think, 'Whatever made me marry that!' " Men looked awful without a shave, she concluded, and even her husband's pajamas seemed slightly repulsive; she resolved to get him new ones as soon as possible.

Her afternoons were spent strolling along the grand shopping boulevards and fussing over her clothes. Although Paris offered much to buy, the process was desperately time consuming. Women trekked endlessly from one dressmaking house to another, from Worth to Chanel to Lanvin, watching parades of haughty mannequins and submitting to interminable fittings, not only for dresses but also for lingerie, those wisps of monogrammed silk edged with real lace and intricate embroidery—pink and white were the colors that year—not to mention the bewildering assortment of hats. Peggy adored hats and owned hundreds, but they were even more trouble than dresses, as one Paris guidebook noted, since "everything that can be said about the anguish of having clothes fitted goes double for millinery because [the] creation goes right on your head."

Evenings began with dinner at the elegant Ciro's, followed by a few hours at a smart spot like the Café de la Rotonde or the Café du Dome in Montparnasse or someplace even livelier and more risqué in Montmartre. On these occasions, Peggy generally drifted off with one or another slick-haired, honey-tongued Continental unknown to her husband. Their bodies pressed tightly together during the inevitable tango, the two of them would exchange whispered endearments just loudly enough so Stanley, seething quietly in a dark corner, could catch the unmistakable drift of their conversation.

The fighting usually began before the Joyces paid their bill. By the time they returned to their hotel they were shouting obscenities at each other and Peggy was lunging at her husband with her sharp nails. Finally, around dawn, they would collapse into bed in a sodden mess, there to remain until it was time to start the whole sordid whirl once more.

One night the battling got so raucous other guests complained. "We had a terrible fight when we got home," Peggy wrote of the episode, "and the manager came in this morning and said he was sorry he would have to move us because the people in the next rooms had been complaining they could not sleep." The Joyces were dispatched to a suite surrounded by concrete walls so thick only the taxi drivers in the street could hear their screams wafting through the open windows. This time Stanley's peace offering was the tiara his wife had admired in Cartier's window. "It is lovely," she wrote of her new acquisition, "only very heavy and quite hard to wear as I have to keep my head up all the time."

What Stanley knew about his wife's dalliances was bad enough; what he did not know was worse. Having decided early on that her marriage was to be largely an arrangement of convenience, Peggy hardly intended to let a honeymoon interfere with her increasingly crowded schedule of amorous interludes. Much of her energy was spent devising ways to sneak off to see the men who really interested her, and with a spouse as dim as Stanley, or as studiously indifferent, the task proved depressingly easy.

Conveniently, she had an ally in planning her assignations, a hard-boiled New Yorker appropriately named Ida Smart, whom Peggy had taken up with during her Ziegfeld days. Officially, Ida functioned as a chaperone, a "stage aunt," as Peggy diplomatically put it. Among other tasks, she had served as a witness at Peggy's marriage to Stanley. But her real job was playing Pandarus, and she performed her duties with a vengeance, helping to orchestrate a series of trysts that took place literally under Stanley's nose.

The first of these capped an affair that had started even before Peggy left America. Shortly after her wedding, she had slipped away for a weeklong vacation with Ida at the Homestead Hotel in the fashionable Virginia resort of Hot Springs. William Barton French, the businessman son of a wealthy New York family, had a house nearby, and he was seated in the mirrored dining room of the hotel the evening Peggy swept in, her jewels glinting in the candlelight. French drank a toast to her reflection, and she sipped an encouraging reply. Within minutes he had learned her name from a waiter and invited her to his home. For the next few days the two rarely spent an hour apart.

Barton, as he was known, was not perfect; his first wife had left him because he wore gray tweed to a formal event. But he was good-looking, amusing, and came from moneyed stock; his father had been associated with J. P. Morgan. Since he was contemplating a trip abroad, the pair decided to rendezvous during the Joyces' stopover in London, with communication taking place via coded telegrams routed through Ida.

On June 13 Peggy received the initial message: "Beer, Lapland, Captain's cabin. Marconi him. Ida." Deciphering the not-so-cryptic wire—Beer was the secret word for French, Lapland the name of his ship—she promptly complied, and the two of them hatched their plans. During the week the Joyces spent in the British capital after their initial stop in Paris, as Peggy babbled to Stanley about her hectic schedule of shopping trips and hairdressing appointments, her maid obligingly whisked her from her suite at the Savoy across town to the Ritz, where the lovers met every afternoon for tea, dancing, and a passionate hour in French's bedroom.

Afternoons at the Ritz, however, were not all Peggy had in mind.

Claiming that the rigors of a honeymoon had left her fatigued and overwrought, she informed Stanley that she was going off by herself to the English resort town of Torquay for a week of absolute solitude. Reluctantly, he tucked her into the $7,000 car he had bought her for the trip, placed her $2,000 gold-fitted traveling bag in the trunk, and pressed into her palm a tiny box of hand-tooled leather containing a $10,000 diamond pendant.

But the day stretched endlessly, and around ten that evening, lonely and rather anxious, he telephoned his wife. "Mrs. Joyce left word not to call her," the unsuspecting night clerk at the Grand Hotel informed him. "She is walking with a gentleman." Stanley slammed down the receiver in fury.

Peggy chatted so freely about her intention of marrying French that newspapers were soon mentioning "the rumor circulating in London and Paris for the last two months that Barton's next matrimonial selection will quite likely be a much-talked-about New York actress, at present the wife of an opulent Chicago lumberman." The only obstacle was French's mother, who controlled the family purse strings and threatened to disinherit her son if he did not break off with the onetime showgirl. He promptly returned home to choose a more suitable wife.

Like most other Americans abroad, the Joyces followed the social seasons, and August was the month for Deauville, the outrageously chic gambling resort on the Normandy coast, a few hours west of Paris. Although *Le Figaro* complained that the women's pearls were longer than their dresses, the titled Europeans and millionaire Americans who congregated there every summer found little to criticize, especially at the waterfront casino where small fortunes were won and lost around the gaming tables.

The debonair French publisher Henri Letellier, whose money and influence had made Deauville the glamorous mecca it was, himself cut an imposing figure. The proprietor of the Paris newspaper *Le Journal,* Letellier was glossily handsome in the Continental manner, with slicked-back hair and a small black mustache, his tie held in place with a tasteful pearl stickpin. Journalists invariably described him as France's second-wealthiest man, able to buy and sell large chunks of Parisian real estate as casually as if they were bonbons.

He also had a richly deserved reputation as a world-class playboy. He owned a string of racehorses and possessed lusty appetites for food, art, and gambling; one observer dubbed him "the uncrowned king of the baccarat salons." His greatest passion, however, was for the female sex; "without a soft bundle of femininity somewhere near him, he was in misery," a French journalist wrote of him. Women gravitated to Letellier, glimpsing something soulful and slightly tragic in his deep-set dark eyes. Over his lifetime he accumulated three wives, one of whom he married on her deathbed, and his collection of mistresses was legendary.

Peggy pretended not to recognize Letellier the evening he strode into the casino—"Do you mean that man over there with the long nose?" she inquired innocently when her husband pointed him out—but in fact the two had been intimate for some time. Soon after catching each other's eye at a Montmartre restaurant, they were lunching together regularly at the Ritz and savoring more intimate moments at the publisher's splendid house on the rue du Bois with its priceless collection of Chinese lacquer. Once, after a dinner party in his home that Peggy had slipped away to attend, the two of them disappeared for so many hours that Letellier's guests began muttering angrily about their host's rudeness.

Nor was Letellier the only man paying court to Peggy in the bracing sea air, for her reputation as one of the golden adornments of the Continental social scene had preceded her. Total strangers telephoned her suite mumbling something about having seen her in Paris or perhaps at the Colony Restaurant back in New York. "Nearly everyone I know in New York seems to be here," she wrote of her visit to

Deauville, "which isn't so good because men will keep raising their hats and talking to me and some even say 'hello, Peggy' which makes Stanley mad. I told him today I could not help it if men admire me."

The old Count Boniface de Castellane kissed her hand the night they were introduced at the casino, his drooping yellow mustache grazing the tips of her fingers. She met Erskine Gwynne, a Vanderbilt relative, "very young and full of fun and thinks he is a devil with the women." Sitting nearby were Solly Joel, the English diamond king, and Manuel, the former king of Portugal, an unimposing character who in her eyes resembled nothing so much as a delicatessen owner. "I think it would be nicer to be married to a diamond king than a real king," she mused, "especially if he looked like Manuel because anyway if there was a revolution or anything the real king might lose everything, even his life, but a diamond king would still have his diamonds."

It was not a king, however, but the tango dancer Maurice Mouvet who precipitated her worst marital crisis. With his shiny hair and his sinuous body, "the high priest of the decadent dance," as the papers called him, dominated his world as completely as Letellier dominated his. Maurice and his sometime partner Florence Walton ranked second only to Irene and Vernon Castle, whose luscious swaying had started the prewar dance craze, and it was said he once broke a partner's neck after a particularly violent dip.

Maurice was just approaching Peggy's table at the casino when Stanley finally decided he had had enough of his wife's indiscretions. As she started to rise from her chair, he moved to block her way. "Sit down!" he barked, and he shoved her back so abruptly her diamond tiara slipped over her forehead and grazed her nose. Stumbling out of the casino with a bloodstained handkerchief held to her face, she rushed toward the hotel, her husband on her heels. Back in their suite, he started to follow her into her bedroom.

"Get out!" she screamed.

Stanley did not move.

"I guess I lost control of myself," Peggy admitted in her account of the incident, "and I just flew at him and I guess he must be quite a sight today. He has not left his room yet and his valet said that he would not go out for a week. Well, all I can say is I am glad. I am sorry I lost my temper but after all he deserved it. My nose is all scratched from the tiara and looks terrible." Before long she was insisting she had been "drenched in blood," and the idea of divorce was looking increasingly tempting. "If there is one thing I cannot stand in a man it is jealousy," she added. "I suppose Stanley will come along with another jewel and expect me to make up with him. Well, all I can say is that it will take more than a diamond bracelet this time."

The episode proved a turning point. When Stanley received a cable summoning him back to Chicago on business, he immediately suggested that his wife remain abroad.

"You will let me stay here all alone?" Peggy reported demanding when he proposed the arrangement. "It certainly is strange to me that you can go away and leave me alone when only a few days ago you could not even bear to see me dance with another man."

"Well, you cured me of that," Stanley replied.

In fact, he had offered her exactly what she longed for, a honeymoon without her husband. On August 14 the Joyces traveled to the port city of Cherbourg, where Stanley's ship was set to depart. As he trudged up the gangplank, Peggy was already racing around the corner and climbing into Letellier's auto, which was waiting just out of sight. Before the boat pulled out of the harbor, Peggy and Letellier were in each other's arms heading for Deauville. They arrived close to midnight, slightly flushed but in high spirits. Letellier's motor, a Farman he had customized himself, had offered all the comforts of home; the backseats pulled out to reveal an entire bed, complete with hot water bottles in case the night air proved chilly. The lovers' passionate week by the sea was interrupted only once, when one of Letellier's girlfriends, incensed by the sight of Peggy parading into the casino on his arm, made a scene by pulling her hair and had to be appeased with ten thousand francs.

Next the couple headed for Italy. As Peggy described the excursion in her memoirs, she behaved with the utmost discretion, traveling in one of Letellier's autos with only her maid as her companion while the Frenchman followed in a separate vehicle. "All through the trip," she wrote of the journey, "I could see him exactly 500 yards behind, never coming any closer and never any further."

It was a touchingly demure image, courtesy of a woman who liked to portray herself, at least publicly, as a model of decorum in affairs of the heart. But, characteristically, the story contained not a word of truth. She and Letellier shared a sleeping compartment during the overnight train journey south, and in Venice they were even more cozily ensconced in a single suite at the intimate Hotel Europe, although in an unexpected bow to propriety Letellier asked Peggy's maid to see if the coast was clear before leaving her room in the morning.

For a while the affair was the talk of Europe's high society. But while there were rumors of marriage, it is doubtful that Letellier ever intended to wed the creature he described as a "gilded butterfly"; this French Lothario had romanced hundreds of beautiful women over the years and would go on to romance hundreds more. Peggy herself was no innocent: she understood the rules that governed Continental courtships. And even after Letellier drifted out of the picture upon their return to Paris, she spent little time mourning his departure. Among the many visitors who trooped up to her suite at the Hôtel du Rhin were a shady Englishman named Edgar James, whose activities were of interest to Scotland Yard, and the dapper Maurice, fresh from his exertions at his cabaret near the Opéra, who quickly changed from evening dress to a more comfortable gray suit before rapping lightly on her door at three in the morning.

Her most celebrated visitor was an Albanian nobleman named Prince Vlora. Sadly, his title was his only regal trapping; he lacked both fortune and kingdom. But Peggy was enchanted by the prospect of a royal union; even for a girl who got around as much as she did, a prince seemed like a nifty catch. "She told me to save her finest lingerie until she was married to the prince," her maid reported, and the lovers spent hours debating how quickly Vlora could dispose of the current princess. Parisian gossips speculated that Peggy had acquired her bejeweled tiara in anticipation of the day she might be the consort of a Balkan monarch, "if his pretensions to the throne should materialize."

Before she could complete her ascent to the throne, however, she received an unexpectedly curt note from her husband, "not full of love and adjectives like most of his other letters and he did not close it with his usual 'Your most loving husband Stan' but just 'aff' yours.'" As she lay in bed pondering the situation, her maid entered with the calling card of an American newspaper correspondent who, upon being invited into her boudoir, asked if she could shed any light on her forthcoming divorce.

"You must be crazy," Peggy replied with a slightly forced laugh, adjusting her negligee around her slender shoulders. "I am not divorcing Mr. Joyce."

"There must be some mistake then," the reporter answered, "and I apologize, but I got this cable from my office in New York." He showed her the slip of paper: HAVE TIP STANLEY JOYCE MILLIONAIRE LUMBERMAN CHICAGO SUING WIFE FORMERLY PEGGY HOPKINS NEW YORK BEAUTY FOR DIVORCE STOP PEGGY NOW HOTEL DU RHIN PARIS GET STATEMENT.

Peggy's initial reaction was that her husband had turned out to be a first-class rat, but she wisely kept her thoughts to herself. Instead she responded brightly, "I only got a letter from Mr. Joyce this morning saying that he has been detained but will be back to join me here in a few weeks."

Next, she received a cable from her lawyers, informing her that Stanley had indeed filed legal papers, accusing her of infidelity with Letellier and half a dozen other men. Much to her fury, he had also removed her jewels from her safe deposit box. "Well, of course, he had a key to the box and a right to open it," she acknowledged in her memoirs, "but I think it was a low trick to take them back like that without even telling me about it. Thank God I have most of my jewelry over here."

By the end of October Peggy was heading back to America braced for battle, and although she left behind a host of admirers, not everyone had been sorry to see her go. At breakfast one morning before her departure, she received an exquisitely wrapped package; when she untied the ribbon and ripped off the shiny paper she discovered to her horror that it contained the body of a dead cat, a farewell gift from one of Letellier's disgruntled old flames.

Still, she was not unduly concerned about the future. "I have a $2,000,000 home in Miami, Florida, given to me by my husband, and a million dollars' worth of jewels besides," she told the *New York Times* reporter who greeted her upon her return to America. "I should worry."

5

"A Vampire with
the Sting of Death"

If any single event marked the apotheosis of Peggy Hopkins Joyce as a celebrity, it was her extended, messy, and incredibly well-publicized divorce from Stanley Joyce. The trial in Chicago, which began in the spring of 1921, reportedly engendered four thousand newspaper articles, not a surprising figure given the saturation coverage the story received across the land and even beyond.

The case offered every guilty pleasure readers could want: tons of sex, much of it occurring in the glittering playgrounds of Europe, not to mention clandestine assignations, coded telegrams, tapped telephone lines, secret informants, stolen furs, smuggled jewels, frantic spending sprees, surprise raids, hidden mistresses, half a dozen illicit affairs, fraudulent divorces, a suicide, bigamy not once but twice, and royalty galore, along with accusations of libel, slander, drunkenness, violence, and brutality—you name it, it was part of the story during the year the headlines blazed with news of Joyce versus Joyce. The press salivated over tales of erotic adventures on foreign soil—her "amorous pilgrimage through the gay capitals of Europe," as one reporter described them—and went wild over the staggering sums of money involved, never tiring of enumerating Peggy's myriad purchases and the price tags attached. The charges and countercharges made the head spin, but there was no denying how engrossing they were.

For weeks at a time newspapers brimmed with reports from the front, scooping up and regurgitating all the drama of Peggy's life thus far, not just the recent bouts of decadence but also the mysterious other husbands and the even hazier early years. The decorous *New York Times* weighed in with some thirty articles, and in view of Peggy's far-flung reputation the event caused a stir abroad. The tabloids, of course, had a field day; a prolonged divorce involving an ex-*Follies* girl, her millionaire hubby, and generous helpings of international sexual intrigue—this was the stuff they were born for.

Day after day the courtroom swarmed with reporters; Chicago alone was represented by eight major dailies. Papers unlucky enough not to have their own man on the scene could stay up to date on the latest developments via the wire services and news syndicates. The result was a blizzard of banner headlines followed by a full page or more of broadsheet coverage and acres of pictures. Often the stories overshadowed accounts of far more significant events, for how could bloodshed in Ireland, the massacre of Greeks, or the inauguration of President Harding compare to the hint of a hitherto unknown prince in Peggy's life? Reporters besieged her so energetically she had to travel from New York to Chicago under cover of darkness to escape the hordes on her trail, or so she complained to the panting pressmen once they finally caught up with her.

Most extraordinary about the frenzied attention was how little Peggy had done to merit it. Admittedly she had gained a reputation for acquiring and shedding spouses at a rapid pace, but she was hardly the only ex-showgirl ever dragged through the courts or the only disgruntled divorcee; one marriage of every seven had fallen apart the previous year. She had not even gotten mixed up in a crime, nor could anyone offer the fig leaf that larger sociological issues were involved. Yet none of this mattered. The press seized upon her and couldn't let go. Her name became so familiar to Americans that a song was written about her—"I'll Be Your Peggy Hopkins If You'll Be My Stanley Joyce"—and it was rightly assumed everyone would get the allusions.

One reason for the blast of attention was her typically impeccable timing. Had she emerged on the national scene during the war, the country would have been preoccupied with far more urgent matters than the transatlantic capers of a faithless wife. Had she arrived a decade later, when millions of Americans were out of work and going hungry each night, tales of $300,000 pearl necklaces and marble swimming pools fringed by orchid-festooned palms would have seemed almost obscene. Had her marital troubles occurred even a few years later, once the ballyhoo era was under way, a jaded public might have asked itself what, really, all the fuss was about.

The year 1921, however, was perfect. Americans had not yet had a big lurid trial to sink their teeth into, and they had not yet gotten swept up in fads like mahjong and crossword puzzles. Legitimate heroes like Charles Lindbergh were still figures of the future. At the same time, the news media that would chronicle the decade's glorious and garish high points had come of age. Presses were rolling fast, and papers spilled onto the street at breakneck speed. Street-smart journalists, photographers, and gossip columnists were poised for action. The endlessly fascinating divorce proceedings of the endlessly fascinating Peggy Joyce unfolded at exactly the right moment.

The preliminary skirmishes had started the previous autumn. Stanley's suspicions about his wife's indiscretions were confirmed by an army of informants, among them bellboys, waiters, chambermaids, and taxi drivers. Following time-honored practice, he placed announcements in various newspapers on October 27 declaring that he would not be responsible for his estranged wife's debts, a resounding opening salvo against a big spender like Peggy. But the real fireworks began in April 1921 in the courtroom of Superior Court Judge Joseph Sabath as Stanley's lawyers laid out his blistering case against his wife and her attorneys hastened to rebut every word.

Branding her "a vampire with the sting of death," Stanley's lawyers charged that during her brief marriage Peggy had committed adultery with nearly a dozen men, a motley assortment that included a prince, a duke, a tango dancer, a French publisher, a barkeep, and a safecracker. The lawyers further claimed she flew into rages against her husband during which she cursed him, scratched him, hurled obscenities at him, and banged his head against the wall so violently she broke his glasses. Peggy, contended Stanley's lawyers, had been guilty of "extreme and repeated cruelty," and they described her as "a woman of great temper" who "frequently indulged in violent fits of passion." What was more, her two previous divorces had been obtained fraudulently, making her a bigamist twice over. In conclusion, they dismissed Peggy as a thoroughly immoral creature who had married simply to get her lovely hands on her husband's considerable fortune.

"Absurdly untrue allegations," she retorted, and her lawyers obligingly fired back with an equally overheated countersuit. They charged that Stanley drank, or as the complaint put it, displayed "violent sallies of passion" and bombarded her with "opprobrious epithets and obscene and abusive language," a course of "continuous and brutal treatment toward her which resulted in a breakdown of her health." They contended that her marriage had interrupted a brilliant career in which she was earning $700 a week and that Stanley "forced" her to open charge accounts at expensive stores. "She was trying to make him a better man," her lawyers told the court, but during their honeymoon in the most expensive resorts in Europe, "he encouraged her to spend, spend, spend!" They claimed detectives had stormed into her apartment and ripped apart the mattresses, that she had grown too attached to her jewels to sell them, and that inasmuch as her husband was worth $40 million she should certainly get alimony, especially since the whole thing was making her a nervous wreck.

Nor were her lawyers quite finished. They insisted that Stanley once had his own mistress, a quiet music student whose tiny Chicago apartment he used to visit. "Her husband brands her with the scarlet letter," stormed Peggy's lead attorney, Weymouth Kirkland, in a typically purple accusation. "This man who came to her warm from the kisses of Charlotte Johnson." When Stanley married Peggy, the lawyer added, he knew all too well what sort of woman he was hooking up with. "He was nothing but a stage-door Johnny!" thundered Kirkland to the delight of the enraptured matinee crowd in the courtroom. "Did he think at that time he was meeting a social debutante at a pink tea? Did he think she never went out at night without a chaperone?" Both parties swore they had been loyal, affectionate, and kind throughout the marriage, claims that seemed far-fetched no matter which side one was rooting for.

Banner headlines started flying, each more sensational than the last. "Joyce Dubs Peggy Huntress; Cites Prince!" "Joyce's Charges False and Cowardly!" "Peggy a Robber, Joyce Testifies!" "Peggy Beat Me, Joyce Testifies!" "Swears Peggy Kissed Five Men!" Newspapers routinely described the proceedings as "the biggest case on the national divorce calendar" or, as the *Denver Post* screeched, "one of the most sensational divorce cases in history."

Even the *New York Times,* which had a man on the scene filing almost daily reports, got swept up in the hysteria. In court, the paper reported, Peggy was depicted as the "dark star of destiny" in the lives of her three husbands. Stanley's attorney, Alfred Austrian, "held her up as a lurid adventuress whose cometlike rise from obscurity into the astral realms of men of wealth was like that of a wandering Melpomene," wrecking and destroying all she came in contact with and "leaving in her path through the heavens a trail of shattered lives and ruined fortunes."

The alimony hearings in early summer, in which Peggy sought nearly a quarter of a million dollars to keep her and her lawyers going for a bit, played as dramatically as theater. At the center stood a fifty-nine-page document—"the instrument of the most merciless legal flailing ever administered to a woman in a divorce suit," according to the *Chicago American*—that fleshed out Stanley's case and sought to demolish his wife's. For days crowds packed the seats, lined the walls of the courtroom, and overflowed into the corridors outside, where bailiffs struggled vainly to keep order.

As the lurid details spilled out, total strangers bombarded Stanley with letters offering further evidence of his wife's indiscretions. A correspondent who signed himself "Veritas" wrote from the Ritz-Carlton in Atlantic City to report that "Peggy is at this hotel with four men in her train—one an 'effeminate' of about thirty, thin, tall, dark, is buying jewels for her." A Long Island man dropped a note to add: "Just a line in regards to your trouble with your wife. I see her picture in the N.Y. papers many times and also yours but you are not the man that stayed here in my gunning shack with your wife for four days. However they made me promise that if any one should inquire after they had gone I should not say who they was. She promised me a auto if I keep my mouth closed forever."

Even Ida Smart came in for her share of attacks. "This bluff 'aunt' is in touch with several girls all the time for high-class men, as she calls them, and Peggy is always called first," a correspondent who described himself as an "old friend" wrote Stanley. "The authorities ought to get after that Smart as she is the cause of many a girl's downfall and she is the one that put Peggy up to get this bunch of cash out of you."

The trial also presented a heaven-sent opportunity for the press to explore the antecedents of this woman whose past was still a mystery to most Americans. "Out of what childhood environment sprang this modern Cleopatra who tossed $1 million to the winds in three months, married three millionaires in almost as many years and lured princes, a notorious crook, and even a hard-boiled bartender to worship at the shrine of her fascinations?" demanded the Hearst papers in the florid prose that characterized much of the coverage. To lay bare "the past of Peggy" the publishing empire dispatched a team of reporters whose research produced a multipart series of articles, the first of which focused on "the childhood of the actress-enchantress."

In tracing her roots, newspapers came up with picturesque if ludicrous scenarios. One was that Peggy's mother had died young. Another was that Peggy and her younger sister, Lucille, had been reared in opulent fashion in Washington. Peggy had been a convent girl, it was suggested, or a telephone operator in Denver. A particularly breathless account began, "The story of Peggy's early life reads like the story of a twentieth-century Cinderella, with fairy godmothers, princes and stepmothers thrown in to add spice."

These colorful versions of her past appealed enormously to her public; why else would there have been so many and with such baroque embellishments? With their rich allusions to the themes of traditional fairy tales—an enchanted childhood, the untimely death of a parent—they did much to burnish what became the myth of Peggy Hopkins Joyce. And they circulated so widely that few reporters managed to unravel the truth, especially since the imaginative creature at the heart of the tales never bothered to set anyone straight.

Countless other morsels emerged during the hearings. One highlight was the suicide in 1918 of an army lieutenant named Alexander McClintock who had taken money from his regiment to satisfy Peggy's craving for jewels and then shot himself to death at the Murray Hill Turkish Bath in New York to avoid disgrace. Police found seven cents in his pocket and empty sedative bottles on the table beside his body. According to the story that had circulated at the time, Peggy had gathered her jewels together, wrapped them in a silk scarf, and handed them to McClintock to help him raise the $7,000 he needed to pay his debts, but the gesture came too late to ease his conscience.

Reporters suggested she had spirited her enormous collection of jewels out of the country so they wouldn't be confiscated by the authorities. "Is Peggy a smuggler?" demanded the *Chicago American*, raising "the possibility of prison bars at the end of her glittering path

of jewels." She in turn insisted she had nearly frozen to death the previous winter because Stanley had taken away two of her warmest
coats—her $40,000 Russian sable, a concoction of fifty-eight paws
and thirty-one tails, and her $10,000 brocade- and velvet-lined chin-
chilla—although, as he reminded the court, she had at least four other
furs stashed away in her closet.

If there was a single moment at which Peggy epitomized the gold
digger she was forever known as, it was the day Stanley's financial
statements were made public, revealing in sensational detail just how
fast and furiously his wife had raced through his fortune. Reporters
offered spellbinding details, enumerating everything from the famous
$300,000 pearls—"the finest luster and quality obtainable"—and two
other strings of pearls ($100,000 for the pair) down to such trifles as
her two automobiles (a Rolls and a Renault, at $10,000 each), a
$6,400 diamond lorgnette chain, a $3,000 electric piano, a $1,000
tablecloth, gold-topped cologne bottles for $130, a $78 shoehorn, and
a $27 gold pencil. In an era in which dinner at a top New York ho-
tel could be had for $2.50, a round-the-world cruise for under a
thousand dollars, a nice wristwatch for five bucks, and scented, gold-
tipped cigarettes for ten cents a pack, such figures were breathtaking.

Stanley Joyce was a shy man who never cared for reporters, but
Peggy more than compensated by making herself generously available to the press, even at this profoundly awkward moment. She
didn't particularly mind the breakup of the marriage, which she had
seen coming, after all, but she desperately hoped to emerge with her
possessions intact. Most of all, she wanted the story told on her terms.

So, although she offered ritual complaints about the blast of attention, moaning that she hated "all this mean publicity," there is no evidence that she ever refused to talk to a newsman. While she revealed
little that was accurate—by now her life was such a patchwork of
concocted stories she herself could hardly keep track of the details—

her intuitive understanding of the uses of publicity helped her realize that, no matter what dreadful things people were saying about her
inside the courtroom and out, the attention of the media could always be turned to her advantage.

Actually, Peggy liked reporters and enjoyed performing for them.
To her they were simply another appreciative audience. She generally
entertained the gentlemen of the press while reclining on a sofa in
her boudoir, wearing some bewitching outfit that sounded even
more amazing in her interviewers' fervid prose. Sometimes her attire
was so scanty she seemed ready to climb into her bath; on other occasions she appeared dressed for a formal ball. One reporter entered
her Chicago hotel suite to find her clad in "a rich black velvet tea
gown trailing a fishtail train lined with cool Nile green silk [that] accentuated the lines of her lithe figure. Against the black depth, her
white skin, pallidly clear, stood out in refreshing relief. Through her
blond bobbed curls glistened every now and then a shaft of reddish
light. . . . A jeweled ankle bracelet shone above the rhinestone and
cut-steel silver buckle of her right foot." One slender finger held a
single ring, "a blaze of small diamonds." The reporter watched mesmerized as she rubbed the nap of the velvet the wrong way and ner-
vously tapped the platinum band of her ring on her chair. No detail
escaped notice. Every gesture seemed laden with significance.

On November 8, the final day of testimony, two surprise witnesses
took the stand. One was Peggy's former social secretary, a trim British
woman named Julia Sawdon, who had traveled all the way from
England to testify and whose modest attire—a blue serge suit with a
lace collar and a gray hat with a black feather—seemed to attest to
her rectitude. The other was Peggy's former maid, a stolid Norwegian
named Hannah Nordstrom. Together they presented so damning a
picture of their mistress's romps across the Continent and sketched
such vivid images of her adventures that the men involved seemed to

have stepped upon an imaginary stage before the packed courtroom. Paris millionaire Henri Letellier, "the central figure in a dozen dueling events and affairs of the heart," entered, bowed, and was gone. Next came Vlora of Albania, the "prince without a principality." Other bit players included the debonair tango dancer Maurice; William Barton French, described as the "poor little rich" New Yorker because of his inability to get his hands on his family's fortune; Spanish nobleman and Parisian dandy the duc de Durcal; and Edgar James, alleged confidence man.

The public learned how Peggy sneaked into the duke's apartment at the Claridge Hotel for clandestine lunches: "We never used the elevator," Mrs. Sawdon testified, "but always entered the back door and walked up a flight of stairs." They heard of the dark night when Hannah, frightened after someone tried to break into her Deauville hotel room, rushed into Peggy's suite and found her and Letellier in "abbreviated raiment," as she delicately put it. Another night Mrs. Sawdon entered Peggy's bedroom at the Savoy and switched on the light to see her mistress and Edgar James entwined beneath the covers, the floor littered with champagne glasses. "All's well," Peggy had whispered to her terrified companion. They heard of the strategy she used to deceive her husband so she could slip away to a dinner party at Letellier's house: "Well, I'll just have a good quarrel with him," Peggy reportedly told Mrs. Sawdon shortly before dashing out the door and into a waiting taxi. The public heard the ardent telegrams from French—"Never let me go again two days without hearing from you. . . . Miss you beyond words"—and they learned of the motoring trip through Scotland during which Mrs. Sawdon kept the impatient French on the line in one telephone booth until Peggy finished talking to her husband in an adjoining one. They even learned that Peggy had persuaded Stanley to change their honeymoon plans from the Orient to Europe so she could carry out her planned assignations with French.

The witnesses also confirmed that Peggy's amorous activities were

hardly confined to the Continent; they had started literally hours after the recitation of her marriage vows. "Flowers and telegrams came
to her in my name," Hannah testified. "Every day there was something." It also emerged that prior to her honeymoon she regularly received flowers from a man named Hudson and spent a week with
him in Atlantic City. "Hudson was in and out of her bedroom at the
Ambassador Hotel," and "he and Peggy acted like lovers," the servant
who had accompanied her had written in a letter that was presented
as evidence. "I frequently saw him in her bedroom where she was in
bed, usually in the daytime—he would sit at the side of the bed and
hold her hand as if he was in love with her."

Nor did the affairs taper off once Peggy returned home; if anything, her schedule grew busier. Even on the boat trip back to
America she was plotting her moves. Hannah told the court that
Prince Vlora had given Peggy an "enormous photograph of himself,"
and, upon landing, the picture was "the first thing she asked for when
her trunks were unpacked in New York." Once she was settled in
New York, her companions included a restaurant owner named Joe
Pani, who drove her around the city in his car while she snuggled in
his lap, the two of them madly drunk. A wool merchant named Evan
Spaulding—"the pauper who expects an inheritance," as he was described—slipped into her Park Avenue apartment so many nights he
had his own key. One afternoon Hannah arrived to find his hat and
coat on a hook and the rooms eerily silent; in her panic, she informed
the court, "I thought someone had died."

The stories told by these two women made eyes widen and
mouths water, and their detailed testimony demolished Peggy's case
in a single knockout blow. Her lawyers acknowledged as much when
they declined to call her into court, thus effectively conceding vic-
tory to the opposition. The official explanation was that the defen-
dant couldn't stand the stress of an extended trial, or, as she explained
to one reporter, adjusting her organdy negligee while lounging on a
sofa at Chicago's Drake Hotel, "It was wilting me." Still insisting the

charges against her were lies, she added: "I suppose I am forever damned by the court proceedings. I've got a black eye, and I suppose I must take it."

Judge Sabath interrupted the mesmerizing proceedings to announce an out-of-court settlement, arrived at quietly the previous day, which decisively proclaimed Stanley the victor and divided up the spoils. Peggy was allowed to keep most of her jewels, which were valued at nearly a million dollars, along with the two disputed fur coats, her Rolls-Royce, and $80,000 in cash. But everything else went to her husband. She gave up her claims to $400,000 in real estate, including the mansion in Miami, and to three prize items worth a total of $150,000—the diamond tiara that had caused her such grief in Deauville, a pearl and gold cigarette box, and a cigarette holder set with emeralds and rubies. As a parting shot the judge rescinded a previous decision to award her $1,350 a month in alimony, a sum that had been intended to cover "theater tickets, taxicab hire, flowers, and new gowns."

Peggy did her best to put a good face on the situation. "I get something like a million out of the divorce," she told a reporter. "That's not so bad." But her defeat represented so humiliating a capitulation that she mentioned barely a word of the experience in her memoirs.

With all the hoopla, people forgot that but for the press there would have been no story. Little of real significance had taken place in Judge Sabath's courtroom, and the response to the trial seemed to prove only that Americans possessed a seemingly insatiable appetite for tales involving the lives and loves of gold-digging blondes. But the interest was not merely salacious; there was more to it. While the bored and restless housewife reading of Peggy's capers pursed her lips in disapproval, the gesture was tinged with longing. How thrilling to actually be Peggy Joyce, she couldn't have helped but imagine. There in her spartan kitchen or her shabby living room, she must have tried to picture herself slipping yet another string of pearls around her neck or awaiting the arrival of yet another Continental charmer. What woman wouldn't have adored wearing the tiara with the two hundred diamonds, settling that Russian sable around her shoulders, or listening to princes whisper candied words in her ear? As for male readers, of course they all prayed devoutly they would never end up in the clutches of such a vixen, but wasn't she a dish with that slinky figure and that knowing smile, and my God didn't she sound like a pistol in bed? What man inside the courtroom and out didn't undress her with his eyes?

Like the best made-for-tabloid tales, Peggy's touched on the most basic of human emotions—love, hate, greed, jealousy—and involved such traditional themes of tragedy as betrayal and deception. It was as if *Othello* had been reworked for the *Daily News* straphanger. Despite a scenario that read like cheap fiction, the sentiments involved were universal and deeply human, which is why accounts of the proceedings touched people in unexpectedly complicated ways. Ordinary Americans found it easy to condemn Peggy, but mixed with their scorn was a powerful current of envy and attraction. Along with offering a titillating glimpse into a world where ordinary rules of behavior didn't seem to apply, her story moved readers for reasons they dared not examine too closely.

For a brief moment Stanley emerged as the hero. Women from around the country deluged him with letters promising to be a proper wife, especially after all he had endured with that terrible Peggy. "If he is ever free to marry again," a woman who identified herself as "a Little Country Church Mouse" wrote his lawyers, "I would be deeply in debt if you could arrange an introduction." But although Stanley won in court, he had lost a great deal. He owed some $700,000 to Peggy's creditors, including $150,000 to Cartier's and $200,000 to Black, Starr and Frost, and the balance of a major bank account stood at $20,000; the gold digger had pretty much picked him clean.

More important, something had happened to Stanley's personality during the ordeal, or perhaps he never was the angel the press made him out to be. He soon found himself back in matrimonial hot water; some years later a second wife sued him for divorce on the grounds of continuous cruelty, claiming he had spanked her with a pair of sandals, thrown her across a dance floor, and held a lighted match to her lips. The protracted case ended only when he suffered a fatal heart attack in 1944. He died alone in Hot Springs, Arkansas, a broken, pathetic figure. His five-million-dollar fortune went to his twenty-one-year-old niece, Beatrice, his only surviving relative.

For Peggy, the official loser, it was another story entirely. All the elements of her life thus far, both real and apocryphal, had been whipped together and served up to a hungry public. The astonishing amount of publicity generated by the trial had transformed her into a full-fledged media celebrity. For more than a decade her name would never be out of the news. Seemingly overnight she had become one of the best-known, if not exactly the most admired, women of her generation; her subsequent exploits simply kept the legend alive. Happily for a nation that loved labels, she was firmly established in the public mind as the "much-married" Peggy Hopkins Joyce, profligate collector and disposer of millionaire husbands, and the term gold digger fit like a French kid glove. For the rest of the twenties and even beyond, her every action, no matter how silly or inconsequential, would make news. In affairs of the heart, every palpitation would merit a story.

To calm her jangled nerves after the trauma of the divorce, Peggy returned to Paris, and by the spring of 1922 her friends were telling reporters she had finally agreed to marry Letellier. "M. Letellier has been pleading continually with Peggy to set a wedding date," one accommodating companion informed a journalist. There were, however, a few complications. For one thing, the French publisher had not brought up the subject of marriage in nearly two years, although as Peggy noted confidently in her memoirs, "I feel that he would do so if I gave him the slightest encouragement." For another, an old flame had reappeared in her life.

The Chilean diplomat Billy Errazuriz, who had been linked with Peggy during her Ziegfeld days, was both Catholic and married, although currently living apart from his wife. But he pursued Peggy as ardently as he had years earlier and had even obtained a French posting to be near her. He may have been one of the few men she actually cared for. "I know that I love Billy more than I ever loved anyone," she wrote in her memoirs, "but I will never let him know. It would only bring unhappiness to everyone concerned."

The crisis erupted as the sun rose one Sunday morning in April. Peggy had dined with Letellier and Errazuriz at Ciro's the previous evening, and the trio continued their revelry over a dozen bottles of champagne at Maurice's cabaret. Peggy danced the tango with Errazuriz and the more sedate fox-trot with Letellier, and at four in the morning the woozy little party headed back for a nightcap at Claridge's, where Errazuriz occupied a room next door to Peggy's suite.

He had spent most of the evening begging Peggy to dump Letellier and run off with him. She may have refused outright or simply waved him off with one of her typically airy gestures; her story shifted during the terrible days that followed. "I was tired out," she told a reporter afterward. "It was six o'clock in the morning— so I said, 'Go to your room, Billy, and wait until tomorrow for your answer.' He turned to me and said, 'There will be no tomorrow for me.' I didn't realize what he meant by that remark until later."

Maddened by jealousy, Errazuriz returned to his room and fired a bullet through his head. Diplomat to the end, and even on his deathbed loath to implicate someone he cared for in a sordid little suicide, he left a letter for the French police saying simply that he was weary of living. He never mentioned the woman who had broken his heart.

The incident made the predictable splash in the French and American papers, especially after Claridge's threatened to evict Peggy because of the unpleasant publicity. The victim's family insisted he had committed suicide because of financial problems, and the grieving widow kindly invited Peggy to the funeral. She did not attend but sent in her place an arrangement of five hundred purple orchids, his favorite flower, which was placed beside his coffin.

World heavyweight boxing champion Jack Dempsey, whom Peggy had met during his recent trip to Paris, was in Berlin at the time, and when disaster struck, she thought of him immediately. "Am in terrible trouble," she wired the fighter. "You remember man I introduced you to; has killed himself."

As Dempsey was a renowned ladies' man, rumors of their engagement began flying moments after his return to the French capital. Interviewed in his bath, the boxer denied reports that the bereaved beauty had summoned him, but he added gallantly: "If I had received such a message, who knows but I might have come? Peggy is a mighty pretty girl." The lady was more cautious, at least publicly. "Jack is a peach of a man with a big white soul," she acknowledged as she headed home, accompanied by a German shepherd that Dempsey had given her as a gift. But she insisted she didn't plan to marry anybody for a while.

For a fledgling journalist from the *Toronto Star*, the Errazuriz tragedy synthesized in a blinding moment the essence of postwar life in the French capital. In a work entitled "Paris 1922," the young American writer Ernest Hemingway wrote: "I have seen Peggy Joyce

at 2 A.M. in a Dancing in the Rue Camartin quarreling with the shel-
lac haired young Chilean who had manicured finger nails, blew a puff
of smoke in her face, wrote something in a notebook and shot himself at 3:30 the same morning." Hemingway had been struggling to
distill the experiences of five months in the city into a few crystalline
images, and the brief explosion involving Peggy and her suave Latin
embedded itself in his imagination.

Nor did the drama end there. Much as the American public had
devoured Peggy's story, Hollywood worried about her potentially
dangerous influence on the nation's moral fiber. The film industry
had been badly stung by the Fatty Arbuckle scandal of the previous
year, in which the actor had been charged with the death of a small-
time actress named Virginia Rappe, and an air of sin seemed to per-
vade the movie colony generally. In response, the major studios had
hired Will H. Hays, Republican Party stalwart and postmaster general
under President Harding, to help elevate its image. In 1922, Hays
started work as head of the studios' new organization, the Motion
Picture Producers and Distributors Association.

The bulk of his actions were cosmetic rather than substantive. But
he did take a number of steps designed to showcase his seriousness
about cleaning up Hollywood. Among his strategies was writing
morality clauses into stars' contracts specifying that any actor involved
in a scandal would be fired. Given her recent behavior, Peggy was a
prime candidate for discipline; the state of Ohio had already banned
all newsreels displaying her face.

Although she seemed far too caught up in her personal life to
make any movies, major forces in Hollywood were taking no
chances. Two weeks after Errazuriz committed suicide, the newspapers reported that "Peggy Joyce will not be permitted to exploit her
sensational love affairs in the movies if the Motion Picture Theater
Owners of America can prevent it." "Acting in the interest of a clean
and wholesome entertainment," the exhibitors had adopted a resolu-
tion that barred her pictures from entering the country and that

pledged not to show such works if they managed to sneak in nevertheless.

The action marked the first time a specific individual had been singled out for censure, but the theater owners had chosen well. Within hours, the Motion Picture Producers and Distributors Association announced it couldn't agree more.

6

"The Most Famous Woman in the U.S."

If ever there was an enduring image from the early days of cinema, it was the mournful face of Charlie Chaplin's tramp, with its black smudges of eyebrows and mustache topped by that pathetic derby. Chaplin was the biggest thing that had ever happened to the movies, a man who transformed a minor branch of cheap amusement into an art form and in the process created the most endearing persona in American culture. By the time Peggy Hopkins Joyce breezed into his Hollywood studio one sleepy summer afternoon in 1922, he was the most celebrated person in America, perhaps the Western world.

The private Chaplin fascinated the public as much as his artistic creations, and to be one of "Charlie's nymphs," as Kenneth Anger dubs them in *Hollywood Babylon,* elevated a woman to a whole new level of fame. Even someone who merely dated him briefly earned a footnote in history. While his affair with Peggy was short-lived— "bizarre, though brief," as Chaplin writes in his autobiography—the event testified to her ability to captivate one of the central figures of her era. She, albeit inadvertently, provided the inspiration for what turned out to be one of his more remarkable works.

The two were introduced by Marshall Neilan, a director who was himself something of a Hollywood legend. A devastatingly attractive

Irishman with curly dark hair and deep-set blue eyes, Neilan had an irreverent sense of humor and a passion for practical jokes; he once planted a cockroach in the soup at Hollywood's posh Montmartre restaurant. His close friend the actress Colleen Moore called him "the greatest beau of them all," and the movie community spent hours dissecting his love affairs with glamour girls like Gloria Swanson. By the age of twenty-six he was also Mary Pickford's favorite director, the boy wonder behind half a dozen of her best films, including *Daddy Long Legs* and *Rebecca of Sunnybrook Farm*. Few in Hollywood were surprised that his name surfaced when Peggy arrived in town to challenge Hollywood's virtual blacklisting of her and to try to pursue a new career in pictures.

Mickey, as he was universally known, initially found his potential leading lady bewitching, so much so that he used to engage the Coconut Grove Orchestra to furnish music for their late-night suppers. But his interest waned as he became aware of her professional limitations. "Though Peggy photographed like an angel, she couldn't act," Colleen Moore recalls in her memoirs. "Mickey was going out of his mind trying to get a performance out of her."

His directorial frustrations, combined with a parallel desire to shift Peggy's interest from him to another important Hollywood figure, may have explained why he brought her to Chaplin's studio that late summer afternoon. "I couldn't understand why, on the way over, Mickey kept telling Peggy how terribly rich Chaplin was," recounts Moore, who accompanied them. "I supposed he thought adding the world's most famous comedian to her collection might not be enough for her, and to help his plan along he threw in the part about the money."

Chaplin was sitting in his studio languidly plucking the strings of his violin when Neilan rushed in to announce that Peggy was about to make her entrance. Still in mourning for Billy Errazuriz, she swept in looking elegant in funereal black, her outfit set off by diamonds, emeralds, and the scent of an intoxicating perfume. "She perched on a table in the center of the room," Moore remembers, "crossed her famous legs, showing just enough thigh to whet a man's appetite, and gave Charlie one of her dazzling smiles." In an effort to impress America's most eligible bachelor, she also trotted out an ultrarefined accent and all the grande dame airs she had acquired abroad. But after an hour of downing glasses of champagne, she gradually shed her veneer of Continental polish, not to mention her plummy vowels, and reverted to her own salty self. When Neilan playfully slapped her on the derriere to suggest it was time to leave, she let loose a shower of obscenities. Chaplin was vastly amused.

In certain respects, the internationally renowned filmmaker and the gold-digging femme fatale were ideally suited to each other. A rich and powerful man who made himself irresistible to women, Chaplin was exactly the sort of person Peggy was drawn to. He in turn lusted after her physically—"In Peggy, Charlie found the greatest sex-lure he had ever encountered," *Photoplay* concluded—and was intrigued by this poor daughter of the South who had transformed herself into one of the sirens of her age. She may have aroused more complex feelings in him as well, emotions stirred by his own humble beginnings and evident in the convoluted attitude toward fallen women so often expressed in his work.

Soon Peggy and Chaplin were having dinner à deux. "Her opener," Anger records, "had a certain showgirl candor: 'Is it true what all the girls say—that you're hung like a horse?'" For a few weeks they were the talk of the movie colony as they dined together nightly and once slipped off for a private frolic on the nearby island of Catalina. "Chaplin and Peggy sought out a secluded cove on the far side of the island where they could picnic and do some nude sunbathing, unobserved—or so they believed," writes Anger. "The presence of the two celebrities on the little island had not gone unobserved, however, and several of the more intrepid native Catalinans had hiked up the mountain overlooking the cove, equipped with powerful binoculars." Soon afterward, the wild goats native to the island acquired the nickname "Charlies."

During their affair, Peggy often amused Chaplin with stories about her various adventures, and her accounts of her tempestuous marriage to Stanley Joyce were fresh in his mind when director Tom Ince entertained the pair aboard his yacht. "It was in the evening and the champagne bottle was in close proximity to Peggy," Chaplin recalls in his autobiography. "As the night wore on, I could see Peggy's interest veering over from me to Tom Ince, and she began to grow a little ugly, reminding me that what she had done to her husband with a champagne bottle she might do to me. Although I had drunk a little champagne, I was sober, and told her gently that if I saw the slightest suspicion of such a notion cross her pretty brow I would toss her overboard."

Headline writers predicted Chaplin would be Peggy's next marital conquest. But as much as she enjoyed his company, she quickly concluded he was not husband material, despite his millions. "Mickey hadn't lied when he told Peggy how rich Charlie was," Moore points out. "What Mickey neglected to add was that Charlie was also one of the biggest tightwads." Nor was Peggy embraced by the exalted circles in which Chaplin moved. Rumors even circulated that Mary Pickford was not "at home" the day he brought his latest flame to visit the hallowed halls of Pickfair.

Although it was never clear who dumped whom, the romance ended as abruptly as it had begun, and, as usual, Peggy's not marrying was as much headline fodder as her marrying. By early September, the *San Francisco Examiner* was proclaiming on page 1, "Peggy, After All, Not to Wed Chaplin." Her explanation of their relationship was typically evasive: "He has been advising me in a business way," she announced fastidiously to the paper's reporter.

Chaplin switched his attention to the exotic Polish actress Pola Negri, and Peggy, temporarily abandoning her desire to challenge the unofficial blacklist designed to keep her off the screen, returned to New York. But her feelings for Chaplin lingered for a time, and at a party the following Christmas at the home of theatrical producer

Oliver Morosco, she boasted loudly of the splendid present she expected from Chaplin. A package did in fact arrive. When she opened
the box, however, she discovered to her fury that it contained only a
tiny plastic figurine, one of the millions of cheap trinkets honoring
the great man that were available at any novelty shop during the years
of his fame. "Instead of being called the world's greatest sheik, Charlie
Chaplin should be called the world's greatest freak," Peggy later
snapped to a reporter. "He is a conceited little rat!"

At the time Peggy met Chaplin, he was poised to make his first film
for United Artists, the production company he had founded with
Pickford, D. W. Griffith, and Douglas Fairbanks. He had been seeking a role that would cap his long association with actress Edna
Purviance, and he desperately wanted to shake free from the comic
image of the tramp. Peggy's vivid stories about Letellier and the unfortunate Billy Errazuriz had resonated in his mind, and he realized
he could make good use of them in his next project. "Peggy told me
several anecdotes about her association with a well-known French
publisher," Chaplin writes in his autobiography. "These inspired me
to write the story 'A Woman of Paris' for Edna Purviance to star in.
I had no intention of appearing in the film, but I directed it." The result proved a landmark in Chaplin's career—his one foray into serious drama—and a breakthrough in the history of motion pictures.

The movie focuses on the bittersweet experiences of a woman
from the French provinces named Marie who sets off for Paris in the
mistaken belief that she has been jilted by the young villager she was
to marry. When next seen, Marie has become the restless mistress
of the sophisticated aristocrat Pierre Revel, a sleek, amoral character
much like Letellier. The villager reappears in her life, but when he
sees Marie and Revel together at a fashionable restaurant, he kills
himself in despair.

Chaplin was so enamored of Peggy's narrative that the original scenario stuck close to her version of events. "In the earliest stages of the story development, the characters are called Peggy and Letellier, and it seems likely that some incidents in the first version of the plot are much as Peggy related them to Chaplin," writes Chaplin's biographer David Robinson. But eventually the director made her stories his own, and in doing so he produced an elegant, sophisticated work remarkable for its allusive storytelling and deft flashes of irony.

When the picture was released in 1923, starring Purviance as Marie and Adolphe Menjou as Revel, critics responded with rapture. "There is more real genius in Charlie Chaplin's 'A Woman of Paris' than in any picture I have ever seen," Robert Sherwood wrote the next day in the *New York Herald*. Although a commercial flop, *A Woman of Paris* was acclaimed the outstanding picture of the year, and for more than half a century, until Chaplin's estate consented to its release in 1977, connoisseurs regarded the movie as one of the great "lost" films, a harbinger of a new naturalism and simplicity in the silent cinema.

With or without Chaplin, Peggy was now a permanent target for publicity. Every event in her life, from a sensational new romance to a thrilling new venture in show business, capitalized on her existing celebrity and ratcheted it up another notch. Each episode generated a fresh round of articles and pictures, which in turn made her even more ferociously in demand. The machine seemed relentless, unstoppable.

And unlike so many of the individuals whose names filled the headlines during those years, Peggy had no need of personal press agents or any other intermediaries to whip her reputation into frothy peaks. "She didn't need a press agent," explains Sol Jacobson, a longtime publicist for the Shuberts. "She generated news simply by existing."

It was true. Once she was anointed, astonishingly little was required to get her name in the papers. New York City had become the headquarters of the country's media and entertainment industries, making it inevitable that her every action, no matter how trivial, would command attention. Gossip columnists never tired of repeating her latest bon mot or cooing over her latest escort. She did not even have to bob her hair or acquire a pet goat, not that reporters ignored such earthshaking events. All she had to do was disembark from an ocean liner—or even from a transcontinental railway train—wearing some sensational frock, dispense a few withering observations about the fecklessness of the male sex, and bat the lashes of eyes invariably described as violet pools. The newsmen did the rest. "New husband? Why, listen; I don't know yet whether I'm divorced from the last one," she replied to a reporter's question as she switched trains in Chicago on her way home from the West Coast. "But give me a few weeks in Paris and New York," she added cheerfully, "and I'll probably have one."

She also found herself in demand for the most outlandish publicity stunts. Typical was an event held in 1924 on behalf of a group called the Citizens Military Training Camps, for which she posed atop a giant beach ball as it was rolled slowly along the sands of Atlantic City.

No matter who else was around, even on a homeward journey of the *Ile de France* when the passenger list included "a Vanderbilt, a Drexel, a grand duke, a handful of counts, a brace of princes, several generations of honorables, to say nothing of excellencies, doctors, and artists," according to the New York *Sun,* it was invariably Peggy's name that led all the rest in the ship's news reporter's account of the arrival. A sampling of headlines from one paper during one period— the *Los Angeles Examiner* during the spring of 1928—suggests the flavor and extent of coverage throughout the twenties: "Peggy Joyce to Marry? No"; "What, Again? Yes, Peggy Will Wed"; "Peggy Joyce Wins Battle of Champagne"(about the evening she hurled a glass of champagne at Erskine Gwynne in response to a satirical piece he had written about her in his gossipy Paris weekly the *Boulevardier*); "Spill Wine Down Youth's Neck? Not Me, Says Peggy" (the account of her denial, or, as she elegantly phrased it, "just a hatful of hooey"); "Petite French Star Thinks Peggy Terrible" (about film actress Lili Damita's feud with Peggy: "She ees terr-ible jealous about me. At Deauville last Easter she see me, and when her escort say I am most beautiful, Peggy get so mad she stamp her feet and walk out of the Casino"); "One More Count for Peggy?"; "Husbands Go, Jewels Stay."

Readers would have been naive to believe most of what was printed about her. Celebrity journalism of the day trafficked as much in fiction as in fact, and when Peggy passed through town, old articles about her were thriftily recycled, with deft touches of updating to reflect her latest exploits and plug whatever city she happened to have alighted in. She herself admitted that few of the words that supposedly emanated from her lovely crimson mouth were hers, and she found it rather endearing that reporters filed detailed personal interviews with her long before having actually laid eyes on her.

But none of this mattered. Having turned her into a household name, the gentlemen of the press had no intention of letting her reputation languish. The only recorded incident in which newsmen broke an appointment with her involved the time Rin Tin Tin came to town and every journalist rushed off to shake the paw of the nation's most famous German shepherd. By the end of the decade, when *Time* magazine proclaimed that Peggy was "easily the most famous woman in the U.S.," its tongue was only slightly in its cheek.

A popular vaudeville routine satirizing life under a Communist regime left no doubt about her main claim to fame: "Comes the revolution you'll all eat strawberries and cream," a soapbox orator promises his audience in describing his vision of the future. "You'll have chicken every Sunday. . . . Why, comes the revolution you'll all sleep with Peggy Hopkins Joyce." A voice from the crowd pipes up: "But I don't *want* to sleep with Peggy Hopkins Joyce." The orator shoots back, "Comes the revolution you'll sleep with Peggy Hopkins Joyce whether you want to or not."

The occasional whiffs of scandal helped fan the flames, and given Peggy's predilection for moving in a fast crowd, the likelihood of her getting caught up in slightly questionable dealings was great. When New York attorney William Fallon—"Bright Light Bill," as he was known—was hauled into court on charges that he had tried to bribe a juror in a mail-fraud case, what reporters and the public alike found most interesting was that Peggy had been Fallon's date at the Woodmansten Inn, the Bronx roadhouse run by her old pal Joe Pani where the incident allegedly took place. Despite the fact that she was a distinctly minor character and her testimony added little to the courtroom proceedings, even the *New York Times* got into the act. In an article headlined "Peggy Joyce Tells of Fallon's Dinner," the paper described her appearance in lavish detail, down to the white turban embroidered with a large *P* that she had worn to court.

When playboy financier John Locke and his brother Herbert were tried in an eight-million-dollar stock-fraud case and Peggy's name surfaced on a so-called sucker's list of women who showed them a good time, her involvement thrust the story onto page 1. Although the newspapers took care to point out that any list that included the name Peggy Joyce could hardly be considered a list of pushovers or easy marks, Peggy was livid about the salacious coverage, and she ripped the *Daily News's* article about the episode into shreds. With her usual eye on posterity, however, she saved the scraps in an envelope and squirreled it away among her personal papers.

Her reputation was such that preachers castigated her from their pulpits. "Peggy Joyce, who is capitalizing [on] her international ill fame for her movie aspirations has [the] nerve to compare herself to Cleopatra," railed one Chicago minister, pointing to her and her ilk as the cause of the city's soaring divorce rate. On the other hand, total strangers seemed ready to die for her. Just days after Billy Errazuriz killed himself in Paris, an American army lieutenant whom Peggy had never met was found near death from an apparent suicide attempt in Nice; in his hand he clasped a newspaper clipping in which she had described her feelings for the young Chilean. Others tucked away clippings about her with very different purposes in mind: a trio of burglars arrested by New York police were found to be carrying fifty skeleton keys and an article detailing the jewelry Peggy had received in her divorce settlement.

Her producer friend Oliver Morosco even made plans to name a nationwide chain of theaters in her honor. The first playhouse was to be in Hollywood, with a design a local newspaper described as "Italian of the fifteenth period." Decorative elements included a life-size statue of Peggy set in the facade and interior murals showing her splashing in a pool. But a freak accident caused the project to run aground before it could get fully under way. Peggy had recently presented the infant daughter newly born to Morosco and his wife, Selma, with a tiny string of uncultured pearls so beautiful they were promptly placed around the infant's neck. But an alarming rash suddenly appeared on the baby's throat, and by the third day she was dead, made fatally ill, or so it was believed at the time, by the lovely beads.

Peggy was not only devastated by the death—"I can never face Selma again!" she sobbed to Morosco—but terrified about how the press would react if the news leaked out. "Louella Parsons hates me," she wailed, "and she'd give her right arm for a story like this." The event marked one of the only times she tried to keep her name out of the papers.

Given Peggy's reputation, the theatrical producer Earl Carroll could not have chosen a better star for the first edition of *Vanities,* a racy new revue set to open in his own Broadway theater in the summer of 1923. What he sought, he candidly admitted, was not someone "endowed with talent" but "the brilliance and power of a well-known name," and Peggy was nothing if not that. Her detour through divorce court had made her an exceedingly valuable property; in a sense, she was New York's answer to Roxie Hart, the heroine of Maurine Watkins's 1926 play *Chicago,* who kills her married lover, revels in the publicity sparked by her sensational murder trial, and eventually parlays the whole experience into a star turn on the vaudeville stage. And for a show dealing mainly with sex, albeit wrapped in fantastically elaborate production numbers, who better than a celebrity renowned for her erotic romps across two continents?

Carroll, a languorous-looking man with a touch of the satyr in his expression, had come a long way from his days as a Pittsburgh youth building theaters out of cardboard boxes and peopling them with images cut from magazines. But he was hardly in the class of a Florenz Ziegfeld; W. C. Fields once dismissed him as a "preacher with an erection." His flamboyant and often offensive behavior led to numerous brushes with the law, most notably for hiring a teenage showgirl to remove her clothes and take a very public bath in champagne, a stunt that undoubtedly would have landed him in prison even if Prohibition had not been the law of the land. Nevertheless, Carroll was a master showman and publicist, with a sharp eye for a crowd pleaser. He had sent Peggy a friendly cable as she was steaming home after a visit to Europe in the spring of 1923. "We dock tomorrow and a wireless has just come from Earl Carroll," she wrote in her memoirs. "He says he wants to engage me as the star in the Earl Carroll Vanities and he will meet me at the pier."

Peggy's return to American soil always sparked a rush of excitement, and to whip up enthusiasm even further, Carroll had arranged a champagne reception for the press. For an hour, cameras clicked as photographers snapped her from every possible angle. "Come on, Peggy, show us those pretty gams!" they yelled, whereupon the object of their attention obligingly pulled up her skirt and flashed her dimpled knees.

Then came the usual fusillade of questions. "Miss Joyce, now that your last marriage to a millionaire has, shall we say, dissolved, what are your plans?" one reporter demanded. "Are you going to get married again?"

"Oh, I suppose so," Peggy replied indifferently. "You get used to being married and you feel kind of undressed single."

"I hear you got a bundle out of that last divorce. How much did Joyce give you?"

"Why, you make me sound like an absolute conniving woman," she answered with a smile. "I have earned that money, you know. I may be expensive, but I do deliver the goods."

Peggy had no illusions about the sort of show Carroll was cooking up for her, but given the state of her personal life she was inclined to consider his offer. Letellier, with whom she had left her precious dogs for safekeeping, was still in the picture. But her time abroad had made her increasingly wary of life with a strong-willed Frenchman. "He might think just because he married me he could shut me up in his Norman castle or something," she wrote in her memoirs. "Well, no man has ever shut me up and no man ever will." A message from Letellier informing her that the dogs had died clinched her decision. "If he cannot take any better care than that of my dogs," she wrote, "how can I expect him to take care of me?" Within days she was in Carroll's office signing her new contract for $5,000 a week.

Vanities opened on July 5, 1923. Hailed as "the most elaborate and daring thing of its kind ever to reach the Broadway stage," it was, at least in terms of the celebrities in the audience on opening night, a star-studded affair. A two-million-candlepower spotlight illuminated Carroll's theater, and the commotion outside became so frenzied that hundreds of police were summoned to maintain order. Yet much had changed in the six years since Peggy had last appeared in a Broadway revue. The Roaring Twenties were in full swing, especially around

Times Square, and the gentility of the prewar years had long since disappeared; playhouses were even installing special lounges where women could smoke.

While the American theater may have been enjoying a golden age, the word *classy* hardly described its typical offerings, particularly the revues that were fast becoming a Broadway fixture. The month after *Vanities* opened, the even racier *Artists and Models* introduced bare-breasted chorus girls to the New York stage, and within weeks Carroll's girls enthusiastically followed suit. "What your weary businessman wants is a show with pep, shapely, scantily clad girls, slapstick comedy, sensuous music," *Theater Magazine* wrote of the audience for the new productions. "They are out to enjoy a 'show' and they prefer it spicy with plenty of undressed chicken."

Nor were revues the only suggestive fare. By 1922 Broadway's farces had become so ribald and even its straight plays so frank there was talk of instituting censorship. A voluntary monitoring organization was hastily established, but it functioned largely on paper, as shown by the 1923 "living curtains" offered by George White's *Scandals* and the Shuberts' *Passing Show:* nude showgirls draped on curtains.

Earl Carroll's latest creation was custom-designed for this bolder, unblushing age. Although the sign over the stage door proclaimed, "Through these portals pass the most beautiful girls in the world," *Vanities* had little in common with Ziegfeld's high-class *Follies*. The emphasis was far more frankly sexual, and increasingly so with each subsequent edition. One sensed the innuendoes before the curtain went up; the opening-night program included advertisements for "lover's-form brassieres" and a fragrance called Pompeia that symbolized the "voluptuous magnificence of ancient Pompeii." Even the names of the chorines on stage—Polly Lux, Dolla Harkins, Flo Tempest, Vera Featherly—evoked the boudoir, and could there actually have been a showgirl named Lota Cheeke? Images of women attired only in garlands of flowers graced publicity flyers, along with an essay by one of Carroll's lissome performers, provocatively titled "Why I Pose Nude."

A famous property like Peggy did not remove her clothes, but she hardly needed to, because reporters were cranking out stories about her even before the first night. Once the show opened, much was made of the $1.5 million worth of jewels she reportedly wore at each performance, and the caption on one picture revealed that she had been photographed "from behind the bars of her dressing room window, which has been especially equipped to protect her gems." Of considerable interest was the "large and supposedly wicked" police dog that had been trained to let no one approach her or her possessions. And every reporter in town rushed to interview the doorman who found her $10,000 diamond wristwatch outside the stage door but who collected only half the promised $1,000 reward because "$500 was all the loose change Miss Joyce had" when she arrived to pick up the watch. It was no wonder advertisers for products like beauty creams were equally enamored of her image.

Although the offerings on the *Vanities* stage included "a hundred and ten beauties" and the gifted humorist Joe Cook, they were intended only as window dressing for the main attraction. Carroll had capitalized on his star's celebrity by taking the essential elements of her reputation and incorporating them into extravagant production numbers whose message was so blatant even the dimmest audience member could get the point. In a tableau called "Mr. Wagner's Wedding March," Peggy posed in bridal finery atop a gigantic revolving wedding cake. In a satirical sketch called "The Cloak," she paraded about in a flame-colored coat edged with white fox and made backhanded references to what the newspapers said about her attire. In a slight song-and-dance number called "Pretty Peggy," she was a vision in white and silver as a chorus line of scrubbed collegians warbled tributes to her blue eyes and her "daring air." And in "The Finale of the Furs," two dozen showgirls wearing squirrel, lamb, sable, and little else paid homage to "chinchilla, queen of all," as

Peggy, swathed in a $20,000 gown—the *Morning Telegraph* said $60,000—that trailed behind her like a giant fishtail, descended the steps of a huge marble pyramid.

The largely male audience was predictably smitten, with the notable exception of a New York jeweler named Randolph Trabent, who had lent her the emeralds, rubies, and sapphires that glittered on her body during the show. "I would suggest that you do *not* raise your skirt so high in the 'Pretty Peggy' dance," he wrote her after his third visit to the show. "It looks a trifle vulgar and I think you would get a much nicer effect to raise it just above your ankle." Displaying more theatrical acumen than might be expected from one of his profession, he applauded her decision to speak her song rather than sing it.

Although critics could not ignore her ethereal presence—"She is delicately formed, has an alluring gaze, and her hair is fair beyond words," as the New York *World* put it—her notices overall were devastating. "Just what qualifies her to head a cast is a mystery," wrote the *New York Evening Post*. "She cannot sing, dance, or act and beyond being a more or less pleasing picture in her blonde slenderness and lovely gowns there was little to commend her." More perceptive observers focused on her real gift, which was simply to bask in the brilliant wattage of her fame. "Her greatest talent, one might say, lies in being Peggy Joyce," concluded the *New York Herald*. "Carroll's showmanship, judging by the huge interest centered on her last night, was never better shown than in picking her for the star of his production." The critic could not resist adding, however, that the producer's showmanship "was also well demonstrated in not having her sing."

Critics who doubted the extent of her talents might have changed their minds had they witnessed the theatrics that took place in her dressing room directly after the first performance. According to an anecdote drawn from an early version of Peggy's memoirs that was syndicated in many newspapers and repeated some in Ken Murray's biography of Carroll, *The Body Merchant,* Peggy had just removed her pink chiffon dressing gown when she heard a knock and the sound of a male voice: "Peggy, open the door. There's somebody who's come all the way from Paris to see you."

Shrugging on her robe, she peeked out, expecting to see Letellier. Instead, there stood Carroll holding the hand of a small ringtail monkey.

"Henri couldn't make it tonight," the producer explained with a slight leer, "so he sent BoBo in his place."

The monkey was shy at first, but when Peggy handed him a banana, he jumped into her lap so enthusiastically her negligee flew open. Carroll untangled the two of them and placed BoBo on the dressing table, which was piled high with corsages, cards, and baskets of fruit. Then he turned to the real purpose of his visit. Slipping his hands under his star's robe, he began kissing her breasts and caressing her body. Within minutes, the two of them were entwined on the couch, moaning softly.

Suddenly the air was punctuated by an unearthly scream. The little monkey, furious that no one was paying attention to him, had begun shrieking madly and tearing up everything in sight, hurling bottles, flowers, and fruit into the air. An overripe orange narrowly missed Carroll's head and landed with a splat against the wall just behind him. A pillow exploded in a shower of feathers. Peggy watched, mesmerized, as citrus juice trickled down the sweating face of her producer, and for a brief moment she marveled at his ability to soldier on, oblivious to the jealous little creature going berserk just a few feet away.

Peggy's stint in *Vanities* brought her something more than the attentions of a leering showman from Pittsburgh and a chance to parade her finery before a Broadway audience. It also brought her a title, the one matrimonial accessory she had not yet acquired, although not for lack of trying.

Marrying royalty had always had great appeal for American

heiresses, a fortunate state of affairs since down-at-the-heels European noblemen were hardly averse to getting their soft, manicured hands on American fortunes. The practice became especially popular around the turn of the century, and by the late twenties a thousand such unions had taken place. Not all were as star-spangled as the 1895 marriage of Jay Gould's youngest daughter, Anna, to Count Boniface de Castellane, a media extravaganza in which everything from the bride's $6,000 veil to the gold boxes that held slivers of wedding cake were duly chronicled by the press. The noblemen involved were not always of the first rank, and many of these couplings came to tragic ends; Henry James knew whereof he wrote in *The Golden Bowl,* when he created Maggie Verver, a tragic heroine made miserable by marriage to a treacherous Italian prince.

But to rich young women from a democratic nation, acquiring a titled spouse had considerable charm. For a woman like Peggy Hopkins Joyce, born into an undistinguished family, such a match would have seemed especially attractive, an encouraging indication of how an increasingly elastic economic and social structure was allowing people to move among various worlds in ways that would have been unthinkable a few decades earlier.

Count Karl Gustav Morner, Gosta to his friends, was not exactly the world's most desirable catch. Although he hailed from one of Sweden's great noble families, had graduated from the national cavalry school, and ranked as a champion discus thrower, by the time he met up with Peggy he was living quietly in Chicago and desultorily running the American arm of a Swedish toothpaste company. But as far as his appearance was concerned, the twenty-seven-year-old businessman seemed ideally cast to play the part of Nordic royalty. "The count is more than six feet tall, well built and looks the part of a Swedish nobleman," the *New York Times* enthused. "His hair and complexion are light and in his immaculate dinner jacket and straw hat with its gay green, white and blue band, he look[s] more like a college student than the president of a corporation."

Peggy and Morner met through yet another nobleman, a Swedish baron to whom she was "practically engaged," as she put it in her memoirs. The baron, a friend of Morner's, had suggested that the count look Peggy up when *Vanities* moved to Chicago after its six-month run in New York, and one spring evening in 1924 he called on her after the show. As usual when Peggy and a presentable young man laid eyes on each other, the chemistry between them was instantaneous. The count struck her as one of the best-dressed men she had ever met, not to mention a dead ringer for the Prince of Wales.

"The baron was a dear, but Count Morner is the finest gentleman and the most gorgeous lover I have ever known," Peggy wrote in her memoirs. "He has a castle in Sweden or rather his family has, but I do not think they have much besides the castle. However a castle is something after all."

After yet another of her brisk courtships—the couple had known each other just a month—she and Morner were married on June 2, 1924, in Atlantic City. Although a typically last-minute affair, the ceremony was slightly less slapdash than Peggy's previous three marriages. Louis Wein, a minister of the Evangelist Lutheran Church, conducted the service, and the bride's half sister, Lucille, to whom Peggy had grown closer in recent years, was alerted in enough time to travel up from Farmville, Virginia, to serve as a witness.

Among the hundreds of myths, half-truths, and outright lies that swirled about Peggy Hopkins Joyce during her lifetime, none was more inflated than the number of rich spouses she had acquired. Had she married five millionaires by the time she met Chaplin, as he claimed in his autobiography and as the public was all too willing to believe? More? Who knew? Who could keep track?

In her memoirs, Peggy claimed she had been engaged fifty times, and perhaps she had. Given her predilection for quick liaisons, not to mention the press's penchant for announcing her betrothal to every man she ever dined with, danced with, or dallied with in the moonlight, it was understandable that in calculating the number of her marriages and near marriages, both public and press literally lost count. Hype overtook reality and became reality. Facts proved irrelevant.

The public's intense preoccupation with Peggy's marital accomplishments was hardly surprising. There was something wonderfully lascivious about multiple marriages, for they offered a tantalizing glimpse behind the bedroom door and reminded people all too explicitly what marriage was really about. Multiple marriages were especially interesting when each new partner was richer than the last. Even in the forties, when marital roundelays became more common, acquiring a long string of spouses was still considered fairly scandalous. When Peggy lurched from mate to mate two decades earlier, such behavior was regarded as shocking in the extreme. In a day when nice girls thought twice about kissing a man—not that they refrained—having collected four husbands by the age of thirty-one was almost unheard of. Not even Fitzgerald's thoroughly modern heroines tumbled into matrimony so frequently and with such abandon.

And despite looser sexual mores and softening attitudes toward divorce, a strict double standard still prevailed when it came to intimate behavior. Conduct by a man that prompted only winks and a few ribald remarks was greeted very differently when it was practiced by a member of the opposite sex. Women of the twenties had won both the vote and the right to rouge their knees, but definite limits restricted how far they could go in most spheres. When it came to changing partners in bed, the limits were clear.

As the most-married person on the planet, or so the world seemed to have concluded, the predictable media circus greeted Peggy's latest nuptials, particularly since this time around she had moved up a notch on the social ladder. Accounts of the wedding adorned front pages everywhere. Once the couple arrived at Peggy's apartment on

East Fifty-second Street in Manhattan, hordes of reporters camped on the doorstep of the building hoping for a glimpse of the happy couple, although they were rewarded only by the sight of the bride's maid on her way to buy breakfast rolls.

The count and his new countess undeniably made a fetching pair. In a photograph taken just after their marriage, they resembled figures atop a sugary Art Deco wedding cake, two beautiful people flanking an enormous bouquet of roses. Peggy wore a long, gauzy dress and a soulful expression; her husband, resplendent in evening clothes, gazed down at her adoringly, having carefully turned his perfect profile toward the camera. For a moment, the two of them seemed deeply in love.

Unbeknownst to reporters, however, the idyll had started unraveling within hours of the ceremony, for despite his royal trappings, Peggy's count was not much of a provider. Even before the couple left Atlantic City, she said afterward, she had begun cashing checks for hundreds of dollars to cover his tailor bills, his entertaining, even his laundry. As they were speeding down Fifth Avenue en route to their new home, they quarreled violently in the taxi, with Peggy claiming that her new husband punched her in the nose when she refused to buy him a new suit. He in turn insisted that, starting the very day of the marriage, she swore at him, called him names, and ridiculed him in public. He further charged that she fast developed a predilection for staying out all night, and when he grilled her about her whereabouts, she spat back, "It's none of your business!"

By July 30, after less than two months together, whatever marriage had existed was over. The count moved out of Peggy's apartment and into the Yale Club, leaving word with a maid that he was "through." Before long, he was evading process servers, selling insurance to make ends meet, and living in Forest Hills, Queens, with a woman the press described as a "raven-haired beauty."

"There was no honeymoon for us," confessed the handsome Swede, who according to his lawyer had married Peggy with only the haziest knowledge of her complicated marital history. "Our happiness was smashed on the day we were married." He had been incensed to learn that she was talking to theatrical agents and demanding several times her normal salary on the grounds that people would be more interested in an actress with a royal pedigree. "She wanted a title," he said bitterly, "and when she got it, she lost interest in me."

In fact, Peggy adored her new status, although she was not likely to admit it. "Titles are the easiest things in the world to get, and in Europe I could have done better than Countess, I could have been a Princess or something," she insisted to a reporter. "I married him because I thought he was a fine, sweet, manly boy, not the pig-headed Swede he has turned out to be." His claims of ignorance about her past struck her as highly dubious. "For him to say that I misrepresented anything about myself is just rot," she told the press. "If he doesn't know all about me, he is the only one who doesn't, for my life has surely been an open book."

Rumors of a reconciliation surfaced briefly, but Peggy was never one to stick around after a relationship soured, and by fall the marriage was a distant memory. "I made a mistake," she admitted in her memoirs. "Count Morner was a very nice boy and very handsome and really quite a good husband, for six weeks, anyway, but he has never worked and I think it would be good for him if he did. Because what is the good of a talent for spending money if you haven't got any money to spend?"

Not until the following year did she file for divorce, and at first she denied having done any such thing. "I am as much in love with my husband as any woman is after she has been married two years," she announced enigmatically in November 1925 to the *New York Times,* which was avidly following the affairs of the woman it referred to affectionately as "Countess Peggy." But even as she spoke, her lawyers were beginning proceedings against Morner in Paris, where relations between a husband and wife were presumed to be a private matter and an alliance could be dissolved far more quickly and discreetly than in the United States. In February of 1926, newspapers reported that a divorce had been granted two months previously, on the grounds that the count "was not faithful, forsook his domicile, and was too fond of his friends."

The whole episode came and went in the blink of an eye. Yet again Peggy had done nothing more than lurch in and out of an ill-fated marriage, leaving a trail of gossip and speculation in her wake. But neither the press nor the public could bear to let a day go by without seeing what new and amazing behavior she was up to. She, for her part, made it easy to track her adventures by telling reporters everything they wanted to know.

By the time her divorce from Morner came through, Peggy had long since moved on to something more compelling than marriage to a ne'er-do-well nobleman. She had become a movie star.

Peggy had made previous assaults on Hollywood, most notably during her brief visit back in 1922, but this time she had come to town under the wing of the powerful independent producer Pat Powers, the current man in her life. Although she didn't approach the stature of reigning Hollywood deities like Pickford or Norma Talmadge, her name recognition now rivaled that of many of Hollywood's bona fide stars. "She is what newspaper men call 'automatic front-page copy,'" wrote the publicity people when her new project was being hatched. The *Pittsburgh Press* added: "If it were announced that Peggy Hopkins Joyce would stop off in the large cities through which she passed on her trip across the country to the film studio and drive through the streets in an open automobile, she could collect greater crowds than either Jack Dempsey or President Coolidge."

Not everyone approved of her career plans. The news that she was heading for Hollywood caused such a stir in Wisconsin, the state legislature hastily introduced a bill advocating censorship of motion pictures. According to *Variety,* the lawmakers feared that "the notoriety she had achieved through her numerous marriages and divorces . . . might be capitalized to sell her pictures."

But most Americans could not wait for Peggy's big-screen debut. Although they had seen her face a million times in the newspapers, relatively few had beheld her in action. Her few previous movies, largely one-reelers in which she had only minor parts, had been made back in the teens, and the reach of shows like the *Follies* had not extended much beyond New York. Now the American public would be able to observe Peggy Hopkins Joyce in the flesh, so to speak. The prospect was awesome.

In late 1924, the year she descended on Hollywood to make her first major motion picture, movies were emerging as the true mirror of the American soul. The fledgling film colony had been transformed into a fabled kingdom by the sea, the place where the nation's dreams and sometimes its nightmares were given shape, reality, and a soaring sound track. Hundreds of feature films were being churned out every year, filling thousands of theaters. Nor were these the drab little nickelodeons of cinema's early days; rather, they were opulent palaces in which stars twinkled in azure ceilings and live goldfish swam in crystalline pools.

By 1926, the year her movie appeared, some fifty million Americans—nearly half the population—were going to the pictures at least once a week. Americans had gotten their first haunting glimpse of Greta Garbo and witnessed such cinematic landmarks as Cecil B. DeMille's *The Ten Commandments,* Erich Von Stroheim's *Greed,* Sergei Eisenstein's *The Battleship Potemkin,* and Chaplin's *The Gold Rush.* And thanks to movies like Fairbanks's *The Black Pirate,* they were enjoying an amazing invention called Technicolor.

Hollywood had come into its own for less savory reasons as well. In the scandal-stained year of 1922, the director William Desmond Taylor was the victim of a sensational murder that destroyed the careers of two famous actresses. After three trials, Fatty Arbuckle was acquitted in the equally lurid death of Virginia Rappe. Valentino was arrested for bigamy, and when he died four years later, rumors would fly that he had been poisoned by a discarded mistress.

For Peggy, this world was as exciting as a new romance. In fact, during this latest visit to Hollywood, Peggy enjoyed one of her unlikeliest romances, a fling with Irving Thalberg, the young genius who headed production at MGM. Thalberg, like Chaplin, was one of Hollywood's mythic figures, not to mention the most eligible bachelor in town, and his brilliance was made more poignant by the sense that his time on earth was short. He had been born with a weak heart, and doctors predicted he would not live past thirty.

A few of Thalberg's playboy friends had introduced him to Peggy, and although the results of a screen test made him reluctant to encourage her professional aspirations, the affair blazed brightly for a short time. Thalberg was drawn to beautiful, sexually experienced women, and Peggy, though not attracted to brooding, intellectual types, was hardly immune to the aura of power Thalberg exuded. Nevertheless, they were indisputably one of Hollywood's odder couples. Thalberg's straitlaced mother, Henrietta, looked with dismay on his glamorous companions, and she was especially appalled by the international sex symbol who towered over her sober, dark-eyed son.

Though intense, the infatuation quickly passed, and after a fling with the actress Constance Talmadge, Thalberg moved on to Norma Shearer, whom he married in 1927. When he confided his feelings about Norma to Frances Goldwyn, wife of producer Sam Goldwyn, she reminded him teasingly that he had once thought he was in love with Peggy Joyce. "Oh, no," Thalberg replied seriously. "That was sex. This is love."

The vehicle by which America would get its first extended look at Peggy, a film called *The Skyrocket,* arrived with an impeccable pedigree. The story was based on a series of articles that Adela Rogers St. Johns, the "world's greatest girl reporter," as the Hearst organization billed her, had written for its *Cosmopolitan* magazine. The powerful Boston banker Joseph P. Kennedy had helped arrange financing. And the director was Peggy's earlier mentor and suitor, the gifted Marshall Neilan, who chose the film as the first project for his newly formed movie company, von Stroheim having declined the honor of supervising Peggy's maiden outing in Hollywood.

The picture starred Peggy as Sharon Kimm, an attractive extra on a movie lot who catches the attention of a world-famous director. With his help, her career takes off, but fame leads to arrogance and eventually the possibility of disaster. Yet there to cushion her fall is an old pal who has loved her all along and who, thanks to one of those amazing coincidences that occur only in Hollywood screenplays, wrote the film that made her a star in the first place.

Neilan thought Peggy perfect for the part of Sharon Kimm, and he anticipated that she would be catnip at the box office. But though the studio's publicity materials had him describing his star as "a screen diamond of the purest water," he had long since recovered from his infatuation.

She too had lost interest in him. "Directors are funny people," she wrote in her memoirs. "They think they are tin gods on wheels and love to keep the star waiting to show how important they are. Mickey Neilan is a very good director, but he is the only man who ever kept me waiting and I will tell him something if we ever get this picture finished. Of course now I must remain friends with him because a director can ruin a picture if he wants to and has it in for the star, not that Mr. Neilan is like that, but I am taking no chances."

Very quickly, the two developed a mutual loathing, and their time together was anything but harmonious. The increasingly influential fan magazines had helped Peggy acquire specific ideas about how movie actresses should behave, and she flounced about the set in a petulant, imperious manner, waving a list of demands that included a chair with her name on it, along with "everything that Mary Pickford has."

Animosity between star and director spilled over even into the area of costumes. Though for most of the movie Peggy was swathed in sumptuous Parisian gowns and a $60,000 sable coat, the early sequences required that she wear the shabbier outfits appropriate for a struggling beginner. Typically, such items were whipped up by the wardrobe department with the liberal assistance of bleach and scissors. But according to Harold Grieve, the art director on the film, Neilan was fed up with Peggy's prima donna antics by now and was eager to teach her a lesson.

"Take her down to the Salvation Army or some of those places where they have secondhand clothes," he reportedly ordered Grieve, "and just buy her secondhand clothes."

Grieve was stunned. "Mr. Neilan, would you do that to a picture star?" he demanded.

"I'll do it to her," the director replied grimly.

Reluctantly, Grieve complied, and the pair set out in a limousine in search of a thrift shop. Perhaps the leisurely drive calmed her down, or maybe it was simply the sight of Neilan's face disappearing in the rearview mirror. In any case, Peggy relaxed to the point that Grieve had a chance to glimpse a very different facet of *The Skyrocket*'s leading lady. As the two of them made their way around the city, he noticed that she was lugging a battered cardboard shoebox, an item that contrasted sharply with her chinchilla jacket and her pearls. She was still clutching the shoebox when they stopped for lunch. Would she like to check it, Grieve inquired.

"Oh, no," she replied. "I couldn't leave that in the checkroom."

After they sat down to eat, he expressed curiosity as to what was inside. "Would you like to see it?" Peggy offered. Removing the thick rubber band, she opened the box to display a mass of glittering diamond jewelry. "This is all my estate," she said simply.

★　★　★

Hollywood publicity campaigns had grown ever more lavish as movies themselves had become more ambitious, and with an international celebrity and certified royalty at the heart of *The Skyrocket,* the push was stupendous, despite the fact that the film had languished for more than a year while Neil pulled together the money to complete postproduction. A few months before the opening, *Moving Picture World* reported of Peggy that the distributors, Associated Exhibitors, were "forging ahead in their plans to make her the biggest star in filmdom" and had organized a special task force to handle the picture. The magazine also ran an eight-page ad touting the movie, with a text that shrieked: "It's big! She is great! Oh-h-h! What a star! What a story! What a picture! What a Wow!" Peggy was compared favorably to Sarah Bernhardt and Lillian Gish, and the press revealed the stunning news that the studio was considering seven hundred properties for her next project.

Newspapers around the country were bombarded with articles in which Peggy dispensed tips on handling men, presumably based on her own vast experience. "No matter how much you disagree with their point of view," urged a typical morsel, "tell them they are right and not only right but wonderful." Her byline appeared on pieces about good grooming, in which she came out fearlessly in favor of henna rinses, clean underwear, and hose that blended with one's attire. Local barbers were advised to offer the fashionable Peggy Hopkins Joyce bob, ice cream parlors were encouraged to promote the "Peggy Hopkins Joyce sundae," and theater operators, who had long since decided not to boycott anything as potentially lucrative as a Peggy Joyce film, were instructed to rope in any stray male viewers by sponsoring Peggy Hopkins Joyce bathing suit competitions, in which contestants would whip up skimpy outfits and model them at a fashion parade when the movie came to town.

In an appeal to highbrow audiences, the filmmakers distributed excerpts from an article by George Jean Nathan, cofounder of the prestigious *American Mercury* magazine, to the effect that "you can't get tens of thousands of people to read about you, write about you and talk about you and pay to see you unless you have something." Potential viewers might have been even more impressed by the rest of his observations: "The truth about this Joyce girl is that, in the midst of a humdrum and prosaic civilization, she is something of a romantic figure," Nathan went on to say. "There is a touch of the French eighteenth century about her. . . . In another day, Peggy Joyce might have made history. In our day Peggy Joyce has merely made cheap journalistic copy. It is not her fault; it is the fault of the age in which she lives."

Movie Weekly featured her on its cover, and *Photoplay*, which dubbed her "the Circe of this age," posed that most tantalizing of questions: "What is that lure of Peggy Joyce?" Ivan St. Johns received the enviable assignment of interviewing the star of his wife's movie in order to provide the answer, and he proved equal to the task. "France had its Dubarry, Egypt its Cleopatra and America its Peggy Hopkins Joyce," he wrote. "The much discussed secret of Peggy's charm is so old that it's new to most of our wise young flappers of today. It's what Lilith taught her granddaughter in the Garden of Eden, and Helen of Troy used to tie up a couple of nations for ten years. Peggy Hopkins Joyce, so-called enchantress, comes nearer to being just an old-fashioned girl than anything I've seen around Hollywood in a long time. . . . She listens with her eyes, and they are big and blue and very sweet and turned up at you in that sort of 'Aren't you wonderful, you big strong man, how did you ever come to know so much' look that is as fatal as raw liquor to anything that wears trousers. . . . And she has a trick of dropping her eyes—the loveliest thing about her is her eyelids, which are like magnolia petals—way down, and then raising them very slowly, almost sadly, wistfully. It would be perfectly easy to understand how any man would say after one of those, 'Here, darling, have a pearl necklace and don't look so sad.' "

No publicity stunt struck the producers as too silly. As Peggy was sailing home from a postfilming vacation in Europe aboard the *Mauritania,* a convoy of planes buzzed overhead, unfurling banners emblazoned with the name of the movie. In a final artistic flourish, the famous French flying ace R. Rex Renee, who had presumably been hired by the Associated Exhibitors sales force just for such dare-devilry, dangled from a rope ladder as the ship steamed into the harbor so that he could pelt the star with roses as she stood on deck.

Next came what *Moving Picture World* hailed as "one of the most novel and brilliant premieres ever given a motion picture," an invitation-only screening in the grand ballroom of the mighty S.S. *Leviathan.* "This is the first time in the history of motion pictures that a premiere has been held aboard one of the world's big floating palaces," the magazine gushed. Peggy and the ship's officers received nearly a thousand guests in the ship's Palm Garden, after which there was dancing to the music of the S.S. *Leviathan* orchestra. Radio station WMCA broadcast the proceedings, and the studio promptly placed Peggy under contract for three more films.

Most remarkable was that the target of all this attention had only the spottiest of professional credentials and had previously earned some of the most dreadful reviews imaginable. But with a bona fide celebrity, such paucity of theatrical talent mattered not at all. People had been hearing about Peggy for years, and they did not want to stop. They couldn't care less whether she could act.

Large and enthusiastic crowds jammed New York's Colony Theater when *The Skyrocket* opened in January 1926. They were not disappointed. Peggy did photograph "like an angel," as Neilan had acknowledged, and publicity photographs from the film revealed that she looked good in cheap clothes and like a million dollars in smart ones. Whether reclining on a settee in a negligee extravagantly trimmed with ostrich plumes, trailing embroidered evening gowns

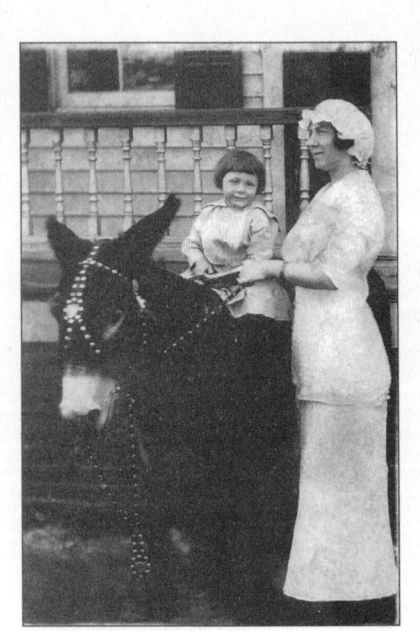

LEFT: Peggy Joyce's maternal grandmother, Emma Jane Sykes Wood *(Price family)*

Dora Wood (right), Peggy's mother. Dora abandoned her husband and ten-year-old daughter, demonstrating that a woman could escape an unhappy marriage. *(Price family)*

Samuel Upton Jr., Peggy's father, son of a long line of Uptons from Camden County, North Carolina *(Upton family)*

The house on Lee Street in Berkley, Virginia, where Peggy spent her early years *(Price family)*

ABOVE: The young Peggy Upton
(Price family)

Peggy at age twelve.
(Museum of Modern Art)

Ziegfeld Follies, 1917. Peggy (far left) donned helmet and gauntlets to portray Great Britain, one of the Allied nations, in an extravagant patriotic number. *(Billy Rose Theater Collection of the New York Public Library for the Performing Arts)*

The star of James Montgomery Flagg's 1918 one-reeler *The Bride* *(Billy Rose Theater Collection of the New York Public Library for the Performing Arts)*

Chicago lumber baron James Stanley Joyce, Peggy's third and richest husband. During their brief time together, Joyce spent $1,400,000 on his gold-digging wife. (*Joyce Foundation*)

In Miami, the $200,000 mansion where the Joyces lived briefly in early 1920 (*Joyce Foundation*)

Peggy in her dressing room preparing for her role in *Vanities*, a racy romp, 1923. Metal bars were installed to protect the $1,500,000 worth of jewels Peggy wore for each performance.
(New York Times Pictures)

Peggy's exquisite image was used to advertise an assortment of products.
(author's collection)

Countess Peggy with Gosta Morner, her fourth husband, a Swedish nobleman, in 1924. The marriage lasted only a few weeks. *(Brooklyn Public Library— Brooklyn Collection)*

VORITE *stars* OF FAMED DIRECTORS

MovieWeekly

OCTOBER 18 1924

10¢

PEGGY HOPKINS JOYCE

an INTIMATE GLIMPSE *of* PEGGY HOPKINS JOYCE

The cover of *Movie Weekly,* prior to Peggy's Hollywood debut in *The Skyrocket,* Marshall Neilan's 1926 film *(author's collection)*

Publicity still for *The Skyrocket*
(courtesy of the Academy of
Motion Picture Arts and Sciences)

An on-screen moment with Owen Moore, Mary Pickford's former husband, who played opposite Peggy in *The Skyrocket (Wisconsin Center
for Film and Theater Research)*

Publicity still for *The Skyrocket (courtesy of the Academy of Motion Picture Arts and Sciences)*

Peggy at the opening
of the Ziegfeld
Theater in New York
in 1927, swathed in
her signature furs
(Museum of Modern Art)

Peggy's $300,000 blue diamond was
said to have come from auto magnate
Walter Chrysler, a token of his
affection presented during their affair.
(Museum of Modern Art)

Edward Steichen's famous portrait, featuring the $300,000 diamond, from *Vanity Fair*, 1931 (© *Edward Steichen*/Vanity Fair, *Condé Nast Publications, Inc. March 31*, Peggy Hopkins Joyce)

"Those Peggy Joyce revelations are rather corking, aren't they?"

Peggy's doings were the talk of the town. A Peter Arno *New Yorker* cartoon, 1931. *(© The New Yorker Collection 1931 Peter Arno from cartoonbank.com. All rights reserved)*

The 1933 Paramount comedy *International House.* At the time, Peggy was better known than W. C. Fields and thus received top billing. *(Marc Wanamaker/ Bison Archives)*

INTERNATIONAL HOUSE

WITH
PEGGY HOPKINS JOYCE
W.C. FIELDS
RUDY VALLEE
STUART ERWIN
george BURNS & *gracie* ALLEN
COL. STOOPNAGLE *and* BUDD
CAB CALLOWAY
AND HIS ORCHESTRA

Publicity stills for *International House*. Peggy was turning forty when the film was released. *(Universal Studios)*

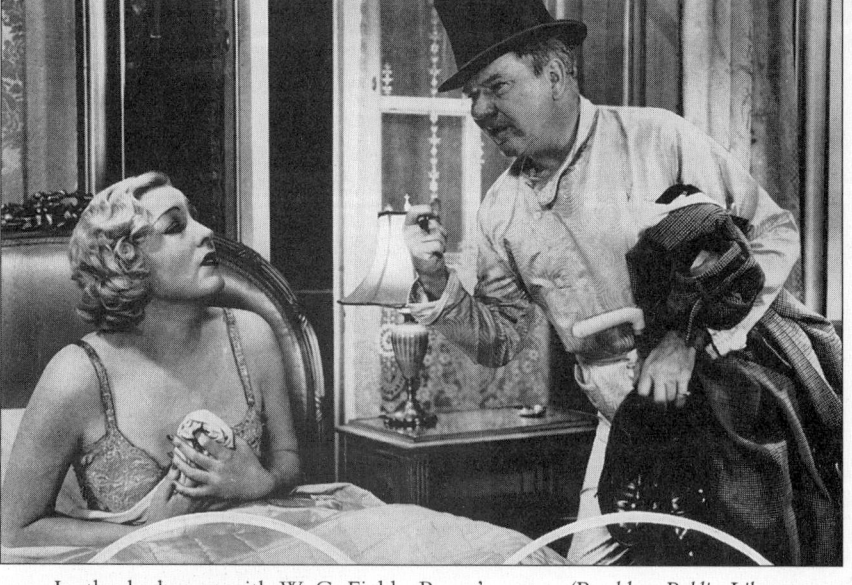

In the bedroom with W. C. Fields, Peggy's costar *(Brooklyn Public Library —Brooklyn Collection)*

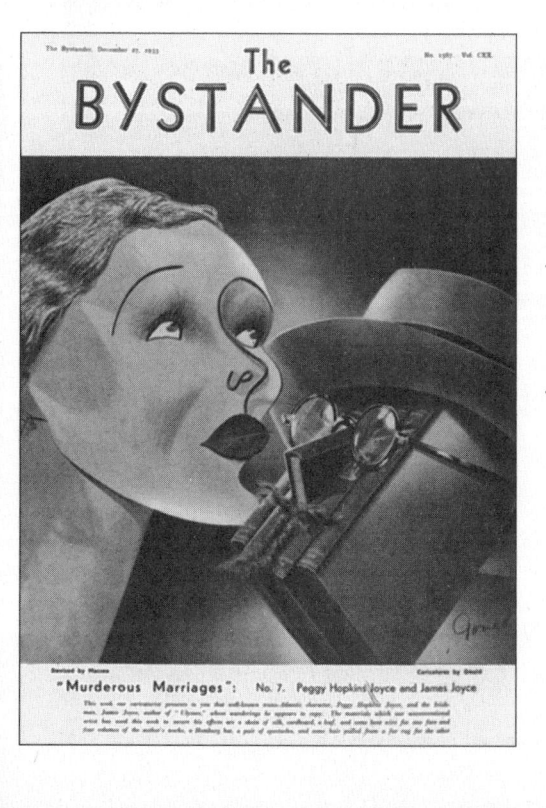

The two most famous Joyces of the day, paired in a "murderous marriage," in *The Bystander*, 1933. *Vanity Fair* also coupled the two Joyces that year: "Think of the fun James Joyce could have with Peggy," the magazine wrote, "teaching her all about the stream of consciousness." *(Free Library of Philadelphia, Theater Collection)*

Nightclubbing with the Clark Gables at the Hollywood Restaurant, New York, 1934 *(Corbis/Bettmann-UPI)*

Peggy with advice-to-the-lovelorn columnist Dorothy Dix in Miguel Covarrubias's caricature, *Vanity Fair,* 1935. The caption read: "Joyce—orchid, green ring, fur brown coat, brassy blond hair, gold ankle bracelet, brite [*sic*] red lips, shadowed blue eyes, with platinum bracelets ... Dix— black dress, lace collar." *(Estate of Miguel Covarrubias, Covarrubias Foundation)*

With Vivian Jackson,
a wealthy amateur
jockey from England
to whom Peggy was
engaged in 1936
*(Brooklyn Public
Library—Brooklyn
Collection)*

With Andrew Meyer,
Peggy's sixth and final
husband
(Corbis-Bettmann/UPI)

A sketch by William Auerbach-Levy, caricaturist to the stars *(Theater Collection, the Museum of the City of New York)*

set off by a fortune in jewels, or simply lounging about in a bathing costume that revealed her very squeezable knees, she never appeared anything less than delectable.

And despite its hackneyed plot, *The Skyrocket* turned out to be "one of the very best films about Hollywood," according to a chronicler of the golden age of Hollywood, ruthless in its depiction of the luminaries of the screen world. Gloria Swanson was identified as the prototype of Sharon Kimm, and many saw traces of Neilan himself in the powerful, womanizing director. The movie even had a hit song, a lilting waltz called "Wonderful One" that had been composed by Neilan, transcribed by orchestra leader Paul Whiteman, and published with Peggy's picture on the cover of the sheet music.

While critics could not assess her performance without taking into account her towering reputation, she collected some unexpectedly strong notices. The *New York Times,* which described her dryly as a woman "not unknown in New York and Paris," allowed that she gave "a credible performance," although it acknowledged that "one is never impressed that she is in want." *Variety* added: "This girl has obtained possibly more publicity than any other woman of her years outside of screen stars. . . . She should mop up at the box office for any exhibitor, and the smaller [the] town the more certain they are of cashing [in], for the smaller towns never had a Peggy Joyce."

Photoplay voted *The Skyrocket* one of the best pictures of the month and singled out Peggy's performance for special commendation, next to John Gilbert's in *The Big Parade* and Valentino's in *The Eagle.* "Every woman in America will undoubtedly go to see 'The Skyrocket' for a look at this most famous 'vampire' of our age, and probably a good many of the men," the magazine wrote, "but the surprising thing is that they are bound to find Peggy Hopkins Joyce not only a beauty but a thoroughly competent actress."

Despite the hoopla, though, *The Skyrocket* barely made back its hefty production costs. A South Carolina theater owner described the opening as "the biggest disappointment of the past year" and said that had he known what a disaster he was in for, he would never have booked the movie, even had it been offered for free. More significantly, *The Skyrocket* proved a last gasp of a world soon to be transformed beyond anyone's wildest imaginings. *The Jazz Singer,* whose arrival would toll the official death knell of the silent era, loomed on the horizon, and a revolution in popular entertainment lay just ahead.

For Neilan, the director who had put Peggy's name on marquees across the nation, the film's troubles were a harbinger of his own fall from grace. His was one of the many careers to collapse with the coming of sound; though a filmmaker of immense talent, he self-destructed early, the victim of hard living and harder drinking. When he died three decades later, it was the song "Wonderful One," a relic from the movie made right before his skid downhill, that was played at his wake.

For Peggy, by contrast, *The Skyrocket* represented simply the latest milestone on her journey through the nation's consciousness, another event that capitalized on her fame and exploited it further. As a result of the film, the press speculated endlessly about subsequent projects, and she regaled reporters with her hopes and dreams for the future, just as if she were a legitimate industry fixture. She was not, of course, and the movie community was aware of that fact even at the time. "She didn't create any sensation here," recalls Adela St. Johns's daughter, Elaine, who was a child when Peggy came to town to star in her mother's movie. "She thought she was from New York and pretty grand. But she just passed through. She never fit in."

Years later, gossip columnist Louella Parsons quoted Peggy as telling someone she was never so glad to leave anyplace as she was to leave Hollywood after the release of *The Skyrocket*. Parsons doubted that such a nice girl would utter something so spiteful, but Peggy was smart enough to know where she shone to best advantage. Her film had done poorly at the box office, and Neilan would have had scant interest in working with her a second time, especially with the forth-coming arrival of sound about to rewrite the rules governing Hollywood moviemaking. She had always felt more at home in the world of the theater; though she dropped out of the cast of the 1927 edition of the popular Broadway revue *Artists and Models* during the tryouts in Philadelphia, she was still on the lookout for a way to return to the stage. It was her great good fortune that not long after-ward, the delightful E. Ray Goetz entered her personal and professional life with the promise of an intriguing project.

Goetz was one of Broadway's powerhouses, the author of such classic melodies as "For Me and My Gal" and, before the twenties were over, the producer of hit musicals like *Fifty Million Frenchmen,* with songs by his close pal Cole Porter. Though hardly an Adonis—Anita Loos once described him as resembling an "overfed Buddha"—he was a world-class charmer, with three wives to his credit. "When he walks into a room," his producer friend Billy Rose often said of him, "it's like turning on a big chandelier." By 1928 his marriage to French actress Irene Bordoni was on the rocks, and Peggy had been named the official "other woman" in the breakup; in her divorce suit, Bordoni claimed, among other things, that Goetz had spent too much money buying orchids for Peggy.

The Lady of the Orchids, the appropriately titled play that Goetz had written and produced specifically for his newest flame, opened on December 3, 1928, and seemed ideally suited for Peggy's return to Broadway. The story focused on the nocturnal adventures of a se-ductive Parisian who is being kept by a wealthy middle-aged lover and simultaneously dallying with a young gigolo and an earnest law student, with predictable confusion in the boudoir. But although the racy French farce that inspired it had been a smash hit in Europe, and despite a certified headline maker at its heart, the project was a disas-ter. Most critics hated *Orchids;* "bosh" and "drivel" were among the kinder descriptions. While reviewers could not ignore the enormity of the star's reputation, and a few even found merit in her performance and concluded that she had not acquitted herself badly, they also could not resist the inevitable wisecracks. "I can always say I've seen Peggy Hopkins Joyce in her pajamas," wrote Robert Garland, who noted appreciatively that the pajamas in question were trimmed with ermine. It was also reliably reported that the star had supplied her own ermine bedspread. Playgoers with any brains headed for *Show Boat* over at the Ziegfeld or Ben Hecht and Charles MacArthur's sidesplitting comedy *The Front Page*. After two and a half weeks and a loss of $50,000, *The Lady of the Orchids* quietly folded before the year was out, one of the undisputed flops of the season.

As usual, the woman Louella Parsons quickly labeled the "orchidacious Peggy Joyce" walked away from the wreckage unscathed. She had had the satisfaction of seeing her name spelled in lights outside the Henry Miller Theater—the title of the play was not mentioned—and she had long since stopped caring about critics. Her dressing room was filled with congratulatory telegrams from Noel Coward, Eddie Cantor, and producer Walter Wanger, among dozens of well wishers. Despite the way she sometimes talked about her professional endeavors, her real career, as she and her audience knew well, was her shimmering lifestyle and the rich men who made it possible. Show business was just a sideline.

7

"Life after the Sun Went Down"

For a glimpse of what it was like to be Peggy during her heyday, the best place to start is with Lorelei Lee, the glamorous, hilarious, and utterly immoral siren who strutted out of Anita Loos's satirical novel *Gentlemen Prefer Blondes* in 1925. As if following in Peggy's delicate, high-heeled footsteps, Lorelei traipsed about Europe in search of adventure, collected diamonds in abundance, married a millionaire, and eventually became a movie star. Both women were shrewd and unsentimental creatures who believed that while sex might have little to do with love, it had a great deal to do with jewelry.

When *Gentlemen Prefer Blondes* became a best-seller and Loos was pressed about the model for Lorelei Lee, the author often cited a pretty featherhead who had caught the eye of Loos's idol and secret heartthrob, H. L. Mencken, "the dumbest blonde of all, a girl who had bewitched one of the keenest minds of our era." Loos loved to concoct such anecdotes, and this one may have even contained a shred of truth. But it is almost certain that a primary inspiration came from Peggy Hopkins Joyce. "I know that Anita looked on her as a key figure," says Mary Anita Loos von Saltza, the author's niece. "Even though they weren't of the same social class, my aunt would have witnessed her behavior. She would have talked about Peggy with amusement and seen her as a type worth writing about."

Peggy was hardly the only gold digger in town during Loos's era, but she was unquestionably the most conspicuous, "the original blonde preferred by gentlemen," as Broadway columnist Ed Sullivan described her in the *Evening Graphic*. An astute social observer like Loos would have been keenly aware of Peggy's reputation and her place in the culture; she acknowledged as much by giving her a walk-on part in *Gentlemen Prefer Blondes*. In one idiosyncratically spelled diary entry, Lorelei explains why her stuffed-shirt companion has snubbed Peggy at the Ritz in Paris: "Mr. Spoffard is a very very famous Prespyterian and he is really much to Prespyterian to meet Peggy Hopkins Joyce." According to film historian Eve Golden, "Loos made no secret of the fact that Peggy had been one of the main inspirations for the character, though she stopped short of claiming that Peggy and Lorelei were one and the same," perhaps to avoid either paying royalties or fighting a lawsuit.

Loos could not have avoided the endless newspaper accounts of Peggy's past, which resembled a souped-up version of Lorelei's story while perfectly capturing its flip, mercenary tone. Lorelei's descriptions of her romps across the Continent sound suspiciously like Peggy's, even down to a series of misadventures involving a diamond tiara. And Lorelei's most famous aphorism—"Kissing your hand may make you feel very very good but a diamond and safire bracelet lasts forever"—encapsulates exactly the sentiment Peggy had been uttering for years.

Like Lorelei, Peggy surrounded herself with opulence. When at noon she would pry open one mascara-smudged eye to greet the day—a girl who had been up till dawn never dreamed of rising earlier—it was to gaze upon a richly appointed setting, courtesy of whichever wealthy protector was footing her bills at that particular moment. Ever since the time she had trudged up to the attic of the Hopkins town house in Washington and been bowled over by the sight of the gleaming antique furnishings, she had nursed a passion for luxurious decor, and once she acquired the means to satisfy her appetite, she did so with a vengeance.

The bedroom in one of her Manhattan apartments so dazzled a writer from *Movie Weekly* magazine that the enthralled journalist could barely keep control of her prose: "Rare inlaid pieces of furniture stood about, lost in the shadows," the visitor wrote. "The lavender curtains were drawn across the windows. A mulberry carpet muffled any footfalls with a white bearskin stretching its generous portions across it. We had expected flowers. But even our acquaintance with the stars did not lead us to expect so many or such flowers. Blood-red American beauties stood about in vases tall as a man. Peggy raised herself from a mound of tiny embroidered cushions as we entered. A soft, shaded light shone beneath the lavender and lace draperies of her bed canopy. And, his slumbers disturbed by our talk, a tiny Pekinese stirred drowsily on his scarlet cushion."

Among the various addresses she occupied on Manhattan's East Side was 423 Park Avenue, at Fifty-sixth Street, the apartment above the Rosary Florist Shop in which she had been ensconced by Stanley Joyce before their marriage; visitors especially remembered the intimate brunches she hosted featuring sautéed calves brains. During another period she lived in a suite on the West Side at the Ansonia, the ornate turn-of-the-century apartment hotel on upper Broadway whose celebrity-studded clientele included her old boss Flo Ziegfeld and her friend Oliver Morosco. In 1926, perhaps feeling a temporary need to nest after her travels across two continents, she acquired a place of her own, a yellow-fronted town house at 158 East Sixty-third Street, complete with servants' quarters on the top floor and a tiled pool in the back garden.

The house also came with a slightly scandalous past. Some years earlier, the single young woman who had owned the place, a dress designer named Edith Bobe, had been terrorized by robbers who knocked out her front teeth and made off with $25,000 worth of diamonds and ermine coats. Given the contents of her own capacious closets, Peggy also worried about unwelcome guests; she once described one of her apartments as "barricaded worse than Sing Sing." And when she cleared out of No. 158 a few years later, among the jumble of expensive items that playwright George S. Kaufman, the subsequent occupant, had to clear away was a solid gold police whistle, "presumably kept for summoning help in the event of intruders."

Peggy's main order of business upon waking was seeing to her attire, a fairly daunting task. Walking into her coat closet was like entering a forest of fur, a thicket of sleek ermine jackets, rich dark mink, and lush silver fox, and she never left home without a solid gold compact and her jade cigarette case encrusted with rubies and emeralds. Her jewels traveled in smart alligator cases, and her fourteen-carat-gold perfume bottles and toilet articles were engraved with the word *Peggy,* copied from her distinctive plump script.

Newspapers delighted readers with lists of her important jewels. A typical rundown from the Hearst organization cited three ropes of pearls, among them the necklace from Stanley Joyce that measured in at three yards, the diamond tiara that had bruised her nose that fateful night in Deauville, and a half million dollars' worth of "miscellaneous" gems. Not even mentioned were such fetching trifles as garnet ankle bracelets, the ruby combs that set off her hair, and a jewel-covered parasol handle worth $3,600. The most famous gloves of the decade were the ones specially made with extra-large third fingers to accommodate her massive diamond rings.

Dressmakers considered her a dream; even whipping up her hats was considered a rare privilege. "It would be a cinch if they came with faces like yours," Rose Saphire, milliner to the city's rich and famous, once complained in a note to Peggy. "But you should see the old bags that have been coming in. Some of them are sunburnt and look like hell. They are all two days younger than god and want to look like Peggy Hopkins Joyce, the sons of b. . . ." Attached to the note was a bill for five suede berets, a white sailor hat, and a blue panama trimmed with currants, with a yellow silk turban thrown in for free.

No matter what the occasion, Peggy's clothes made news. The day she swept into a New York courtroom with two lawyers and a maid for a four-minute appearance at the closely watched stock-fraud trial of bankers Joseph W. Harriman and Albert M. Austin—as a client of their institution, Peggy had been called as a witness—all the reporters took note of her tailored gray suit, her matching knitted beret, the jeweled pin that secured her white stock collar, and especially the enormous corsage on her lapel. "Peggy Hopkins Joyce and Her Orchid at Bank Trial," one headline summed up the event, although when pressed on the source of her flowers, Peggy snapped back, "That's my business!"

Not everyone was enamored with her spending sprees. The day she walked into a New York department store and bought thirty-two pairs of shoes, an undertaking that put the store's entire fleet of shoe salesmen at her command, a dozen customers who had been impatiently waiting for service stormed out in a fury, canceling their charge accounts on the way; a "terrible rumpus," the *Daily News* called the scene. And her conspicuous consumption was sometimes the object of ridicule, as it was during a theater party hosted by Oliver Morosco at New York's Claridge Hotel. When Peggy excused herself to visit the powder room, actress Charlotte Greenwood gathered up all the jewelry worn by the other women guests and draped it around herself in mocking fashion. Peggy returned to the table, took one look at Charlotte, and burst into tears. "Please," she begged between sobs. "I'm a regular girl."

But usually her purchases and her possessions prompted gasps of amazement, and newspaper readers never tired of the tantalizing glimpses into her boudoir, her closets, even her garage, which for a time housed an auto designed for Rudolph Valentino. The $25,000 Isotta-Fraschini, a pale blue palace on wheels outfitted with red upholstery and sparkling with nickel accents, had been built according to specifications furnished by the actor but was completed only after his death, at which point financier John Locke bought it and presented it to Peggy for Christmas.

The nation uttered a collective sigh when the *Los Angeles Times* revealed under its "Helpful Hints Department" that "Peggy Hopkins Joyce says she avoids taking cold by tucking herself into bed under an ermine bedspread." Did she travel with five trunks, as the papers insisted, or seven, as her studio bio claimed? Descriptions were inevitably couched in superlatives: reporters routinely described Peggy as "the best-dressed woman in the world," and her $65,000 Russian sable coat as "the most perfectly matched coat of its kind in America." Or was it her $80,000 sable that was "the finest in the world," as *Daily News* columnist Sidney Skolsky suggested? There were so many items it was hard to keep track.

Sable coats and jeweled parasols did not come cheap, and like many other women raised in modest circumstances and thrust suddenly into great wealth, Peggy had developed complicated and often contradictory feelings about money. She was extremely generous with other people's fortunes and always made sure her escorts did well by the swarm of chauffeurs, waiters, and doormen who buzzed about her. "She was famous for getting money out of the men who went out with her," fashion journalist Diana Vreeland recalls in her memoirs. She'd have her driver waiting, Vreeland remembers. "She wouldn't drive in your car. You'd leave the Ritz in her car, go right to her place for supper or something and then, back at the Ritz, as you got out again, she'd look at you. 'Now what are you going to do for George.' . . . Anything less than a hundred-dollar bill, forget it!"

When it came time for Peggy to dig into her own bejeweled evening bag, however, she proved unexpectedly tightfisted, a surprising trait, considering that she had never gone hungry or lacked for rich benefactors. On the few occasions she found herself between suitors, there was always the largesse of previous donors to draw upon, carefully invested by her army of bankers and financial advisers. Yet a lingering fear that her means might not keep pace with her desires made Peggy deeply reluctant to part with what money she had, regardless of the sum.

Her stinginess did not go unnoticed. "Money flows like glue from Peggy," the gossip sheet *Broadway Brevities* sniped, alluding to the meager tips she doled out to stagehands during her time in *Vanities*. *Confidential* magazine wrote of her behavior: "If any man recalls seeing this elaborate lady pull so much as a dime out of her diamond-studded purse . . . he was merely watching her transfer it to a safer place. Even when she went to the little girl's room in the fashionable clubs and restaurants, she asked her date in advance for the tip to give the attendant. When she ordered cigarettes at a table, she would usually pick up a sufficient supply for the following week."

For special occasions, Peggy frequently "borrowed" frocks from her favorite stores and shipped them back the next day without explanation. After one such incident the owner of an exclusive dress shop wrote her pointedly: "The wrap which we sent you has been returned to us without notifying us what you want done with it. We hope you will not ask us to take it back, as the embroidery of the gown you had worn under it is pressed very plainly into the velvet."

Peggy's reluctance to part with her money brought her onslaughts of dunning letters—alternately pleading, cajoling, and threatening—from furriers, jewelers, and other impatient creditors. "Unless we receive a check by Monday I shall simply serve you with a summons," one attorney stormed after a series of entreaties failed to produce any response. Peggy even stiffed her old friend Madame Frances, ignoring an invoice for $11,000 worth of dresses for so many months the matter finally ended up in court.

Her own flesh and blood felt the sting of her pinchpenny ways. Occasionally Peggy would take a few days off from her busy life to pay a visit to Norfolk, to bring a bit of big-city glamour to her small-town relatives and press a few desperately needed dollars into the hand of her mother, who had divorced her second husband and moved back home to Lee Street. But the trips were brief and the assistance grudging. "Peggy sent her mother a check every month for groceries and stuff," her cousin Francis Price recalls, "but only if she begged for it."

Long-suffering servants like her maid Bea fared little better. She constantly had to beg Peggy for money, too, particularly since her mistress was sometimes as much as three months behind with her salary. Only Peggy's beloved dogs were assured of her generosity. On them she lavished the best money could buy, like the $3,000 gem-encrusted green leather collar snapped around the neck of one lucky pup, with "Pal" spelled out in tiny diamond chips and the legend "I belong to Peggy Joyce" engraved on a gold plate.

To satisfy their readers' hunger for the outsize and extravagant details, journalists would dredge through the most prosaic aspects of Peggy's life. "Her bath salts come in champagne bottles," wrote Sidney Skolsky in a *Daily News* column purporting to draw back the curtain of Peggy's private existence. "Before going to bed, no matter where she had been or what time it is, she drinks a glass of milk. . . . Is godmother to her housekeeper's child and visits her every Sunday. . . . Her favorite foods are waffles, veal stew, and corned beef and cabbage. . . . Smokes Ed Laurens' Prince de Monaco imported cigarettes [and] continually switches the cigarette from her left hand to her right so that the nicotine won't stain her fingers. . . . Wears socks when she sleeps because has cold feet.

There is a crucifix hanging from the top of her bed. She touches it whenever she feels nervous."

These frothy disclosures sometimes contained nuggets of truth. But more than the tabloids' feverish reportage, it is the bills and invitations and telegrams, the scraps of paper that drifted around Peggy like so many pieces of colored confetti, the odds and ends stuffed in the drawers of her little writing desk or tucked in the corners of her innumerable beaded purses, that suggest the real texture of her life during the years of her reign. These documents, scattered about her various apartments and eventually crammed into a trunk for safe-keeping, paint a true picture of her daily life at its peak.

From a swank Manhattan establishment called the Hotel des Artistes came an invitation to a New Year's Eve costume ball: "The glory of old Versailles and the Villa Trianon will be revived in pageantry. . . . Masks must be worn until midnight." From a photographer representing a West Coast news service came a letter that began: "Do hope we can make an appointment for your picture soon but am glad we waited because we have just installed a wonderful spot that will bring out your hair much better than anything I ever dreamed of." From a realtor who catered to New York's carriage trade, an inquiry regarding an eight-room duplex: "The owner does not want it to become public property and it must be a quiet exclusive sale." An admirer from Pennsylvania who identified himself as a "scientific horseshoer" sent a gift accompanied by a gracious note: "Your ladyship, please find enclosed a little hand-forged good-luck horseshoe."

From her friends at Black, Starr and Frost, an announcement of the arrival of imported Christmas cards, "exclusive designs never before shown in this country." A woman who described herself as a "beautifier" sent a request for prompt payment for "swan puff and other items." From a Mme. Naftal, a notice "to those who contemplate the disposal of their slightly used street and evening gowns, wraps, furs, and general attire, also diamonds. . . . Strictest privacy." From an enterprising young Irish chauffeur who had caught a glimpse of Peggy outside the Ansonia, a letter urging her to rent one of his Packard limousines, "in beautiful shape, clean and looks first class." From Delmonico's, a bright orange invitation to a Halloween party on the restaurant's newly enclosed roof. From a glossy magazine, a fragment of an advertisement touting bronze gates, "for burglary protection." From the Animal Hospital, a receipt for seven dollars. One man wrote inquiring whether she might care to purchase "two beautiful Bengal tiger skins fully mounted and one brown Bear Skin, rather large size, unmounted."

On notepaper from the Ansonia Peggy had jotted a typical memo to herself: "Six bracelets. Two string pearls. one sq. Diamond ring, one breast-pin." On another scrap was a hastily written Christmas list: "Mother, Arthur, Aunt Evelyn, Selma, Olie, Clara (bracelet), Colonel and Mrs. Figel, Bill Fallon (clock), Earnest (robe or handkerchief), Jimmy (evening charm), John Perry (ties), chauffeur (cigarette case), cook (dresser set), Mamie (umbrella), Cathleen (stockings)." She had penciled the lyrics for her *Vanities* number "Pretty Peggy" on the back of a menu from the Hotel Chatham on an evening when the offerings included baby partridge on toast for $1.75, filet mignon for $1.90, lobster for $2, and mock turtle soup for forty cents. On a corner of an envelope she began a draft of a love letter: "Darling I am happy that you are coming back to me. Life won't be an empty dream when you come back, sweetheart."

With a telephone that never stopped ringing, despite an unlisted number, there were endless jotted messages: Mr. Raoul Walsh at Plaza 1740, Mr. Rippley at Plaza 4600, Captain Mattet at Vanderbilt 6453, Mr. Hart at Bryant 3280, Mr. Eyre at the Ritz-Carlton, Perry at the Elysee Café, Mr. Cluik at Metropolitan Trust, Mr. Eyre a second and third time, Mr. Brooks, John from the hat shop. Notes from men were scattered everywhere. "Hello, Peggy. Have you anything to do?" scribbled an unidentified admirer named Joe. "If not, have supper with me." From a Maine resort came a postcard bearing the cryptic signature "Bob—guess which one." On a magazine page plastered with photographs of luminaries living it up at El Morocco, a desperate male had pleaded: "To my darling Peggy. I love you so much— why don't you?! The same." There were scores of telegrams from celebrated admirers like Milton Berle and Mark Hellinger ("You've been terribly sweet. I was far from sweet.").

Swan puffs and turtle soup, baby partridge and famous directors, rooftop parties and Packard limousines. Pieced together, the thousands of bits of paper Peggy stashed away for posterity form a mosaic of endless, perpetually amusing bustle. Lorelei Lee could not have done better.

In the twenties, New York after dark was a giddy place, part Gershwin, part Cagney. The crowds on Broadway were thicker than anywhere else on earth. The women looked ravishing beyond words, their beaded dresses shimmering in the light, their knees and pearls flying in the ubiquitous Charleston, and the men looked gorgeous, too. Everyone seemed terribly rich. Thanks to the official start of Prohibition in January 1920, New Yorkers were also drinking harder than ever. They were rubbing elbows with one another in unprecedented fashion as well, not just society millionaires and chorus girls but also gangsters and butter-and-egg men, *Scandals* stars and ballplayers and Park Avenue hostesses and prizefighters. The jostling melange that quickly became known as café society—"a society a little livelier than the solid mahogany dinner parties of Emily Price Post," according to F. Scott Fitzgerald—moved through the city's clubs night after night, bouncing about to the strains of "Bye, Bye, Blackbird" and chugging down the last of the vintage champagne before starting in on carbonated cider laced with alcohol that had been bottled somewhere in New Jersey.

The New York tabloids and especially their newly muscular gossip columnists were as integral to this world as the hot jazz and the frosty gin, for as much as anyone, they created and nurtured the new soci-

ety. Without the columnists, a breed that club-hopped as vigorously
as any patron, who would have known which starlet's career was pffft
now that her sugar daddy producer was looking elsewhere for thrills?
Who would have known which of the princely Mdivani brothers,
those Russian siblings who called themselves royalty and always
seemed to be marrying, had snagged an American heiress? Without
Winchell and company, who would have known about the couplings
and uncouplings, the rifts and the tiffs, the great and shabby moments
that punctuated an evening on the town and made for such delicious
reading over coffee and toast the next morning?

Nowhere did all these worlds come together more explosively
than at Texas Guinan's place. Like Chaplin, Fitzgerald, and Peggy herself, the New York nightclub hostess Texas Guinan ranked as one of
the era's great figures, a woman who epitomized the decade that had
produced her. "Jimmy Walker rules New York by day, Texas Guinan
by night," one journalist wrote of her, and the conceit was close to
the mark. No one could match her magnetic smile and her throaty
laugh, her flair for making the night come alive and her ability to
turn every evening into a party. Few even came close.

Starting in 1922, when Texas began infusing the Gold Room of
the Café des Beaux Arts on West Fortieth Street with her distinctive
energy and salty humor, her club was the hottest hot spot in town.
She moved around a lot—with federal agents on her heels, eager to
close down whichever illegal speakeasy she happened to be operat-
ing at the moment, she had to be nimble—but each location offered
the same seductive warmth, the same throbbing vitality. A typical
night brought out the cream of café society: Mayor Walker, his current flapper on his arm; nightclub host Sherman Billingsley; Mae
West; Harry Thaw, now out on the town after serving time in a mental institution for the murder of Stanford White; a few girls from the
Follies; perhaps a Vanderbilt; and of course the journalists—Winchell,
Sullivan, Heywood Broun, Mark Hellinger.

Reminding one observer of "a gorgeous tamer who has just let herself into a large cage of pet tigers," Texas stood on two chairs set side by side in the center of the room, her generous figure encased in a rose-colored cocktail dress, her thick blonde hair pushed into rigid waves, mascara dripping from her lashes, and ropes of pearls dangling around her neck. As she kept a practiced eye on the crowd, near-naked dancing girls stuffed cherries into patrons' mouths, pelted them with felt snowballs, and playfully ruffled their hair. The click of wooden noisemakers and the pop of champagne corks punctuated the air, and from the moment the stars came out until they faded in the morning sky the action never flagged.

Peggy herself was a creature of the night: "She personified life af-ter the sun went down," a former press agent says of her. Although she was never a member of true high society or the intellectual cir-cles that clustered around the Algonquin Round Table or certain bo-hemian Greenwich Village haunts, she was nonetheless a fixture on the New York scene during the twenties and thirties. And these hide-aways were her favored milieu. In later years she haunted El Morocco and especially the Stork Club, where she could join the exclusive throng that slipped past the velvet rope and sidled up to the power-ful Winchell, but during the twenties she spent practically all her free evenings at Tex's. The brassy hostess and the fun-loving blonde got along well, and one of the first things Texas did after setting up shop at the Gold Room was throw a party for her friend. "Texas Guinan desires you to meet and know personally Miss Peggy Hopkins, star of many Broadway successes, who will be her guest of honor at supper," read the invitation, which went on to promise that late-night festiv-ities would feature "Joe Fejer, violin virtuoso," followed by "im-promptu entertainment by famous artists."

Peggy was such a regular at Tex's various clubs that caricaturist Wynn Holcomb included her among the celebrities he sketched for the back of one of the menus, along with Gloria Swanson, Eddie Cantor, and John Barrymore. Her name also surfaced in the raucous songs that were an inevitable part of the evening: "Peggy Joyce is a vegetarian, so I understand," began a typical lyric. "Anyone can tell that by the carats on her hands."

With her flair for outrageous behavior, Peggy could be depended on to help keep things lively, as she did the night she set out to pull a fast one on Rudolph Valentino and his current wife, Natacha Rambova. The matinee idol had agreed to stop by Tex's for a few hours on the condition that there be no trace of his first wife, an actress named Jean Acker who had taken to hissing whenever she saw her ex-spouse. Having reserved a front-row table for the evening, Peggy sailed in with a creature sporting a bright red wig and décolletage down to her navel. The stranger introduced herself as the countess of Itch, and the two women sat down directly opposite Valentino. The actor did a double take and promptly exploded. "That's Jean Acker!" he shouted angrily. For a moment Tex was furious, too, but when she caught Valentino's eye, the two of them burst out laughing. Even when tinged with malice, Peggy's silliness was hard to resist.

As in the past, when Peggy was not living it up in New York, she was doing much the same thing on the other side of the Atlantic, where social mores were increasingly fluid and, more important, booze was legal. A growing number of affluent Americans had adopted the Continent as a second home, and rarely was Peggy absent from the pack of international celebrities—everyone from Thomas Mann and Ignacy Paderewski to Tallulah Bankhead and the queen of Romania—that milled around the piers as the great liners prepared to sweep off into the sunset.

Judging by her press clippings, Peggy seemed to be setting sail every week. By now, Paris felt as familiar as New York; London and Venice, too. One memorable night on the Italian Lido she joined William Randolph Hearst and Marion Davies aboard Cole Porter's celebrated music barge, a splendid craft, equipped with a dance floor and a jazz band, that had carried many an illustrious passenger around the Venetian waterways. The two ex-Ziegfeld girls sat out most of the dances so they could reminisce along the sidelines, their blonde heads close together as the boat glided through the old canals in the darkness.

In Peggy's eyes, however, nothing compared to the Riviera. By the late twenties the south of France had established itself as a year-round playground, and the legendary American expatriates who had been the resort's pioneers—the Fitzgeralds, the Cole Porters, the Gerald Murphys—had been joined by a wave of Algonquin stalwarts, among them Robert Benchley, Dorothy Parker, and *New York Times* drama critic Alexander Woollcott. Peggy arrived as part of a third contingent, a more social and moneyed crowd that included Coco Chanel, an assortment of low-rent royalty, and such minor show business figures as Rosie Dolly of the Dolly Sisters.

Although not quite the neighbor Fitzgerald might have envisioned, she took to the place instantly. "Peggy Joyce became a constant visitor," Pamela Harriman, then Pamela Churchill, wrote some years later in the London *Evening Standard,* during a period in which she was contributing articles to the paper on a regular basis. "Everyone knew her. She had that careless, confident walk which women acquire when they know that all eyes turn toward them when they enter a room." Indeed, Peggy felt so at home she would even take an occasional snipe at her fellow arrivistes, much to the amusement of insiders and journalists alike. "Miss Joyce, who had arrived in Monte Carlo in one of her statelier moods, confided to a friend a few days later that she had simply decided to *leave,* because Monte Carlo was full of such *dreadful* people that season," the writer Margaret Case Harriman recalled in the *New Yorker.* "When the friend protested mildly that a good many attractive people seemed to be around, Peggy drew herself up and loftily inquired, 'For ninstance, whom?' "

Despite her protestations, she had no intention of leaving, and in

February 1929 she plunked down 350,000 francs—about $80,000—to acquire a house of her own, a toylike pink villa charmingly named the Little Blue Dog. The house nestled in a cluster of fig trees, bougainvillea, and umbrella palms atop a rocky outcropping on Cap d'Ail, just west of Monte Carlo. Intrepid guests could thread their way down the winding stairways that led to the garden and the sea while less adventurous visitors relaxed on the balcony, sipping cocktails in the afternoon and brandy in the evening as they scanned the horizon for a glimpse of the Monte Carlo casino, glistening in Belle Epoque splendor across the inky water.

Peggy was between husbands when she made the purchase, and there was considerable speculation in the press as to which of her many admirers had actually put up the cash. But in the eyes of at least one observer, there was no doubt as to the merits of this latest acquisition. Pamela Harriman, a woman whose string of male conquests would dwarf even Peggy's, described the house as an oasis of "unique charm," and in the sympathetic opinion of that observer, both villa and owner had much to recommend them, the latter for having chosen so well. "Small and unpretentious," it was clearly the abode of "a woman of great taste," Harriman wrote. "No detail, however extravagant, was overlooked. It was placed among the rocks as carefully and as delicately as the setting of a precious jewel."

Peggy's enjoyment of her new plaything was made even sweeter by the fact that she had snatched it out of the hands of a rival. The actress Irene Bordoni had fallen in love with the place when she and her husband, Ray Goetz, had visited the Riviera in 1927, but at the time the owner refused to sell. By 1929, after Peggy had elbowed Bordoni out of Goetz's life, he proceeded to describe the house to his latest conquest. She promptly made a more tempting, and ultimately more successful, offer.

Being a property owner was not without its problems, as Peggy quickly discovered. For weeks at a time, her orchid-colored car was almost hidden by a swarm of workmen who labored mightily to refurbish her new acquisition. If this was not enough, a terrible scene erupted the day the painters dripped lime into her fountain and killed all the goldfish, leaving their carcasses floating on top of the water as an unsightly reminder of their ignominious end. "Well I said some things to those painters which they did not understand, but they could see that I was in a rage," she wrote of the episode in her memoirs. "But all they did was shrug their shoulders and jabber away in their patois, which is more Italian than French and they all threw down their tools and quit."

Pamela Harriman's opinion notwithstanding, the results of the renovation were hardly unpretentious. "I have four bathrooms, including one for the help, and mine is done in black marble with gold and onyx fittings," Peggy wrote. "The rooms are mostly done in genuine Louis XV, which I adore. The decorator said Italian Renaissance would suit the style of the house better but I do not like Italian Renaissance it is too ornate, besides, one is never sure of Italian Renaissance.

"Of course," she opined, "one is never sure of any antiques." But sounding like the ultimate expatriate, she knowledgeably insisted that "I think one can be more sure of French Antiques than Italian."

Although she amused a local journalist by briefly claiming she intended to forswear Monte Carlo's liquor and gambling in the interest of leading a more monastic existence, the reality was quite the opposite. At a typical party she hosted at a fashionable Cannes hotel, more than two thousand champagne cocktails were consumed, or so the papers reported. Nor did she lack for diversion in other areas. She and a friend raced along the corniche in their respective Hispano autos—hers was red, his black—her French chauffeur, François, at the wheel of her vehicle. She claimed she had been presented to the Prince of Wales. And thanks to Harpo Marx, she found herself at an improbable venue—a farewell dinner party Alexander Woollcott threw at Villa Galanon, his place on Cap d'Antibes, for George Bernard Shaw and his wife.

Harpo, with his taste for practical jokes, had invited a few extra guests to liven up the proceedings this particular evening, Peggy among them. She was "easily the most popular broad on the coast of France," he notes in his autobiography, "although not at literary dinner parties." The evening passed without incident, and to Harpo's great delight Peggy reciprocated. "It'll be informal, just the two of us," she promised when she asked him to dine on a subsequent night. "But I don't think you'll be bored."

As Harpo recalls the evening, he arrived promptly at seven to find his hostess attired in a skimpy Oriental outfit. The two of them adjourned to the sitting room after dinner for brandy, and a few minutes later they were being fanned by a servant as they reclined on an enormous sofa. Snuggling into the satin cushions, the lady of the house gave a wriggle of anticipation and whispered meaningfully: "Peggy wants to have a little fun, Harpo. Will you help Peggy have a little fun?"

Her companion didn't hesitate for a second. "You name it, honey," he replied.

She dimmed the lights and summoned her butler: "You may bring the books now." The butler returned with a stack of fat leather-bound volumes, which he deposited with a thud on Harpo's lap. Nestling closer, Peggy rested her head on his shoulder. "Read to me, Harpo," she purred.

The books did not contain the pornography he expected but rather collections of *Mutt and Jeff, Bringing Up Father, Krazy Kat,* and other of the latest funnies, and his hostess was so familiar with the contents she corrected his every mistake. "No, no!" she howled at one point. "You didn't read it all! You didn't read the 'Bam! Bang! Sock! Pow!' part!"

Whether Peggy really behaved in such a bizarre fashion or whether Harpo simply concocted the tale to underscore his hostess's anti-intellectual bent is hard to say. But the event he describes as the capstone of the evening sounds more in keeping with her personality, especially her appetite for publicity. After Harpo finished reading, she ran to a massive chest and pulled out a drawer overflowing with newspaper clippings. Scooping up an armful, she shoved it toward him. "Look!" she exclaimed. "They're all about me! Here, start reading these." The proceedings were rapidly turning into a Marx Brothers farce, with Peggy offering up a star turn in the madcap Thelma Todd role. Before things could disintegrate further, Harpo quickly made his escape. Dashing out the door, he fled into the night, back to the safety of Woollcott's Villa Galanon.

8

"That Strange Art
of Being a Woman"

Peggy acquired only two husbands during the twenties and thirties, but judging by the newspaper coverage of her matrimonial activities she seemed to be tying the knot every week or at least seriously considering the idea. Most of the prospects arrived well endowed with money, power, and social standing, and reporters usually heard the sound of wedding bells in the not too distant future. By the height of the Jazz Age she had truly become "the national symbol of marital prodigality," as Emile Gauvreau, editor of the *New York Evening Graphic,* described her, and the roster of men who had been linked with her was starting to look, as one quipster put it, like "the seating arrangement of a public dinner in the Waldorf."

Inevitably, there was much speculation about what made her so desirable to so many rich men. In a day when every chorus girl longed to marry a millionaire, how did she pull off, seemingly again and again, a feat others only dreamed of? Was it true she possessed a repertoire of exotic sexual tricks designed to drive men wild in bed, that, as one of her contemporaries suggests, she used "a certain muscle" to send her lovers into paroxysms of ecstasy? Was she really one of the great beauties of her day, as the papers routinely claimed? To be honest, no. Among her contemporaries, Mary Pickford and Lillian

Gish had more riveting faces, as did Marlene Dietrich and Greta Garbo, to name just a handful of the gorgeous women Hollywood produced during her era. Still, if not beautiful in the traditional sense, Peggy was nevertheless a knockout. She radiated a sultry glamour that proved a powerful aphrodisiac. Her model was not the impudent flapper; Peggy was a little old to be Clara Bow, parading about in short skirts and pursing her bee-stung lips. Her appeal had a riper quality: hair so perfectly waved it seemed sculpted, nails so lustrous one could almost feel them grazing a rough male cheek, skin so flawless it looked enameled. She was famously slender at a time when Americans were beginning to tire of rounded figures—110 pounds on a five-foot-three frame, according to one studio bio—and she selected every stitch of clothing, from her jewel-toned dresses to her luscious furs, with men in mind.

Peggy's many mouthwatering qualities were on view in a famous color photograph of her taken by Edward Steichen and published in *Vanity Fair* in March 1931. Steichen captured her at her haughtiest, her head held high to display an enormous expanse of throat. To a modern viewer the portrait seems a parody image of a woman about to be ravished. But with her golden skin, the creamy satin of her low-cut gown, and the diamonds glinting on her fingers, wrists, and neck, the pale tableau accentuated by her blue eyes, her bright blonde hair, and her brilliant red lips, she struck her contemporaries as the epitome of erotic allure.

Beneath the costly exterior lay even more to tempt the senses. Robert Deacon, a young neighbor who visited Peggy near the end of her life, remembered seeing a set of "artistic" photographs taken in her prime, a packet of gauzy sepia prints that depicted her in various states of undress. "And she was just gorgeous!" Deacon recalls. "You can see what those dirty old men saw in her."

Still, Peggy was hardly the only glamorous creature to turn heads during the twenties and thirties. Her appeal lay deeper still. As Ivan St. Johns had summed up her talents in *Photoplay* during her *Skyrocket* days, "She understands that strange art of being a woman," and what that "art" applied itself to, of course, was the cultivation of men. "She knew how to handle them," recalls Herman Klurfeld, a longtime ghostwriter for Walter Winchell who saw her often at New York nightspots like El Morocco. "She not only liked money and wanted it, she also liked men and she liked sex. She was very forthright about it. And as a result she got a lot of money and she had a lot of fun."

Peggy had mastered a million formidable ways to flatter men and nourish their egos. Parting from a man, even one she had just met, she would sidle up to him with the plea: "Don't say good-bye. Give me a hug and a kiss." She laughed when a man told a joke, a seemingly simple act but one that men found unexpectedly endearing. She had also perfected the adoring gaze, the ability to stare worshipfully at a man as if he were the only creature in the room.

"She has the art of simulating the tender passion down to a science," a *Brooklyn Eagle* reporter wrote. "She has practiced the downward glance, the sigh, the upward gleam of a tender eye until she can do it without trying now. And when a pretty girl breathes deeper as she shakes your hand when introduced—one of Peggy's pet tricks—when she confides some little intimacy to you and says, oh, so softly, 'Don't tell,' when she gives a man the impression that her flinty little heart is stirred by his presence"—well, the reporter concluded, it would take an exceptionally strong man to resist her attractions.

Men found it equally hard to resist her buoyant personality. The cheerful little extrovert from Norfolk had matured into a happy-go-lucky adult who took neither life nor herself terribly seriously. "She had a terrific sense of humor," remembers Jackie Olson, whose mother, Madeline Copeland, was Peggy's friend for many years. "She was delightful, very outgoing. There was that sparkle about her, a twinkle in her eye. She did silly, outrageous things." One long-running joke involved her penchant for answering the telephone with a clearly fake French accent and pretending—not that she ever fooled anyone—to be her own maid. Another involved a half-finished wool scarf she liked to pull out whenever a new boyfriend appeared on the scene. "Darling," she invariably announced with a broad wink, "I'm knitting this for you."

Most of all, in her sleek, elegant way she radiated a powerful and earthy sexuality. When she strolled up to a potential admirer flashing her inviting smile and exuding a megawatt charge of warmth and sensuality, no man in his right mind could mistake her intentions. And unlike many women of her day, she got a kick simply out of talking about sex; a man could say anything in front of her, and she responded in kind. "Using obscene words wasn't too common back then," notes Klurfeld, "but she used them. Doity words, like Tallulah. When a man hears that sort of talk, he thinks a woman is easy. And she was, for the right price."

"She genuinely liked the boys," Diana Vreeland said of Peggy, and she made sure they knew it in the most blatant way possible. "I know this is terribly personal," she wrote of her affair with Earl Carroll, "but Earl loves me because I have frequent orgasms. It makes him know he is thrilling to me. What he doesn't know is during love affairs with all men I have frequent orgasms."

Peggy's palpable appetite for carnal pleasures combined with the daunting erotic repertoire she had acquired at home and abroad to make her the ideal sexual playmate. "She knew her way around the bedroom," says John Kenley, an assistant to Lee Shubert who heard endless tales of her prowess. "She wasn't a hooker, but she'd do things wives wouldn't do"—in other words, less conventional, more imaginative modes of coupling. "She had special talents and she used them. And the man was flattered. It was a feather in his cap."

Unlike a wisecracking Mae West, whose sexuality was so exaggerated she became a caricature of herself, or a Marion Davies, who insisted to the very end that she and William Randolph Hearst were simply good friends, there was nothing coy or ironic about her persona. Others may have called her a tramp and regarded her as a high-priced call girl, but Peggy fit more easily into another mold, that of a full-blown courtesan whose approach to the opposite sex was frankly strategic. The critic George Jean Nathan, who had discerned "a touch of the French eighteenth century about her," was right: had she lived in another time, in another land, she might have taken her place in a long and distinguished line of women for whom being a courtesan represented an honorable and often prestigious way of life.

As author Cornelia Otis Skinner noted respectfully of the legendary courtesans not of the eighteenth century but of Belle Epoque France, those visions of loveliness wreathed in clouds of ylang-ylang who drifted from the races and the polo matches to the Opéra and the Comédie Française and onward to late suppers at Maxim's: "The leading cocottes were in an upper echelon not to be spoken of in the same breath as the status of an ordinary prostitute. They were celebrities as firmly established as the top stars of the theatre. They were the talk of the smart set. Boulevardiers quoted their bon mots. . . . Even the press rated them as important news."

In that world, Peggy might have rivaled La Belle Otero, the fiery Spaniard whose diamond bolero stopped traffic on the rue de la Paix when it lit up Cartier's window and whose provocative music-hall dancing intrigued a young Colette. Or Laura Hayman, a mistress of Proust's great-uncle Louis, who helped inspire the author's memorable love object Odette de Crécy. Or Emilienne d'Alençon, who performed on stage with bright pink rabbits and wrote a book of poems called *The Temple of Love*. Almost certainly she would have reminded people of Zola's Nana, blonde, dimpled, and good-natured, who like many other courtesans with links to the theater found little difference between performing for an audience of many and entertaining an audience of one.

For Skinner, these women, though part of a long and glorious tradition, were often misunderstood and their achievements underrated. "They had to be clever and levelheaded at gathering the primroses," she wrote. "It took intelligence, style and perseverance for an ordinary demoiselle to promote herself into the extraordinary position of grande courtisane." In many respects these sumptuous, clear-eyed creatures were Peggy's true forebears, and like them she excelled at her chosen endeavors.

Because Peggy's real career was her love life, the list of her many conquests became part of her official biographical file in newspaper morgues, organized methodically under husbands, fiancés, and "possible fiancés." After a while, fact and fiction were inseparable. Did she really have an affair with King Gustaf VI of Sweden, whom she mentioned discreetly in her memoirs as a friend and who reportedly put up the $80,000 for her villa? Was there any truth to the gossip, courtesy of "a member in good standing of Café Society at the time," about Prince Christopher of Greece, who allegedly gave her a priceless heirloom diamond necklace said to be part of the Greek crown jewels, or railroad magnates Averell Harriman and Reggie Vanderbilt, who "put at [her] disposal a railroad car," or merchant prince Hiram Bloomingdale? Theatrical producer Arthur Hammerstein, uncle of composer Oscar Hammerstein II, had provided the auto that whisked her from New York to Chicago during her big divorce trial—at least that was the conclusion of reporters who traced the license plate. Was he another of her admirers?

What of the rumors about the maharajah Gaekwar of Baroda, reputed to be the second-richest man in the world? Would she not have fallen hard for an Indian potentate whose assets included ceremonial herds of elephants and gold-plated plumbing and who reportedly presented her with a "priceless ruby necklace" that was surely part of the state jewels? The papers were constantly dropping names of various royal figures to whom she was reportedly engaged or about to be, among them a Prince Lubermirsky, son of a former Russian am-

bassador to France; a Medici variously identified as an Italian nobleman or a Spanish grandee, depending on which publication one followed; and a Prince Ibrahim, an Egyptian nobleman.

Her flings with her bosses in Hollywood and on Broadway barely
raised an eyebrow, for nowhere were the boundaries between work
and sex more porous than in the world of entertainment during the
twenties, and it was the rare producer who failed to find a place on
stage for his current sweetheart, even if she had crossed eyes and two
left feet. But any man in show business was fair game, even the openly
gay Hollywood actor William Haines, who in 1930 was voted the
number-one box-office attraction in America. Haines was just beginning his rise to stardom in 1924 when Peggy told *Screenland* magazine that he had delivered "the best screen kiss" she had ever seen,
in *The Midnight Express*. Since the suggestion of a romance with a
woman like Peggy would go far to establish any man's heterosexual
credentials, studio publicists saw in her comment a potential publicity bonanza and promptly arranged a meeting. Nothing came of it, of
course, but it made good copy.

Peggy hardly confined herself to show-business types. She edged so
close to marrying Stanford Comstock, a portly realtor from Miami,
that many newspapers listed him as her fifth husband. Forty-eight
hours after the pair met at Texas Guinan's nightclub, he headed for
Cartier's to buy her a $19,000 bracelet studded with sapphires "as big
as large marbles," according to the *Daily Mirror*. Unfortunately, there
were complications. Comstock's current wife objected that her husband was not legally divorced; Peggy, dismissing her comment as "sour
grapes," added philosophically: "Ex-wives always act that way." Three
months later, the whole thing was off. "Changed my mind," Peggy ra-
dioed the Associated Press from the *Homeric* as she headed for Paris.
"Woman's privilege. Not marrying anyone." By the following winter
the *Daily News* was describing Comstock as "last season's fiancé."

She also came close to snagging a few other noblemen. For a time
she was reportedly engaged to a French count named Frédéric de

Janze, to whom she had been introduced by the marquis de Falaise, Gloria Swanson's husband. Then, in 1928, Peggy discovered an even more enticing royal prospect.

"I have just met quite a wonderful boy who also has asked me to marry him," she wrote in her memoirs. "In fact he asked me five times and the first time just five minutes after he met me, at the Ritz Towers, but of course I laughed at him. His name is Earl of Northesk and he is getting a divorce. He is a little young, only 26, but he is a Scottish nobleman and has one of the oldest titles in Edinburgh. He drinks nothing but champagne except when there is no champagne and altogether is a very nice boy. I have not decided if I will marry him. For one thing he is a Scottish nobleman and I am not sure how a Scottish nobleman would be for a husband. Besides, I have only known him for three days."

David Ludovic George Hopetoun Carnegie, the eleventh earl of Northesk, did boast an impressive pedigree. The *Evening Graphic* revealed that he sprang from the same lineage as the industrialist Andrew Carnegie and owned a respectable ten thousand acres of real estate in his native land. He had also nearly killed the king of Belgium during a bobsled race. Although Northesk was clearly enamored of Peggy, it is questionable whether he was genuinely interested in matrimony. And there was a bigger problem. For the first time in years the public interest in Peggy's love life seemed to be flagging. Something had to be done.

"The thin-worn standing headline 'Peggy to Marry Again' is being wooed more scientifically," the *Brooklyn Eagle* wrote in July. "Peggy has taken a press agent." A young journalist turned author who had written about her extensively in the past had been selected for the role, and the two "began a campaign to whipsaw the press of the world into the proper state of suspense." The press agent informed various newspapermen in Deauville—in strictest confidence, of course—that Peggy and the earl were planning to wed and even alerted them to possible photo opportunities.

The strategy worked brilliantly. For months newspapers over-flowed with stories as the pair swam, danced, and played baccarat in Deauville and along the Italian Lido, where Peggy's ravishing blue and white satin beach pajamas were the talk of the resort. Much was also made of the green crepe de chine rompers that matched her emeralds and of the fact that Northesk had allegedly proposed by the artful device of asking the band to play the song "When I Marry You" one evening as they were dancing. Their idyll was interrupted only by the appearance of Northesk's soon-to-be-ex-wife, Jessica Brown, another blonde former *Follies* girl, who followed the love-birds around the Continent and glared at them from the sidelines as they caroused at various fashionable nightspots.

The foreign press charted the byzantine progress of the affair as avidly as the American papers, and everyone, it seemed, was rooting hard for Peggy and her lord. "Northesk Free for Peggy!" exulted the *New York Journal* in a bright blue banner headline when the earl's divorce came through that fall, and journalists on two continents jubilantly predicted he would be the next Mr. Peggy Hopkins Joyce. But twenty-four hours after the divorce was granted, Peggy confessed that yet again the idea of matrimony had begun to pall. "I can't marry everybody," she wailed to one reporter. Besides, she added, she would be busy with lessons in elocution, singing, and graceful posture in preparation for her appearance in Ray Goetz's new play, an under-taking for which the producer had wisely drafted a document speci-fying that "Miss Joyce is not to marry anyone until after her contract has terminated." The prospective groom was described as desolate, al-though he promptly showed up at a club and downed his trademark magnum of champagne. Peggy responded to the news of his behav-ior with her usual aplomb. "I didn't see why he acted so sentimental and broken-hearted and made a fool of himself at the night clubs," she told the *Daily News*. "It certainly wasn't very flattering to me. But anyway, I am through."

A few years later, she made a play for what passed as American royalty. John L. de Ruyter Jr., a well-connected young New York stock-broker, was America's closest equivalent to a noble scion. An aunt, described by the *Daily News* as the "all-powerful society dowager Mrs. Moses Taylor Campbell" of the Staten Island Huguenot Campbells, claimed as her bosom friend the inimitable Mrs. Cornelius Vanderbilt. One night Walter Winchell informed radio listeners throughout North America that Peggy felt a marriage coming on, and a few days later she herself announced from her suite in the Waldorf-Astoria Towers that the social registerite would be her next spouse. "New York society sat back with mouth agape yesterday," gasped the *Daily News,* "as it tried to swallow the realization that Peggy Hopkins Joyce is about to crash its sacred portals." The world waited breathlessly for the moment when de Ruyter and his intended would approach his aunt to announce their plans. But long before wedding bells could chime, his family raised the predictable objections and the affair ended as abruptly as it had begun. In keeping with her belief that few men were worth losing sleep over, Peggy took this news in stride, too. "You can't eat the Social Register," she told the *Daily News* the following day.

Phil Payne, managing editor of the *Daily News,* was neither royalty nor society figure but someone who stood at the opposite end of the social spectrum. A short, stocky fellow whose horn-rimmed glasses dominated an open, guileless face, Payne was a creature of simple tastes; he rarely even bought a new suit. He had married his childhood sweetheart, and for a time the two of them lived quietly in New Jersey. Her premature death left him devastated.

His friends, however, persuaded him to spruce himself up and get back into circulation. Given his job and Peggy's reputation, it was inevitable their paths would cross. The two soon became a couple, and they might have become something more had it not been for the evening Peggy paid a visit to Payne's office with the intention of seeing how a newspaper was put out. Drifting around the building, she stared in wonder at the reporters banging away on their battered Remingtons, the clicking Linotype machines, and especially the lumbering black presses. Could she turn them on, she begged Payne? Somewhat reluctantly, he agreed. Extending one slender finger, she gingerly pushed the button that set them in motion. Then she sprang back and clutched her companion, terrified by the thunderous noise. Payne immediately pressed the stop button, but Peggy had had enough of industrial machinery. "Take me out of here!" she screamed.

Payne's boss, Joseph Medill Patterson, imposed few rules on his subordinates, but he did forbid them to associate with judges or actresses, presumably on the assumption that either of those species would corrupt the morals of his minions. Upon learning of the incident that had taken place in the newspaper office, Patterson promptly fired Payne, not for letting an outsider fool around with the paper's expensive machinery but for fooling around himself with an ex-chorus girl.

The extent of Peggy's powers was perhaps most evident in her greatest catch, one of the country's most prominent industrialists and a man whose wealth and power assured that he would never lack for female companionship.

Auto magnate Walter P. Chrysler had a wife and four children when he took up with Peggy in the late twenties. He was also nearly twenty years her senior. All things considered, she was hardly the most appropriate paramour for a person of his stature. Although family members on both sides knew of the liaison, both Peggy and Chrysler tacitly agreed the affair would be conducted with the utmost discretion. Years later she confided to friends that his family had paid her a considerable sum to keep her mouth shut about the relationship, and she happily complied. "I have a very ardent admirer just now who is showering me with gifts," she wrote in her memoirs of the man who would soon set her up in an apartment at the Dorset. "He is quite prominent and I dare not write his name but I will call him Mr. Z."

It is unlikely Mr. Z erected the Chrysler Building in her honor, as Anita Loos suggests in her book *The Talmadge Girls,* although the silvery Art Deco skyscraper at Forty-second Street and Lexington Avenue in Manhattan did bear a certain resemblance to the sparkling creature spotted frequently on his arm. What is certain is that his largesse knew no bounds. According to a famous story that made the rounds during their time together, he telephoned Peggy one morning and ordered her to look out the window of her town house: parked in front were two Isotta-Fraschinis, one an outsized town car, later used by Gloria Swanson in the movie *Sunset Boulevard,* the other a canary-yellow roadster garnished with black patent leather upholstery and sterling silver trim. The total cost: some $45,000. The tycoon was so crazy about Peggy, *Confidential* magazine wrote in its account of their affair, "he didn't even think his own Chryslers were good enough for her."

Nor did his generosity stop at fancy autos. The discreet jewelers of the period rarely kept records of transactions, a wise move considering how many lavish trinkets were bought for women other than wives, and Peggy was alone the wintry day in 1928 she walked into a private office at her favorite jewelers, Black, Starr and Frost. But even *Time* magazine identified Chrysler—"someone said to be prominent in the automobile industry"—as the man who presented Peggy with her most famous piece of jewelry, a breathtaking $300,000 diamond.

Whether Chrysler really was her benefactor is debatable. Other accounts of Peggy's acquisition of the stone suggest that she received it as part of a swap for which she gave Black, Starr and Frost a $350,000 string of pearls—presumably the necklace Stanley Joyce had given her nearly a decade earlier—and $23,000 in cash. But it was a measure of the intensity of her relationship with the auto tycoon and his penchant for swathing her in luxury that his name was widely associated with this latest offering.

Stories eventually circulated that the diamond had been found in Brazil in the eighteenth century and became part of the Portuguese crown jewels; more probably it was dug up in South Africa two centuries later and owned by no one in particular. The 127-carat octagonal stone, set on a flexible Egyptian-style platinum choker studded with hundreds of lesser diamonds, was nonetheless an extraordinary work of art and nature, "the largest and finest of its kind," according to the *New York Times*. Plump as a walnut, it was so brilliantly faceted the surface seemed to pulse with a life of its own. A 1924 advertisement for the stone had described it as "the largest blue diamond in the world," and indeed, when exposed to ultraviolet light, the diamond glinted a dazzling blue and was literally bright enough to read by.

Not surprisingly, when the newspapers got wind of the purchase, they went wild. The *Brooklyn Eagle,* which ranked the stone with such legendary competitors as the Hope and the Kohinoor, concluded: "Cleopatra, the Serpent of the Nile, who made such a fuss over drinking her dissolved pearl, never wore anything as lovely." Gossip columnists called the bauble "Peggy's skating rink," and *Time* magazine described it as "the largest perfect diamond in the world." Even slicing away the journalistic hyperbole, there was no question of its magnificence.

Caring for such a treasure was a mixed blessing. "I sometimes think it is more worry than a husband," Peggy complained to one journalist. "The insurance company sends a detective along, like Mary's lamb, to follow me wherever I go. . . . It bothers me no end." When she sailed for Paris the following month, reporters duly made mention of the burly guard who had been hired to hover along the sidelines each time the diamond made an appearance.

But as readers of *Photoplay* learned from the article "Why Women Love Diamonds," she had come to see that in the long run the diamond was worth the trouble it caused—at least that was her official story. "I knew that nothing I had accomplished in life would live beyond the grave," said the story that appeared under her byline. Nothing, that is, except possession of the jewel. "I was under no delusions concerning this 'fame' which newspaper headlines had thrust upon me. Ten days after the mortal remains of Peggy Joyce were carried to their last resting place I should only be a memory, growing fainter with the years." She was especially taken with the idea that the stone's history would include the words "first worn by Peggy Hopkins Joyce," and since the jewel had no romantic past of its own, she determined to call it the Peggy Hopkins Joyce diamond.

While the litany of Peggy's lovers and the gifts with which they showered her was impressive, more impressive still were the letters she received from the men who fell under her spell. Like latter-day Swanns obsessing over their faithless Odettes, many wrote several times a day, stuffing pages and pages of love-soaked declarations into fat envelopes and growing increasingly frantic as their entreaties went unanswered. "How many times I have telephoned I cannot say but often two or three times in an hour," confessed a wretched Englishman who had met her in Monte Carlo. "This very morning I telephoned, first no reply, then I came to the hotel, knocked on your apt. door, no reply, then I went downstairs again and tried for the third time in your hotel. Then phoned and phoned far into the night, knocked on your door without success." Desperately they kept trying, for Peggy haunted their days, their restless evenings, their anxious dreams.

"Dearest," began a suitor who signed himself Grisha and wrote her from a series of exclusive addresses on two continents. "Before I indulge in a feverish slumber, I want to tell you some of my thoughts about our great and unique love. You are the only woman who could render me soft and bold at the same time. I know I am an outlaw but you are my princess who can lead me either to the throne or to the scaffold. I hate everything and everybody but you, who talk to my soul and body as a pledge of the life I am going to live."

"Darling my own love!" he wrote on another occasion. "You do not hear me over the phone—cables only give us glimpses of our thoughts and feelings—letters are too long to reach. Darling, I have been so lonely at this time. People don't mean anything to me anymore. All men are bores and all women are frumps to me now. O darling love—please be with my heart and soul, for never have I been so close to a person in my life. Never did I think that one could suffer so much. Without you my love there is nothing within nor without me. Everything has gone wrong—business, life, thoughts— and I do not know where fate is leading me. I really would prefer death, and who knows, maybe it's not too far away, but only to see you again still gives me strength to hang on to this miserable little path we call existence. Life is hell to me now. Please come and save me."

From an abject Englishman named Archie, writing on crisp notepaper from his home in Lower Bisildon, Reading, came the following confession: "I wonder very much whether my presence on this earth means anything to you. You have everything in the world, and just a man, when they are all in love with you, can mean very little. Of course he is nothing. He is only a stupid fool for flattering himself that he does."

These yearning wooers, whether real-life lovers or men who crossed her path only briefly, could barely contemplate life without her. "My darling baby Peggy," a tormented soul who apparently belonged to the first category wrote from the Ritz in Paris, filling sheet after sheet in his neat, precise script after his beloved had departed for Cannes. "You must know dearest that from a worldly point of view I'm no longer an infant. I've been almost everywhere and met all sorts of people and had the chance to fall in love with many different types of women but baby dear I swear to you that never in my life have I felt anything to compare with the love, the longing I feel for you my darling.

"After you had left Friday I felt that you had taken with you all my life and everything that could ever mean anything to me. My darling child, I have been in this room for five hours trying to stop myself from writing to you because I felt that I could not write sensibly and would only succeed in making a fool of myself. When I did start this letter, I thought that I had got myself well in hand but it is no use trying to be sensible. I'm just like a crazy man tonight. I can't think reasonably. I can't talk to anyone without being rude. I can't sit still and I just feel that I'm going mad. I want you madly and I don't know what I'll do unless I get you. I would welcome all kinds of physical pain but the mental pain and the heartache that I'm now suffering is more than I can bear. I'll do anything in the world that you want or can suggest in order to be with you but I just can't bear this any longer."

Even the devastating Lou Tellegen, one of the great matinee idols of the early twentieth century, proved putty in her exquisite hands. Tall and broad-shouldered, with eyes routinely described as blue velvet, Tellegen had such a magnificent physique that Auguste Rodin used him as the model for a marble nude titled *Eternal Springtime* that ended up in the Metropolitan Museum of Art. The cover of his memoirs, *Women Have Been Kind,* proclaimed him "the perfect lover." He associated with all the glamorous creatures of his day—Caruso sang for him, Isadora Duncan danced for him—and he toured the United States with Sarah Bernhardt. He was married briefly to the American-born opera singer Geraldine Farrar, one of the era's biggest celebrities, and before he had untangled himself from Farrar, headline writers were predicting that he and Peggy would wed. Yet even after he set Peggy up in an apartment on East Fifty-seventh Street in Manhattan, where she lived for a short time in the early twenties— "our little home," as he tenderly described their love nest—he was maddened by her indifference to his entreaties and feared she had moved out during one of his extended tours in the West.

"Peggy darling," he wrote from a Winnipeg railroad hotel one blustery December night, the words streaming out in his strong masculine hand. "I have written you about every day and sent you wire the same. I addressed them all to the apartment. Are you not there? Why don't you write to me? I know I am a hell of a distance away but I sent you my note so I would get your letter. It is enough to drive a man crazy."

Peggy saved all these letters, for she always relished lavish compliments. But she herself rarely displayed such depth of feeling. The love note she once scribbled on the back of an envelope—"Life won't be an empty dream when you come back, sweetheart"—reeks with empty sentiment. Outbursts of unbuttoned passion might have made her cringe. She liked to keep things light; when a conversation grew too intense, she would have been the first to suggest adjourning to the nearest dance floor.

Maybe she simply never loved as passionately as those who loved her. In 1932 Ed Sullivan claimed in his column that Peggy "never, apparently, had a deep passion," and unexpectedly she wrote back to say he was right. "I've been fond of various persons and I've had flirtations but I've never been deeply in love," she admitted. "At least I have never been willing to sacrifice anything, and they say that the willingness to sacrifice things is the index to real love."

In a remarkably candid moment she told a *Photoplay* reporter three years later: "I haven't been in love with anyone for years and I don't think anyone has been really in love with me. But it doesn't matter because no one would believe it—and so my box-office goes on just the same!" It was a poignant admission from one of the world's most famous brides.

Peggy's feelings about her admirers were probably inseparable from what they had to offer, but in this, surely, she was no different from generations of women before her who had been raised to accept the fact that their lot in life was determined by the economic status of the men who paid court to them. She knew the conventions and, perhaps unwittingly, revealed them for what they were. Each time Peggy acquired a new lover and especially a new husband, she would say the politic thing, announcing to the world that she was truly besotted. "I'm in love—terribly, madly in love," she fluttered to the *Daily News* after her wedding to Count Morner. "This is my last and only real marriage." Nevertheless, the amount of time she spent with most of the men in her life could be measured in months, sometimes weeks. Though she talked a great deal about love, what she really seemed to crave was a bubbly concoction, sweet and intoxicating as a gin fizz, composed of equal parts glamour, romance, and sexual high jinks. What she treasured were the breathless rituals of courtship: the murmured endearments, the stolen moments of passion, and especially the extravagant gifts. For Peggy Joyce, true love was a heavy diamond bracelet, preferably one that arrived with its price tag intact.

9

"The Most Preferred Blonde"

"Marguerite Upton Archer Hopkins Joyce, the ex-Countess Gosta Morner, is that rarest of phenomena, a living person who has become a legend," *Vanity Fair* magazine wrote in March 1931, the year its subject was savoring some of her greatest fame. "Her marriages and her sables, her dimple and her diamonds have been the talk of two continents for a decade. Although Miss Joyce (as she chooses to be known) has tried the movies, and even, as an actress on the legitimate stage, won occasional plaudits from the critics . . . it is rather because of her philosophy of life than her artistic achievement that her name has passed as a symbol into current thought. Her successful development of this philosophy, which combined high-powered sex-appeal with native shrewdness, and a total indifference to public opinion with a sure instinct for self-promotion, has made her the perfect representative of a type of womanhood peculiar to the century. Best known as a lady of property, she is nevertheless one of the most romantic figures of our generation, one to arouse much philosophical speculation on contemporary manners."

When the country's most sophisticated and influential periodical proclaimed Peggy a legend, the magazine was simply stating the obvious. Starting in the twenties and cresting by the early thirties, she had become a larger-than-life figure, an emblem of her times. As with John D. Rockefeller and Charles Lindbergh, Marie Antoinette and Cleopatra, individuals whose particular achievements revealed something significant about the worlds in which they lived, the mere mention of her name unleashed a flood of vivid images among a vast audience. She had become an icon.

Her place in the culture was sharply illustrated by the frequency with which her name cropped up in the songs of Cole Porter. In their range, their specificity, and their penetrating observations on modern life, his lyrics provided a running commentary on the kind of nation America was becoming during his era, and they were rich with references to the people and products that defined the times. To be mentioned in a Cole Porter song signified a great deal about the reach of one's reputation.

Starting in 1928 with "Quelque-Chose" and "Which," both written for early versions of the show *Paris,* and continuing until 1950, Porter drew wittily on Peggy's predilection for collecting husbands and living large, twisting his ingenious rhyme schemes around her signature possessions and deportment. The narrator of "Quelque-Chose" mulls her own particular appeal while acknowledging reluctantly that "Mrs. Nash may have more cash, and Peggy Joyce, more clo'es." In "The Queen of Terre Haute," from an early version of *Fifty Million Frenchmen,* the status-conscious title character happily crows, "My string of Rolls-Royces is longer than Peggy Joyce's." The catalog song "They Couldn't Compare to You," from the 1950 musical *Out of This World,* finds Peggy taking her place among the memorable sirens of history—Eve, Brunnhilde, Nefertiti ("a perfect sweetie")—as the narrator giddily confesses, "I became so confused I was even amused and abused by Peggy Joyce." Along with Garbo and Cleopatra, she joins another roster of charmers in "Let's Not Talk about Love," from the 1941 show *Let's Face It:* in a meaningful aside the narrator admits that "Peggy Joyce was once a pupil of mine."

The lyrics are imaginative, if slightly strained—it was evidently not easy to find a variety of rhymes for *Joyce*—but particularly revealing is how a songwriter concerned with the mysterious, bittersweet complexities of love played with Peggy's attitude toward romance. In mulling the question of fidelity to a single lover in "Which," the composer's alter ego poses the question: "Should I make one man my choice and regard divorce as treason, or should I, like Peggy Joyce, get a new one ev'ry season?" In "Why Shouldn't I?," a wistful ode to love that proved one of the memorable songs from the 1935 musical *Jubilee,* he finds himself wondering more seriously: "Miss Peggy Joyce says it's good, and ev'ry star out in far Hollywood seems to give it a try so why shouldn't I?" In the composer's deft hands, the gold digger was transformed into an emblem of the quest for connection, or at least unromantic love, in a fragile, unpredictable world.

Porter was not the only major composer to find her an apt reference. Rodgers and Hart tipped their hat to her mercenary ways in their jaunty "I've Got Five Dollars," the one enduring number from their 1931 show *America's Sweetheart:* "Peggy Joyce has a bus'ness; all her husbands have gold." The irrepressible Eddie Cantor, her old colleague from the *Follies,* acknowledged the peculiar nature of her fame in one of the endless encore verses of "Makin' Whoopee," his light-hearted treatise on the vicissitudes of modern romance:

> *Take Peggy Joyce*
> *With little voice*
> *She soon became*
> *The nation's choice!*
> *I tell you, buddy*
> *She's made a study*
> *Of makin' Whoopee*

Among the many listeners on whom the verse made a lasting impression was Winston Churchill, who rasped out the lyrics verbatim when he and Cantor met at London's Savoy Hotel nearly a decade after the words had been written. Even as late as 1940, the greatest tribute that could be paid to a woman's charms in Irving Berlin's musical *Louisiana Purchase* was to claim she "takes two men away from Peggy Joyce." Another song from that same year—one that drew inspiration from *Harper's Bazaar's* popular upscale advice column, "Why Don't You?," and underscored what had become not just the salient point to be made about Peggy but by now the only point—suggested: "Why don't you have a stag line composed of ex-husbands of Peggy Hopkins Joyce?"

More literary types also found Peggy's name a convenient shorthand to evoke the prototypical playgirl. A young lawyer character is meant to get a laugh in Elmer Rice's 1931 hit play *Counsellor-at-Law* when he announces as he leaves his office, "If Peggy Joyce calls me, I can be reached in my box at the opera." In the story "Sense of Humor," Damon Runyon paints Joe the Joker as a real card by noting that he "calls up Mindy's and imitates a doll's voice, and tells Mindy he is Peggy Joyce or somebody and orders fifty dozen sandwiches sent up at once to an apartment on West Seventy-second Street for a birthday party although of course there is no such number as he gives and nobody will wish fifty dozen sandwiches if there is such a number."

When novelist Dawn Powell was jotting down notes in her diary for a satirical study of New York bachelors, she envisioned a scene showing "young brothers quarreling over their Peggy Joyces." No less an eminence than Eugene O'Neill recognized Peggy's special place in the culture when the publicity-shy playwright wrote in a letter to a friend in 1930 that he had acquired "too much notoriety for too many years and '[Strange] Interlude' topped all that and put me on a par with Peggy Hopkins." Will Rogers regularly offered wry observations about her matrimonial proclivities. In a typical comment, made in one of his weekly articles in 1925, he wrote: "We want Scandal, but we want NEW Scandal. The familiar faces who have been committing various forms of moral, political and social scandal are out of date with us. For example, if Peggy Joyce picks up a wayward Millionaire and, explaining coyly that no one has ever really understood her but him, heads him into a Justice of the Peace's office, why that's not news. That's what we in Editorial parlance call inevitable." Even the notorious madam Polly Adler, no piker herself when it came to collecting headlines, acknowledged the size of Peggy's shadow when she wrote in her popular memoirs, *A House Is Not a Home,* "Like Jimmy Walker and Texas Guinan and Peggy Joyce and Scott Fitzgerald, I played a conspicuous role in the comedy melodrama of an already legendary decade."

To Harlem Renaissance novelist Zora Neale Hurston, Peggy represented the ideal of confidence and self-possession—the white woman's ideal—against which to measure her own image. "At certain times I have no race," Hurston wrote in her 1928 essay "How It Feels to Be Colored Me." "I am *me.* When I set my hat at a certain angle and saunter down Seventh Avenue, Harlem City, feeling as snooty as the lions in front of the Forty-second Street Library, for instance. So far as my feelings are concerned, Peggy Hopkins Joyce on the Boule Mich with her gorgeous raiment, stately carriage, knees knocking together in a most aristocratic manner, has nothing on me."

A new breed of caricaturists also found Peggy a potent signifier of the times. Like many other comely women of her day, Peggy frequently sat for her portrait, not only for the ubiquitous James Montgomery Flagg, the prolific illustrator who had directed one of her short films back in the teens, but also for lesser-known figures like Nicola Michailow, who described himself as the Bulgarian court painter and insisted he had never seen a figure in Europe that compared to hers. In calibrating one's position in the hierarchy of the famous, however, sitting for a portrait signaled far less than catching the caricaturist's eye.

Drawing on a bold modernist aesthetic and brilliantly isolating and exaggerating the traits that defined a particular individual, hundreds of sketch artists worked in this medium during the twenties and thirties. In a tabloid culture that placed primacy on image over text, their stylish, acutely observed depictions of the famous and occasionally infamous did an enormous amount to satisfy the voracious public appetite for celebrity. Any well-to-do society matron could be painted by Flagg. But to capture the attention of a William Auerbach-Levy or an Al Hirschfeld or an Alfred Frueh was an achievement of a much higher order, for the whole point of caricature was that its subjects were so familiar as to be instantly recognizable from a few broad strokes.

The Mexican-born artist Miguel Covarrubias shrewdly realized that his real subject was not individual celebrities but the system that created them. In the early thirties, he and American humorist Corey Ford, writing under the pseudonym John Riddell, joined forces to invent what would become *Vanity Fair*'s most popular caricature series, the "Impossible Interview." Covarrubias's witty pairings of high-cult and low-cult figures—a shriveled Prince of Wales (the future duke of Windsor) and a glowing Clark Gable, both vying for the title of world's greatest heartbreaker; Chief Justice Charles Evans Hughes and Public Enemy Number One Al Capone, the two faces of Prohibition; a soignée Martha Graham and a befeathered Sally Rand, "just a couple of little girls trying to wriggle along"—underscored the fact that a person's social status mattered less than the drawing power of a name. An appearance in an "Impossible Interview" was one more sign of Peggy's prominence.

Covarrubias teamed her with Dorothy Dix, the straitlaced author of the book *How to Win and Hold a Husband* and creator of a widely read and desperately prim advice-to-the-lovelorn column. The two sit side by side on a swing, Dix a portly figure in black, her white hair piled unfashionably on top of her head, Peggy a symphony of ravishing color—brassy curls, blue-shadowed eyelids, bright red lips and nails, and glossy brown fur coat. A huge orchid is pinned to her bo-

som—she had not starred in *The Lady of the Orchids* for nothing—
diamond bracelets wink on her wrists, and her legs are crossed seductively.

"Dear Dorothy Dix," she purrs. "I am twenty-one, pretty and in
love with a young man—"

DOROTHY: You should never go out with a man unless his "inten-
    tions" are honorable because marriage is worth more than fur-
    coats and orchids and jewels—
PEGGY: He wants me to marry him, dear Dorothy Dix. . . .
DOROTHY: (sternly) I am afraid you are interested only in the
    "flighty" things of life and that your love is mere "infatuation."
    Forget about marriage for awhile and sooner or later the Right
    Man will come along—
PEGGY: That's just the trouble. I'm married already. In fact I've been
    married heaps of times.

An even more irresistible combination were the two eminent
Joyces of the day. On December 27, 1933, the *Bystander,* a prestigious English magazine, featured a witty collage of the novelist and
the husband hunter on its cover. The Joyces were also ideal candi-
dates for the *Vanity Fair* feature "Married in Name Only" which
included such other unlikely couples as Pierpont and Helen Morgan
(the prototypical Jazz Age torch singer) and Alfred and Kate
Smith. "Think of the fun James Joyce could have with Peggy,"
the magazine fluttered, "teaching her all about the stream of
consciousness."

New Yorker cartoonist Peter Arno offered a pithy comment on
the fascination with tales of her exploits, a fascination that
consumed all social classes. "Those Peggy Joyce revelations are
rather corking, aren't they?" one of his raffish straphangers
observes to the bewhiskered nob who has been surreptitiously
peering into his tabloid. As much as anyone else in those years,
Arno had his finger on the public pulse. To be immortalized by

the cartoonist whose subjects were, by definition, the talk of the town proved the reach of one's reputation.

Peggy also managed to insinuate herself into the Queens, New York, courtroom where one of the most sensational trials of the decade was playing daily to packed houses. At center stage stood Ruth Snyder, a hard-eyed housewife from Queens Village who turned out to be the mastermind of a complicated plot involving adultery and revenge. With her married lover, Henry Judd Gray, a New Jersey corset sales-man, she found herself in the dock for the murder of her husband, Albert, who had been bludgeoned with the weight from a window sash, then chloroformed and strangled to death with a piece of wire. Lust and treachery in a peaceful suburban neighborhood proved a powerful draw, and the trial held much of America spellbound dur-ing the spring of 1927. To heighten the drama, the *Daily Mirror* had the inspired idea of asking a string of luminaries to record their im-pressions of the proceedings. Its roster included historian Will Durant, film director D. W. Griffith, playwright Ben Hecht—and Peggy, on the assumption that what a woman who had acquired four husbands did not know about passion was not worth knowing.

On April 21, reporting on its "reporters," the *Mirror* noted that "Peggy Hopkins Joyce, the most preferred blonde of them all, radi-ant and charming, arrived in court yesterday afternoon." Taking her seat at the press table and gazing at Ruth Snyder, she whispered to one of the press people: "How can she avoid looking at Judd Gray? I couldn't keep my eyes off a man who had been as close to me as he has been to her and who was tangled up with me in a mess like this."

What interested her were not the knotty sociological implications of the crime but the love angle. Referring to the concept that ro-mantic novelist Elinor Glyn had just popularized (and Clara Bow would epitomize), she wrote after her first day in court: "Henry Judd Gray simply hasn't got IT! What Mrs. Snyder saw in him is absolutely beyond me." Nor could she picture the illicit pair as "red hot lovers" who went to such extraordinary lengths to indulge their passion. "I can't see poor Judd Gray's appeal at all," she wrote. "If he were present at a tea or dinner where I was, I don't believe I would even be interested enough in him, just looking at him today, to remember him afterward."

She suggested that both parties be put to death as quickly as possible so all concerned could get on with their lives: "I wonder if it would be best for their poor relatives, who have to bear the burden of all this, if these two people were electrocuted so that the great public would forget about them in time and the children, at least, be given some kind of chance to get away from their parents' mistakes." Presumably, she was gratified by the most famous tabloid image of the decade, the photograph that appeared the following January on the front page of the *Daily News* showing Ruth Snyder, strapped into the electric chair, at the moment the switch was being pulled.

Not everyone was impressed by Peggy's performance during the trial. "Peggy Hopkins Countess Morner and whatnot Joyce, the famous grass widow, came again to dazzle all the beholders with the magnificence of her display," Damon Runyon wrote in the *New York American* after her second appearance in court. "Probably she didn't believe her eyes and ears on her first visit that a lady had seemed to have some difficulty in getting rid of her husband. Peggy never did, you can bet on that."

In addition to news stories and column items, the dailies also devoted considerable space to Peggy's own writings about herself. Starting in the spring of 1922, when her sensational divorce from Stanley Joyce was fresh in millions of minds, newspaper readers from coast to coast were treated to weekly helpings of succulent information, thanks to a four-month-long series of first-person articles distributed by Hearst's International Feature Service.

A few years later a similarly hefty package of revelations appeared in the *Evening Graphic*. "I will begin with the startling statement that I have been married only three times," began one breathless installment. "Extraordinary and unbelievable, isn't it. But this only goes to prove again that truth is stranger than fiction. Almost every well-regulated family in this country boasts of at least two marriages, and numerous prominent matrons would not faint at the thought of possessing their fourth decree. So you see I have not been such a menace to the young debs aspiring to millionaires as you might think."

Around the same time, a New York news syndicate ran a ten-part series offering Peggy's "Ten Commandments for Winning Men," of which the first was the cryptic but impassioned statement "Thou shalt love but love." In the author's opinion, even the famed Cleopatra did not comply with this directive. "I have never felt she was a great lover," Peggy wrote in dismissing the queen of the Nile. "She had too many other interests. She did not even hold Antony all the time. She could not win Caesar as she wanted to. . . . If she had really loved love, she would never have killed herself."

Peggy's articles, especially for Hearst, went a long way toward honing the persona she strove to project to the world, that of a spunky madcap enchantress out to get the most she could from the men in her life as she glided from one sumptuous setting to another. She was hardly the first celebrity to craft a seamless version of her life, abetted by a team of nimble-fingered rewrite men. It was the rare individual in the limelight who did not concoct a fanciful biography for the delectation of his or her fans. But Peggy understood that telling her tale in the newspapers offered a heaven-sent opportunity not only to burnish her image but also to settle a few scores.

Her accounts for Hearst of her progression from innocent daughter of the South to worldly-wise globetrotter read like pulp fiction, with Peggy as the triumphant, if slightly battered, heroine. "The Famous Beauty Who Married and Divorced Three Immensely Rich Men and Was Named in a Series of Romances with a Dozen More,

Stripping the Secrecy of Her Long Silence from the Intimate Details of Her Spectacular Career and Divulging the Truth about the Charges That She Is a 'Vampire of Millionaires,'" trumpeted a typical headline.

The prose was the best Hearst's money could buy. "Like a glad bird loosed from a golden cage into a garden of the gods to sing and frolic and strut gay plumes and fly free and high," one passage began, "I live into the day life and the night life of the world's fastest and most furious metropolis of frivol and carnival." To underscore the authenticity of the tales, the opening chapter was accompanied by a photograph of the "author" seated at her ornate little writing desk, along with snippets of the monogrammed notepaper—textured buff with her initials in a tiny circle—on which she had allegedly preserved her thoughts for posterity.

While many of the articles lamented the price of fame—"It is a fearsome thing to become too well-known," she complained at one point—she was realistic enough to acknowledge her role in the media circus. "Goodness knows that I contribute enough to it," she wrote of the flood of material that had been published about her, "and these pages are among my voluntary bit of it." She also took aim at the "dastardly lies" that had circulated about her during her divorce trial, to the point of comparing herself to other famous martyrs of history. "I have been no Joan of Arc," she admitted modestly, but she did see a few parallels. She had also inflated the size of her divorce settlement to a whopping two million dollars.

Hearst had been wise to capitalize so energetically on the interest in Peggy's life story, and the articles proved enormously popular. Most remarkable, however, was the wellspring of feeling they aroused in women across the country, women who had little if anything in common with the teller of these extravagant tales. These readers hungrily devoured Peggy's ruminations and felt such an intense connection with her it seemed inconceivable she would ignore them in their time of need. The articles made no mention of any particular acts of kindness or generosity on the part of their author, beyond the sweeping statement, "I intend to devote the rest of my life on this earth to making others happy," a goal she felt would be satisfied by her plans to start a chain of theaters with Oliver Morosco. But some very human and sympathetic quality seemed to shine through the overheated prose. And so, late at night, writing with stubby pencils on ruled paper torn from cheap writing tablets, in letters that were riddled with misspellings and sometimes almost illiterate, her readers poured out their hearts and made their pitches.

"Dear Mrs. Peggy Hopkins Joyce," began a young Cleveland woman named Flora in a round schoolgirl hand. "I hope you will excuse my boldness in writing you. I have been reading your story in the Cleveland paper every Sunday. I work in a laundry and this hot weather I think of you and picture myself in your shoes. Oh, what would I do if I could have beautiful clothes like you and everything my heart could wish for. I have often thought of a little cottage for two or three, but I have a dear mother to look after so I haven't time to think of marriage. So I thought I would write this letter and ask if you would help us a bit. I can earn enough to keep from starving and a good bed for mother dear. But it is hard to buy clothes for us both and if you had anything in clothing, underwear, coats, I would be so glad. I would be willing to pay a little each week. It wouldn't be much. But I would show you how much I would thank you. Even if you won't send me things I will think of you always."

A desperate Colorado housewife wrote: "I know you can help me out of my troubles. We are poor and haven't any money to pay our bills. We are paying $30 for a two-room house and it is more than we can afford. We have two babies, one is two years and one is one year old. My husband works but earns very little, only $85-$90 a month. If you could only give us $200 or $300 to get our things paid. The reason we got that much to pay is that my husband was in the strike in 1920. The man was out of work for a year. Please, Mrs. Joyce, open your heart and let us have that much money. It will look like a million dollars to us. If you'd like to have it back we could pay you $10 a month. That's the best we could do, as babies and myself need a little clothes. I hate to bother you with this, but I know you will help me."

From a dutiful daughter living in Lancaster, Pennsylvania: "I am a maiden lady 47 years old, and have lived at home with my parents all my life as it was a duty to them, until a year ago when the home was broken up by death. Father died in 1912 and mother in 1921. She was 87 years old when she passed away and the house had to be sold. But for all that I would not think of writing this if I were strong and able to do any kind of work but that is not my lot as I am subject to nervous headaches. Oh, Miss Hopkins you don't know what it is to be without a home. I tried to picture this before the home was broken up, but oh, it is much harder than I realized, and I thought it would be dreadful." The writer closed with the forlorn confession: "Now I have written this letter but don't know if I have the heart to mail it or not."

A Chicago woman wrote: "Dear Mis Hopkins. I hope you wont be anoid of this my letter. It is the first time I beged for anything. I ask you because I think you are kindhearted. I am married and have 3 children. The oldest are 4 years old. My husband are only making 23 dollars a week so I am not able to get much clothes. I was thinking you might have a suit and a waist you don't care for. I would apreciate any kind of clothes you could spare and would be pleased to do som crosheting for it if you wanted me to."

Particularly poignant were the notes from young girls, who worshiped Peggy as ardently as they did the stars of the silver screen. "Dear Peggy," wrote a teenager from a small town in Pennsylvania in a note so smudged the words were barely legible. "I am an orphan and have no mother or father nobody. I stay with a lady friend. So if you are so kind please send me some of your old dresses and hats and stockings. I never had a pair of silk stockings yet I wear 10 cent stockings. And my birthstone is April a diamond if you can spare one for me. And also send me one of your pictures. Every time I get the paper and your picture is in it I cry so hard I don't know what to do. I wrote this letter with tears."

From a Colorado teenager named Helen, a long letter dotted with inkblots: "I am a girl living in Denver and find it very hard to get along. My father died four years ago with heart failure and I had a little sister and brother born three weeks after he died. My mother was just operated on her stomach a short time ago and is not even able to do her working. My mother says I am not very strong and will never be able to do heavy work and on account of that one reason I wish to get two years of high school at least. And the carfare is awful high out here and I don't think my mother can send me to school.

"I wonder if you would send me enough money to send me to school. I certainly would think you was my dearest friend. I read in the Post that you was going to build a theater in Denver. Of course I never have money to go to a show. And I also read that you have been in the Rockies. Aren't they beautiful? I haven't no auto or nothing so I can't enjoy even those because I can only look at them from a distance." She concluded with the words: "I often wish my name was Peggy. It is such a sweet name and you are a beautiful girl."

The writers of these letters occupied the margins of an increasingly prosperous era. Far from the penthouses of Park Avenue and the mansions of Miami, far from the glitter that defined the decade, they spent their days caring for sickly children, watching over aged parents, struggling along in poverty-level jobs, or taking the place of husbands who had been laid off by strikes or maimed in horrible industrial accidents. Uncertain where to direct their pleas, they did the best they could. Fortunately, the object of their requests was so well known that a letter sent care of "Postmaster, NYC" or addressed to Peggy at "her famous Park Avenue Bachelor Apartment" immediately got through.

The recipient of these heartfelt notes apparently did not think highly of her fans. She complained to one newspaper that she received "trunkloads of letters," adding with some annoyance, "Half the letters I get are begging ones." She found her correspondents whiny, greedy, and slightly contemptible, and she scanned their messages only briefly before stuffing them back into their envelopes and tossing them into the old trunk where she kept her papers. Except for a girl who shared her initials and to whom she claimed she sent a set of monogrammed pillowcases, there is no indication that Peggy ever gave any of her fans a second thought; even that story was probably apocryphal. But these heartbreaking scraps of letters offer eloquent testament to the desires and fantasies Americans projected onto the girl from Virginia who had risen to such lofty heights.

Given the overwhelming response to Peggy's newspaper memoirs, it did not take an enterprising publisher long to realize what a smart move it would be to package her life between hard covers. The twenties, after all, were an age of memoirs. Everyone was writing them; hostess Elsa Maxwell seemed to turn out one a year. In 1929 the New York firm of Macaulay and Company contracted with Basil Woon, an English journalist and travel writer with a flair for waxing poetic about the sophisticates of Hollywood and Europe, to help Peggy tell her story.

The aptly titled result, *Men, Marriage and Me,* was allegedly based on the author's childhood diary, although Peggy was the first to admit she never kept such a sentimental thing. "It's my diary," she confided to one reporter with a broad wink. "That is, my diary and a little fiction." In a series of chatty, loosely connected anecdotes written largely in the present tense, the book traced the string of impetuous romances that had catapulted her from her modest Virginia home to the glitter of Monte Carlo, a journey in which she perpetually seemed to be not a minute over sixteen. The style was vintage Lorelei, down to the blizzard of exclamation points, capital letters, and forced misspellings, and the text was studded with pungent one-liners regarding the artful handling of the male sex.

"A woman should never give her husband credit for too much generosity, it makes him complacent," a typical kernel suggested. "If a husband gives me a diamond ring I thank him very sweetly of course but I let him see that what I really wanted was a pearl necklace."

As for her prescriptions for a happy home life: "You show me a man with his stomach full of his wife's good cooking and his slippers on the rug and his pipe in his mouth and his newspaper in his hand while his wife sits by sewing, and I will show you a man who is too happy to be in love." Her primary counsel was charmingly hard-headed: "Tell a man you love him but say it in such a way to make him doubtful and think you are lying."

Like her newspaper memoirs, the book did a great deal to buff her public image as the quintessential twenties hedonist. Particularly enticing was her definition of the perfect husband: "He must get up first thing in the morning and go out and not let me see him until he is shaved. It is very tiring to have to look at a husband early in the morning. . . . He must be a passionate lover but not a mauler, especially in public or when I am all dressed and made up to go out. . . . He must not be a teetotaler, because teetotalers generally have something else wrong with them, and anyway, it is not much fun to go out with a man who will not even drink champagne."

A great deal of her saga bore only a glancing relationship to the truth—every romance was whirlwind, every lover an Adonis, and every Adonis a cad in the end. But that was no surprise, coming as the book did from an individual who was so much a creature of her own invention, whose life was such an artful blend of fact and fancy. *Men, Marriage and Me* was a masterful concoction, self-serving, savvy, and thoroughly fun. And in truth, it took no more liberties with the truth than most such creations. Peggy's own jaded view was that "there is not a woman living who is physically or mentally capable of telling the true story of her life."

Despite the lavish embellishment of the facts, the book contained some revealing, if calculated, insights into the author's personality. "I am fond of pretty clothes and jewels," she acknowledged at one point. "What girl isn't? Is it surprising that I like to have such things bought for me? Do these things make me happy? Are they all I want? I'm being honest now. I may as well go on. Happiness means peace and contentment. And with all that I have I am not peaceful and contented. I worry. I fret. I am irritable.

"I suppose I am vain," she continued. "And I have been selfish lots of times. Yet God knows I help plenty of people out when they are in trouble. I can't be all wrong. Chance made me the sort of person I am and I suppose I have been spoiled by too much attention. But I have a heart and feelings as well as anybody."

In a typically savvy move, the work was dedicated to Walter Winchell, "my great friend," as Peggy described him in the front of the book. She and the country's premier gossip columnist were hardly intimates, but she knew better than most what sort of person drove the publicity machinery that had helped make her what she was.

The parodies of *Men, Marriage and Me* began spewing forth even before its official publication in February 1930. A newspaper spoof entitled "My Husbands I Have Met" suggested that the author would leave her collection of husbands—"one of the finest in the world"— to the Smithsonian and said of a particular conquest: "I don't recall who I married next. But I loved him! Loved him passionately! Madly! . . . I don't know what in the world became of him but I must have mislaid him or lost him during a continental trip."

Once the book arrived in stores with a drawing of Peggy, red quill pen in hand, on the deep purple cover, Corey Ford amused *Vanity Fair* readers with an even more extensive riff on Peggy's literary efforts: "I have decided hereafter to keep a filing cabinet of my husbands. It is getting to be more than one girl can remember. It would take all her time. I decided to do this today after a most embarrassing incident. I went downtown this afternoon to get a divorce from my husband and after I got into the divorce office I found out that in my haste I had neglected to marry him." The trouble with a diary, the narrator continues, is that "you forget to write things down as they happen and afterward you cannot remember them properly, especially if you have had more than one husband the same day."

Macaulay, Peggy's publishers, shared her belief that there was no such thing as bad publicity, and the firm launched the author of *Men, Marriage and Me* with a lavish caviar tea at the Ritz-Carlton Hotel, an event that proved as newsworthy as the work that had prompted it. "Peggy Hopkins Joyce, the famed blonde, was brought out as an author yesterday afternoon at the Ritz in one of the most extraordinary literary events experienced by the local literati," the New York *Sun* reported. The Spider Web Orchestra and the Washboard Serenaders played soft jazz in a private suite bedecked with ferns as the woman of the hour, wearing a short black velvet dress and a matching turban, mingled with the mostly male gathering.

"I hardly know what to say to you," she murmured to proletarian writer Mike Gold, who had donned a flaming red tie for the occasion.

"And I hardly know what to say to you," replied the famous leftist.

"Well," his hostess chirped brightly, "let's have a drink."

The poet Hart Crane not only showed up but danced repeatedly with the guest of honor. "I danced and danced until finally she said that she had to turn to some of the others and do the courtesy act," Crane told a friend afterward. In the spirit of the afternoon, he also proposed marriage, an offer that fazed Peggy not in the slightest. "There are at least two ahead of you," she replied with her usual archness. "I hope you have the patience to wait."

Nor was the press campaign quite over. Hardly had the last caviar canapé been cleared away before the news spread that Peggy had been rushed to the Harbor Sanitarium on Madison Avenue for an emergency appendectomy. "Though cancellation of her passage to France helped to make the operation seem dramatically sudden, it was not," *Time* magazine revealed. "Authoress Joyce's room at the hospital had been engaged for weeks." Nevertheless, reporters and photographers dutifully trooped to her hospital suite, where they were rewarded with descriptions of the patient in her sickbed along with pictures of the offending organ, which the surgeon had thoughtfully preserved in a little cut-glass bottle.

Despite the blasts of publicity that accompanied its publication, *Men, Marriage and Me* was not a critical success. An English reviewer complained that the book made him physically ill, and he compared Peggy's observations to "the babblings of a depraved nursery or the jungle." But the work helped keep its creator's name in the public eye. When the *Evening Graphic* was casting about for a woman to lend her name to a weekly advice-to-the-lovelorn column, the editors decided to look no further than Macaulay's latest literary find.

"How to Get Your Man" was the unambiguous name of Peggy's column. In it, she offered a series of parables, complete with morals, about life in treacherous modern times. She lamented the tragic fate of Cissie, an otherwise lovely girl who did not take proper care of her skin; "I hope she comes to her senses very soon," Peggy wrote. She told of the unhappy Florence, who made a career out of chasing minor celebrities while rejecting the love of an unassuming but steady man. "She had happiness within her grasp, but ignored it to chase will-o'-the-wisps," Peggy concluded. "Don't you think she is rather pathetic?" Sounding prissier than Dorothy Dix, she came down firmly against petting and extramarital flings, on the grounds that "no matter how fascinating the man who proposes a love affair to the restless married woman, she will find, in the end, that her husband is more fascinating." Perhaps drawing on whatever wisdom she had gained from the suicide of her Chilean lover Billy Errazuriz nearly a decade earlier, she even offered hints on how to keep a man from killing himself after rejecting his advances. "All these unexplained suicides one reads about!" she lamented. "A cruel word delivered at just the right psychological moment can drive a young man, terribly in love, to drastic measures."

As an added attraction, the *Graphic* threw in "The Peggy Joyce Love Chart," which invited readers to answer a series of questions—"Have you a jealous disposition?" "Do you love children?"—whose answers would enable "the world's most seductive woman" to determine their "love magnetism" and their chances for "love happiness."

Taken as a package, these morsels didn't sound as if they had emanated from the free spirit Peggy's audience had come to know and adore. But the editors of the *Graphic* understood better than most people what sold newspapers. They realized that tidbits of information purporting to be about sexual behavior, even when clothed in moralistic language, had an undeniable appeal, especially when they allegedly came from the pen of an internationally famous figure and showed up faithfully in each Saturday's paper.

By the early thirties, Peggy had begun to regard herself as something of a writer—the contributions of the hardworking Basil Woon were rarely mentioned—and given a life that so resembled a picaresque novel, it seemed appropriate that she actually write a novel or at least contribute a few details to a novel to which her name could be attached. Her European travels had given her considerable knowledge about the high life abroad and provided more than enough grist for a dramatic yarn. Whether or not *Men, Marriage and Me* had been "one of the best sellers," as the Associated Press insisted, Macaulay decided to take another chance on her.

The result was *Transatlantic Wife,* the steamy story of an American charmer named Evelyn Russell, she of the forget-me-not blue eyes, who takes leave of her loutish businessman husband and sets off for Europe to taste the amorous pleasures of the Old World. The motley cast of characters includes a gangster's widow from Chicago, whose specialty is recruiting unscrupulous gigolos to service footloose American wives, and a black-eyed Spaniard who makes women "quiver with passion from head to toe" and tries to steal the heroine's priceless pearls while guzzling her creamy neck—biting them first to make sure they are genuine.

With settings ranging from the elegant Ciro's in Paris's richest quarter to the seamy cabarets of Montmartre, with its faked suicides, spying maids, and the occasional nightclub raid by the French police, the narrative sounds remarkably like the testimony in Peggy's big divorce case. The only unfamiliar note is struck by the relentlessly upbeat ending, in which a sadder but wiser Evelyn—"Take me back, George dear, across the Atlantic to America . . . your home and mine!"—returns gratefully to her husband's arms.

Macaulay did not throw another party—by this time the Depression was in full throttle—but in urging booksellers to jump on the Peggy Hopkins Joyce bandwagon, her publishers took pains to underscore the reputation of its famous author. "Whatever she does is national news in thousands of papers," the firm pointed out in an advertisement directed to the trade. "Her new novel will have reams of publicity, double-barreled promotion, supercharged advertising, and a popular acceptance that is eager—like an issue of new currency to the book trade. She is the American queen of perennial publicity." Rumors were even floated that the novel would be made into a film, although Peggy quickly denied that she had any designs on playing her heroine. "Of course, she's a charming lady," she told the *Los Angeles Times*. "But I don't like this thing of a film coming out, its forward reading, 'Peggy Hopkins Joyce, starred in Peggy Hopkins Joyce's novel, scenario by Peggy Hopkins Joyce, costumes by the same, dialogue by Peggy Hopkins Joyce, incidental music ditto'—and then maybe introducing the Joyce pants or something."

In most other respects, however, Peggy took to her new role with considerable zeal. Even before the book was published in May 1933, she had started presenting herself to the world as a woman at home in the world of letters and both comfortable with and enamored of those who dwelt there. "Millionaires may be all right," she told a reporter in Paris as she lounged about her suite at the Crillon in a pink satin negligee, her bright pink toenails much in evidence. But, she insisted, "they can't compete with the man who is interested in human nature and who is also clever enough to make money at it."

A short time afterward, she confessed to Joseph Mitchell of the *New York World-Telegram:* "I've been so busy. My novel is finished. I work with a secretary, of course, and I have to use the blue pencil a lot." She also admitted she had been finding inspiration in other people's work, although she drew the line at comparing herself with the greats. "It would be silly for me to make out that I am literary," she acknowledged to Mitchell. "I read novels. They give me ideas."

Despite Basil Woon's help, *Transatlantic Wife* was so excruciatingly awful as to be extremely, though inadvertently, funny. The plot leaped feverishly from one outlandish episode to the next, finally fetching up with the heroine in hot pursuit of an Austrian archduke who has taken up chicken farming along the Riviera. And overblown as the story was, it could not match the excesses of the prose, which grew especially fiery when exploring the secrets of the boudoir:

"Mario quivered. He was singularly thrilled by the undulation of this supple body beneath his sensitive fingers. And a night of champagne and fine liqueurs sharpened the edge of his lust. His black eyes dipped their fever in Evelyn's blue ones which the visions of the diving sin rendered provocative and pleasantly vicious. . . . [He] allowed his hot, heavy head to fall on the throbbing breast of the lovely woman whose desire, tantalized by this terrible teasing, was rendering her momentarily insane. All Evelyn's body was convulsed by the touch of those scorching lips on her half-naked breast. Furiously she tried to draw to her this marionette of vibrant flesh and pulsing blood which every nerve within her craved to possess."

Critics could barely keep a straight face. "Naturally in a Joyce book there are some startling bits of philosophy which even James Joyce (no relation) couldn't improve on," the reviewer Norman Klein wrote in the *New York Evening Post,* pointing out that most of the author's literary experience had come from endorsing alimony checks.

When Basil Woon's next book was published, the *New York Times* turned the knife a bit further. "There are parts when it all seems very mixed up," the paper's literary critic wrote, "as though Peggy Joyce was ghosting for Mr. Woon."

Peggy even had a final fling in vaudeville. In April 1931 she was tapped for a brief humorous skit at the Palace in New York. The sketch designed for her was entitled "Rings on Her Fingers"—by now an all-too-apt description—and she had been chosen solely in an effort to capitalize on the drawing power of her name. Exactly why she bothered to take part in such an inconsequential effort is unclear. At the Palace and every other vaudeville house in the country, the art form was dying; the year 1931 also saw such unlikely acts on the Palace stage as columnist Heywood Broun and a pair of Siamese twins. The nicest thing that the *New York Times* would find to say about Peggy's appearance was that it surely was a sign spring had arrived.

The one medium Peggy never penetrated was the world of radio, despite its enormous power in the new celebrity culture. As a force in American society, it crested a little too late for her to take full advantage of it. And although she represented a "lovely menace to American home life," as a reviewer noted after one of her rare performances before a microphone, "her chief charms were lost to her hearers." Nor was unscripted banter her strong suit; when Fox Movietone filmed a brief newsreel segment in which Peggy extolled the joys of European living, she needed half a dozen tries to produce a usable snippet of footage.

But if celebrity could be achieved without radio, it could not be maintained without Hollywood. And so, in early 1933, accompanied by seven trunks, fifteen traveling bags, a maid, a secretary, and a French chef, Peggy headed west again, this time to star in a major comedy called *International House* for Paramount. Thanks to the arrival of sound and the maturation of the studio system, the business of producing stars that had begun in the silent era had come of age. Norma Shearer, Jean Harlow and especially Joan Crawford were truly goddesses of the screen, and the dramatic photographic portraits by such masters of the genre as George Hurrell presented these mortals as the deities the American public believed them to be.

The movie industry, which at first seemed unaffected by the Depression, had by 1933 proved no more invulnerable than the rest of the economy. After a decade in which the moviegoing audience had virtually doubled, by the early thirties it started to decline. But as economic chaos turned the country into a shambles, Americans discovered that one of the few things that took their minds off their troubles was the largely escapist fare churned out by Hollywood. Every week, tens of millions of moviegoers descended on the nation's theaters, where they could laugh at the Marx Brothers, wince as James Cagney shoved a grapefruit in Mae Clarke's face, and gasp as Johnny Weissmuller leaped from vine to vine to prove himself lord of the jungle.

International House, one of the glossy comedies that Paramount had become known for, was designed to appeal to just such an audience. The flimsy plot was intended merely as a device for getting the roster of stars under one roof, in this case a hotel in the fictional city of Wu-Hu, China, where all parties are involved in an intrigue surrounding the rights to an invention that sounds suspiciously like television. In addition to Peggy, the eclectic lineup of performers, many of whom were drawn from the world of radio, included W. C. Fields, her old chum from the *Follies,* along with George Burns, Gracie Allen, Bela Lugosi, Baby Rose Marie, Rudy Vallee, and the Cab Calloway Orchestra.

The film, which was directed by Edward Sutherland, did a great deal to advance Fields's career. The actor had suffered through a series of silent flops during a previous assault on Hollywood back in the twenties, and only after *International House* proved successful did

Paramount offer him a coveted multiyear contract, leading to the string of comic masterpieces like *It's a Gift* and *Man on the Flying Trapeze* that he created over the next few years. But while Peggy was chosen for the movie solely for her celebrity value, she was the better-known figure, which was why Paramount awarded her star billing.

She played herself with a vengeance, a sophisticated blonde on her way to Wu-Hu because she knows that whoever buys the new invention will become rich and she intends to marry him. Her misadventures begin when she spends a night with a strange man during an unscheduled stop in the desert. Despite the presence in Wu-Hu of one of her many ex-husbands (Lugosi, as a jealous Russian general), she winds up sharing a bedroom with an eccentric American professor (Fields). Under the impression that he is already a millionaire, she quickly sets her cap for him. The two finally end up together, and after a wild chase scene in his little auto, they take off in a helicopter amid a flurry of slightly blue one-liners.

Lest anyone forget why Peggy had been selected to portray a vampy gold digger, the script was laced with not-so-subtle reminders as to the nature of her reputation. One woman remarks to her fiancé in incredulous tones, "You were perfectly platonic with Peggy Hopkins Joyce?" At another point, Peggy confronts her ex-husband by demanding skeptically, "Didn't I get a divorce from you in Paris?"

With Peggy as a drawing card, not to mention the general array of talent—"More stars than you saw when you fell down the cellar stairs," one ad promised—Paramount had high hopes for the movie and pushed it hard. As always with a Peggy Joyce production, the studio hatched an endless series of promotional gimmicks, complemented by the usual avalanche of hyperbole-drenched articles in the fan magazines. *Motion Picture* proclaimed itself especially taken with the tender way the star slipped a pink rosebud into the lapel of the photographer who had snapped her picture, the charming compliment she paid to the hairdresser who had set her wave, and Peggy's professed amazement at the banner headlines her foray in movieland was engendering.

At that particular moment, however, Hollywood had a great many other issues on its mind than the success of a sometimes actress. Three years earlier, in 1930, the Motion Picture Producers and Distributors Association, by then known as the Hays office, had adopted its Production Code, a formal set of guidelines indicating what was unacceptable in such areas as violence, religion, and most of all sex. Pressure had been building for decades; the first municipal censorship ordinance had been passed a quarter century earlier, and efforts to blame a great deal of the licentiousness of the freewheeling twenties on the cinema had quickened the pace. By 1933, after years of desultory attention to the morals of the American public, the Hays office, pressed by the well-organized and increasingly vocal and influential Roman Catholic Church, no longer considered voluntary compliance sufficient. Self-regulation was on the brink of becoming mandatory. Lewd behavior and suggestive language were especially frowned on, not to mention loose-living women who failed to receive their proper comeuppance. With the size of the movie audience shrinking precipitously, Hollywood could not ignore the pressure from outside forces.

The result was a power struggle that roiled the entire movie industry and echoed far beyond it. As production began on *International House* early that year, one of the hottest issues in town was exactly what constituted an acceptable picture. And a movie pairing one of the most promiscuous women on the planet with a comedian who made a raised eyebrow look like an indecent proposition had trouble written all over it.

International House presented various offenses. The censors bristled especially over the scene in which Peggy and Fields share a bedroom, albeit in twin beds and oblivious to each other's presence, and another in which Peggy loses her skirt in a car door, revealing a brief glimpse of underwear. By the time filming ended, the pressure had increased. "As you are doubtless aware, this is a type of picture with which censor boards recently have been dealing severely, with particular reference to double-meaning lines and gags," the Hays office wrote Paramount. Reluctantly, the studio agreed to one of six recommended cuts, and the film was readied for its May opening.

Though not one of the big movies of the year—*King Kong,* Mae West's *She Done Him Wrong,* and the Disney cartoon short *The Three Little Pigs* were among the more popular films of 1933—*International House* did respectably at the box office. And considering the hodge-podge Paramount had whipped together, the reviews were not bad. The *New York Times* described *International House* as "wild fun," and *Variety* noted appreciatively that the star "wears a whole fox farm and gives 'em a one-gal fashion show from the panties up."

But despite the picture's relative tameness—one industry source deemed it "suitable for children, adolescents, and Sundays"—reports from local censors around the country revealed that the double entendres exchanged by Peggy and Fields were affronting moral sensibilities in the hinterlands. Of special concern was a scene in which Peggy sits on a mysterious object in Field's car, whereupon Fields replies with one of his famous leers, "It's a pussy."

The Hays office was furious, especially since no one could remember the episode from the original script, and there was considerable debate about the presence of an actual cat. "It seems apparent from what a number of people have said to me that the studio 'pulled a fast one' by changing the scene between W. C. Fields and Peggy Joyce in the Austin," a Hays office representative exploded in a memo. "From several people who have spoken to me about this scene, it is my understanding that it has been changed radically and in such a way as to make it offensively vulgar."

A subsequent memo fumed: "The whole picture is vulgar and borders constantly on the salacious." As for the line about the alleged cat, "the dirty-minded lout who put it in the picture knew perfectly well . . . what he was doing and undoubtedly felt he had gained something by getting away with it."

Overseas, the film ran into problems as well. Japanese audiences objected to a scene in which Peggy removes a pair of men's shorts from her suitcase and announces innocently, "I packed these by mistake in the desert." Sweden rejected the picture entirely, although on aesthetic rather than moral grounds: "Considered unsuitable—story too artificial and absurd," the country's censors ruled. Two years later, when Paramount sought permission to rerelease the film, the studio was informed that approval would probably be denied on the grounds of "gross vulgarities in both action and dialogue." As late as 1950, the censors were still asking Paramount to reedit the movie, and to lose the scene about the cat, to make it more acceptable for the American public.

Peggy continued to look ravishing in the profusion of studio photographs released in connection with the film, decked out in smart little coats set off by wing-tip sleeves, voluminous fur wraps, slinky black gowns that trailed the floor, and snug berets tilted rakishly over one eyebrow. One particularly sultry image showed her with her head flung back and her eyelids lowered, her strapless dress cut deep to reveal the tops of her luscious breasts, and her arms clasped around her shoulders as if she were enjoying a private moment of ecstasy.

But no one could deny that she was fraying around the edges. She was forty years old, and even the most artful retoucher could no longer conceal the spread of her hips and the spidery lines that laced her face. The studio biography that listed her weight as 110 pounds was badly out of date. Her expression had turned harder, her brilliant smile more forced, her hair less springy. One riding costume made her appear distinctly plump; when caught off guard, she almost looked her age. Although still regularly described as "the most alluring of all American women," she was no longer what she had been.

Fortunately for her, the current man in her life felt honored to be seen in her company. The smiling, round-faced actor Jack Oakie was as boyish and bouncy as his name, and while he was something of a bumpkin, even down to the price tags Peggy noticed clinging to his suits when the two of them dined together in the studio commissary, she liked him very much. "He is the most charming man I've met here," she told the press during her stay in Hollywood. "He is the *only* man who can amuse me." When she listed the qualities that defined the perfect husband—Clark Gable's dimples, Gary Cooper's physique, Maurice Chevalier's personality, Jimmy Cagney's energy— she paid her newest flame the compliment of including "Jack Oakie's sense of humor."

He in turn squired her around town, posed cheek to cheek with her when photographers were on the scene, and rushed to her side when the massive Long Beach earthquake sent cast and crew fleeing from the *International House* set. Oakie had been at work on an adjacent lot when disaster struck, and he raced next door through a shower of plaster, shouting, "How's my girl?" Peggy emerged from her portable dressing room with every hair in place. "I'm just fine, Jack, thank you," she replied calmly.

Peggy almost ended her Hollywood days with a plum role in Twentieth Century Pictures' *Broadway thru a Keyhole,* and the gritty, unsentimental film would have provided a fitting capstone to her career. The movie, which was based on a story by Walter Winchell and drawn from the real-life romance between Al Jolson and his future wife, onetime chorus girl Ruby Keeler, offered a caustic glimpse into the worlds of show business, organized crime, and the gossip press and explored the messy and potentially dangerous way they intertwined.

The cast included Texas Guinan playing a brassy nightclub hostess much like herself and featured Peggy as "a fading blonde with all the shrewdness of the ex-Broadway showgirl," a woman whose life "could be summed up in the next drink and the next dress—and the next man to provide her with both." Peggy would undoubtedly have loved everything about the part, not only the furs and jewels but also the opportunity to portray a world-weary femme fatale who still possesses a great deal of magnetism. But on the third day of filming she collapsed on the set and was rushed to the hospital. Within hours, the studio announced that she would not be appearing in the picture. The official explanation suggested that she had been weakened by a previous attack of tonsillitis and that her condition had been exacerbated by the California humidity, whch had proved unexpectedly enervating. Given Los Angeles's desert climate, the idea that the city's humidity could be harmful to anyone struck the movie community as doubtful, so much so that studio head Darryl Zanuck took pains to insist publicly that Peggy had not been fired from the picture but had left solely due to ill health.

The full truth never emerged. Perhaps she hadn't performed as well as Zanuck had hoped, and he found a graceful way to ease her out of the movie. Perhaps she simply turned out to be a prima donna on the set and more trouble than she was worth. Whatever the real story, her departure marked the end of her days in show business. More important, it marked the beginning of the end of her time in the sun.

10

"The Last Generation's Celebrity"

A celebrity's glow rarely begins to dim at a single moment. But the announcement in the late summer of 1933 that Peggy would not be appearing in *Broadway thru a Keyhole* seemed to mark a definite change for her. A line she would have recited had she remained in the cast—"Fifteen years from now they won't remember you any more than they remember me"—has an oddly prophetic ring. More than a decade had elapsed since her affair with Chaplin and her first romp around the Continent. The divorce trial that had catapulted her into the headlines was an increasingly distant memory, as were her heady days with Ziegfeld. Though she was still a household name and would remain one for a while, people were forgetting exactly why she was famous. All they could remember was the endless parade of husbands.

Both she and the times were changing, and not in ways that complemented one another. Peggy herself was no longer young and exquisite—a serious problem for a woman whose reputation so hinged on her looks—nor was she as given to deliciously bad behavior. And as the exuberance of the twenties faded, her life no longer spoke to the public as powerfully as it once had. The Depression had dealt a body blow to the nation, and before bad times lifted, the clouds of

another ordeal, a world war, had begun to gather. An anxious, belea-
guered country in which millions were limping from one dreadful
day to the next had scant interest in the antics of a forty-year-old
gold digger, even if she still looked delectable in her ermine and
pearls.

Americans had certainly not lost interest in celebrities. On the
contrary. Irving Berlin and Moss Hart's *As Thousands Cheer,* a musical revue that took great delight in skewering the public obsession
with such larger-than-life figures as Mahatma Gandhi and evangelist
Aimee Semple McPherson, triumphed on Broadway when it opened
in 1933, showing that the American obsession with fame and the famous continued unabated. It was merely the case that, as with many
a long-running show, the cast had to be changed to keep it fresh.

As historian Daniel Boorstin notes in *The Image:A Guide to Pseudo-
Events in America,* "No one is more forgotten than the last generation's celebrity." Famous folk were proving less than durable, and new
faces invariably replaced old standbys. If the public was to lose its
heart to a glamour girl, she had to be someone different and splashy,
like Woolworth heiress Barbara Hutton, whose 1930 society debut
had been an extravaganza featuring eucalyptus trees and an appearance by Rudy Vallee, both imported from California, and whose collection of husbands eventually rivaled even Peggy's.

The sharply declining number of articles about Peggy in the *New
York Times* offered a revealing indicator of her flagging reputation.
Back in the early twenties, during her divorce trial, the paper had run
dozens of reports on her escapades, one right after another. But the
daily spate of stories was a thing of the past. Not coincidentally,
Peggy's own maintenance of the flame, as reflected by her voluminous collection of personal papers, faltered. With a sharp eye on posterity, she had spent the previous two decades diligently stuffing
newspaper clippings, letters, telegrams, and other documents into her
trunk, a portable archive that she carted around as she shuttled from
country to country, man to man, adventure to adventure. By the

midthirties she abandoned the effort; she simply packed up what she had in a big carton and shipped everything off to Poughkeepsie, New York, to the home of a man named Frank Williamson who was engaged to marry her cousin Myrtie Price, the daughter of her Aunt Evelyn. There was little left to collect—no reviews, no fan mail, no ardent love letters. And as the owner of the memorabilia understood better than most, the situation was unlikely to reverse itself.

Peggy nevertheless continued to merit headlines throughout the thirties, especially in the tabloids. For one thing, she rode out the worst of the Depression in style, thanks to canny investments of her generous marital settlements and the size of her bejeweled nest egg. Even F. Scott Fitzgerald had been struck by her propensity for putting her money into those things whose value would endure: in his notebooks he mentions the "instinct of Peggy Joyce collecting jewelry instead of bonds." Not every American was laid low by the crash and its aftermath—the very rich were often notable exceptions—and when Peggy's bank balance dipped, there was always another emerald to sell. In Europe, where she continued to spend much of her time, the effects of economic collapse were less harrowing for a comfortable American, and she was spared the sight of a stock market that was racking up one dismal day after another. Although she periodically moaned to reporters that she would soon be reduced to clerking in a dime store or even hawking apples, "if somebody'll donate a box," the sight of her full-length mink and glittering lorgnette emphatically suggested otherwise, and she always emerged smiling after talks with her broker. Even the news that a California bank holiday had forced her to borrow taxi fare from the gatekeeper on the Paramount lot was greeted with skeptical amusement.

In Peggy's eyes, national economic collapse boiled down to decisions about her appearance. "The famous Peggy Hopkins Joyce jewels, worth a king's ransom, have never been seen in Hollywood,"

Louella Parsons noted in 1933. "I don't think it is wise to wear them during a Depression," Peggy explained to a reporter, sporting only a modest diamond circlet atop her sleek blonde head. "And I'm not buying any new clothes, wearing out my old ones instead. I even turned down a little French hat the other day because they wanted $35 for it. But it was cute on me."

Still, in the light of the Depression, tales about the luxurious trappings of Peggy's life no longer sent the press into such paroxysms of ecstasy—and certainly not when Peggy appeared to be accumulating debts. In the summer of 1934 newspapers reported that seizure notices had been plastered on the door of her Riviera villa stating that the contents would be sold to cover bills she had left behind when she returned to America. Much to the disappointment of souvenir hunters hoping to snatch up pieces of her silver and her antique furniture at bargain prices, the sale was postponed when Peggy grudgingly agreed to return to Europe and settle her affairs in person. "I think it was for a chair or some other absurd piece of furniture," she told a reporter as she set sail for France, making little effort to conceal her irritation. "You know how it is over there. Let some tradesman become worried about a trifle of a bill and the next thing you know there is an attachment."

Around the same period the federal government announced plans to sell items of her clothing and bric-a-brac it had seized years before in connection with a customs dispute. Back in the early twenties, Peggy had disembarked from the *Mauritania* without declaring all the newly purchased contents of her luggage—the culprit, she insisted, was a careless maid; now the government decided it was time to assess taxes and penalties and auction off her belongings.

The sale took place amid stacks of dusty packing cases at the Brooklyn Army Supply Base, the auctioneer perched atop an old soapbox. But the greatest ignominy was not the tawdry setting but how little people cared about Peggy's precious things; interest was so desultory that at one point bidding started to go down rather than up. "Auctioneer Dan Greenwald, an old-timer at his job, handled his gavel with the dexterity of a maestro," reported the *Sun*. "But for all his pleadings and his hammerings he failed to arouse the bidders from their lethargy." A $12,000 plaque studded with two hundred diamonds went for $1,000; offers for an embroidered silk Spanish shawl worth $480 started at twenty-five cents. Peggy's wardrobe trunk, valued at $700, went for $64; the contents included an ermine-trimmed frock, a lace-embroidered lilac number, and a bedraggled lavender negligee. The total sale netted just over $1,000, a sixth of the duty levied and an even smaller fraction of the estimated value.

Still, faithful reporters kept an eye on her comings and goings. Nor did interest flag at her favorite haunts. At El Morocco, the band struck up "Pretty Peggy," her old song from *Vanities,* every time she marched through the door on the arm of one or another companion. Café society still hummed with tales of her outrageous behavior, like the time she and entertainer Harry Richman made elaborate preparations to fly to Europe. "She had a gold lamé jumpsuit designed," her friend Billy Livingstone, a fixture of the nightclub world, recalls with a laugh. "And they bought twenty-five thousand Ping-Pong balls, in case the plane crashed," presumably in the hope that their lightweight raft would keep them afloat if they ended up in the Atlantic.

The newspapers continued to run her picture as well: Peggy draped along El Morocco's famous zebra-striped banquettes; enjoying a drink at the Mayfair Club one Saturday night after the repeal of Prohibition (this made the front page of the *Daily News*); dining with the Clark Gables at New York's Hollywood restaurant; sipping champagne with a balding Argentinian, a current millionaire flame, at Mario's Mirador Roof; kicking up a storm on the conga line at Le Conga along with Dorothy Kilgallen, Errol Flynn, and Peter Arno.

A *World-Telegram* photographer caught her and bandleader Artie Shaw at Jack Dempsey's restaurant when the prizefighter stopped by their table to get autographs for his young daughters. Broadway columnist Louis Sobol was scribbling away at the Stork Club when

Peggy, upon learning that William Saroyan was sitting nearby, announced, "Well, Mr. Sarong, or Strong or Soybean or whatever your name is, you are a beautiful man." The celebrated playwright thereupon leaned over, kissed her hand, and replied with a flourish, "You are undoubtedly someone about whom a play must be written, perhaps by myself."

She still made waves at big-ticket benefits and at celebrity-studded occasions like the party marking Eddie Cantor's twenty-fifth anniversary on Broadway. She still graced the guest lists of posh affairs like Dorothy Kilgallen's wedding and, rather amazingly, Franklin D. Roosevelt's birthday ball, a gala event that brought thousands of the nation's political, diplomatic, and business elite to Washington's Shoreham Hotel in 1934. The list of guests who gathered to help the president blow out his fifty-two candles included Cornelius Vanderbilt Jr., Treasury Secretary Henry Morgenthau, the president's wife in peach satin—and Peggy, resplendent in green velvet and white orchids. Exactly how she came to be included among such impressive luminaries, or what she discussed with them, was never reported, but there was no lack of comment about her appearance. "Ah, Peggy!" sighed the *Washington Herald* the next day, noting that she had been "the cynosure of all eyes at the ball—especially her diamonds."

Reporters continued to find her good copy, especially when it came to observations about men. Chatting with a journalist from the wire services, she announced that "it is not enough for a man merely to have good looks, charm, and a talent for hand-kissing, although it helps. Now a man must have brains to be attractive." Even as the years took their toll, she could dazzle when she was in the mood, although with time the dazzle sometimes contained a hint of desperation. "She was like a marvelous drawing, something you don't forget," remembers Miles White, a costume designer who could barely control his elation the afternoon that his milliner friend Rose Saphire took him to the Delmonico bar to meet her famous client. "She was wonderfully over-made-up, with bleached frizzed hair, lots of bracelets, very over the top," he recalls of that visit. "It was like seeing the Statue of Liberty."

Although Peggy's name was linked with fewer men during those years, she did embark on one great love affair. In November 1936 newspapers in America and abroad throbbed with the news that she had chosen Charles Vivian Jackson, a thirty-year-old amateur jockey and professor of astrophysics at the University of London, to be her fifth husband. Word of the romance had leaked out at an English racetrack when she kissed Jackson for luck as he set off astride Russet, one of the dozen racehorses he had given her. When the man from the Associated Press clamored for details, Peggy demurely deferred to her fiancé, who explained of their meeting: "We both love horses. That is what set us going."

Shortly thereafter, the newspapers backtracked from their original report, now claiming that Peggy's newest suitor was not a distinguished university professor but simply an occasional lecturer at some lesser institution. The truth was never made clear. But Jackson unquestionably came from a wealthy family—his twin brother, Derek, married one of the Mitford girls—though with his boyish face and dimpled smile he looked more like Peggy's nephew than her fiancé. And as usual when Peggy began an affair, the two were photographed everywhere, not only at the races—Jackson clutching a saddle with one hand and his intended with the other—but also at his ancestral manor house in Surrey, complete with a coat of arms over the ancient oaken doorway, where the pair planned to set up housekeeping.

The fairy-tale romance seemed too good to last, and it was. Before the two could marry, Jackson was killed, the victim of a freak accident in the Swiss Alps. An article that made page 1 in the *New York Times* reported that a horse-drawn sleigh in which he and Peggy were riding had overturned in a little village just outside Saint Moritz. The couple had been returning from an afternoon drive the day before New Year's Eve when the brakes failed at the top of a hill and their graceful red sleigh lurched forward. Jackson sprang up and tried to halt the terrified animals, but they bolted into the main street, hurling their helpless passengers against a pair of stone pillars. When the clouds of snow subsided and doctors had untangled the bloodstained fur robes, they discovered that Peggy had broken her hip and her fiancé had fractured his skull. He was pronounced dead a few hours later.

It seems unlikely that Vivian Jackson was the love of Peggy's life, as she often claimed. The age difference between them was considerable, and given her abysmal track record when it came to marriage, the romance would probably have sputtered and died even had he survived the crash. Still, his death marked a turning point. Starting in the late thirties and picking up steam through the forties, the same forces that propelled her rise now governed her fall. Behavior that once seemed adorably daring now appeared tedious. All that cavorting with one man after another suddenly grew tiresome. Styles had changed, and her diamonds and furs now struck her audience as more than a little vulgar.

Nor could anyone deny how the years had tugged at Peggy's fabled loveliness, loosening the taut skin until everything seemed to sag—her eyes, her cheeks, her chin, her breasts—thickening what had been lithe and firm, dimming the incandescent glow that once emanated from her face. And while she was not exactly fat, no man in the world would have bothered to give her figure a second glance. "She used to be a beautiful showgirl," remembers Anna Sosenko, a New York theatrical producer who knew Peggy during the late thirties, "but as the years went by she began to lose the wondrous beauty she had when she was young and it became a burden."

Around that time, tactful saleswomen at the exclusive dress shops Peggy patronized discreetly changed the tags on her purchases to screen her from the knowledge that her once svelte figure had swelled to a size sixteen. But no stratagems could disguise how baggy and puffy her body had become. She also grew careless about her appearance; the immaculately groomed fashion plate of the twenties had become unkempt, sloppy. Even her voice changed; too many cigarettes had turned it hoarse and whiskeyish.

Having been such a dish in her day and having acquired so much of her plush lifestyle by dint of her glorious appearance, Peggy took the experience of growing older harder than most. Although she usually managed to dig up an escort for a night on the town, she could hardly pretend that men still grew weak in the knees at the sight of her. So she began to drink, downing scotch after scotch, straight, and starting earlier and earlier in the afternoon. She had always enjoyed the buzz of champagne; by the late thirties she found liquor necessary just to help her make it through a day. "By the end," says Billy Livingstone, "she was almost an alcoholic."

"It was all terribly sad," adds Jackie Olson, Madeline Copeland's daughter. "She still pictured herself as the glamour queen. She was used to having all the attention, and toward the end, she wasn't getting it. She simply couldn't stand the idea of getting old."

In 1937 Peggy's name appeared in a flurry of newspaper articles when she was sued in superior court in Los Angeles for money she allegedly owed Celebrity Pictures, a studio involved in the making of *The Skyrocket*. Back in those days, she had evidently signed a document at the direction of the studio's head, Pat Powers, requiring that she work for a longer period than she actually had. The suit was especially haunting in that it was a reminder of her past life; Peggy had reportedly been engaged to Powers a decade earlier.

She garnered more publicity, none of it favorable, in 1940, when her maid, Louise Grimaldi, dragged her into a Manhattan court claiming she had been attending Peggy for years and, as reporters noted meaningfully, "implied it had been a trying life." Specifically, Grimaldi contended she had never been reimbursed for $8,000 in cash that she had given Peggy to pay the gardener and the caretaker at the Riviera villa. Peggy, who had fired Grimaldi more times than she cared to remember, only to beg her sheepishly to return, promptly branded her maid a common thief and countersued for $20,000.

On other occasions, Peggy's name appeared in the papers as part of embarrassing publicity stunts, like the time she turned her hand to musical composition. The title of her creation was "I Love You, Oh Yes I Do," and the lyrics—"Our hearts will rhyme, you are my dream so divine"—were worse. Her bandleader friend Bob Knight did his best to put a good face on the situation—"To think that Peggy Hopkins Joyce of all people should have enough talent to write a song," he gushed to reporters—and perhaps to indulge an aging warhorse, he played it nightly for a time at the Café Pierre. But plans for publishing the work were vague, and to the relief of the music world no more was heard of it.

Her encounters with others became increasingly poignant, even pathetic. Typical was an episode that took place at the Savoy-Plaza Hotel on Fifth Avenue and Fifty-ninth Street in Manhattan. One afternoon in 1942 Billy Livingstone discovered Peggy sitting by herself in the hotel's Café Lounge, and the two struck up a conversation. She asked him to call her at ten that night, but he was scheduled to leave at dawn the next morning for army camp in the South and promptly put the matter out of his mind. Arriving home from overseas a year later, Livingstone found himself back in the same hotel, only to discover Peggy sitting alone in the identical spot where he had left her twelve months earlier. "I'm not speaking to you," she announced coldly, looking up with glassy eyes. "The other night I waited an hour and a half for you to call."

Peggy was acquiring a reputation for inappropriate, even bizarre behavior, and more and more often during these years, a night out ended in a scene. One evening at El Morocco, she went after a minor celebrity named Mabel Boll, whom reporters had recently anointed the "most jeweled woman in America." Furious that another woman seemed to be poaching on her territory, Peggy marched up to the banquette where Boll was sitting. "Darling," she drawled in a voice that could be heard well above the music of the band, "I hear you had such a horrible time with your last face lift." As a final gesture, she leaned over and tipped a glass of wine into her rival's lap.

Another night at El Morocco, as a waiter tried to seat her in a cramped area near the entrance, Peggy prompted giggles but also a few winces when she bellowed, "I refuse to sit in Siberia!" She once greeted the owner of the Manhattan nightclub Armando's by yanking a ring off his finger and refusing to give it back. "She just said, 'I like that. I want it,'" Jackie Olson recalls. "She eventually returned it, but not without a struggle." At the Stork Club, even Walter Winchell took note of her propensity for using the men's room—why she did this no one had a clue, unless it was simply to turn heads.

Peggy precipitated a real brawl at Le Conga when a slightly tipsy makeup artist from Hollywood leaned over and hissed in her ear, "Hey, babe, how about marrying me?" Her date on that occasion, comedian Joey Adams, responded by punching the offender in the eye. "I've never been in a fight before in my life," Adams told the *Daily News,* "but when I saw the look on Peggy's face, I had to do something."

Another evening Peggy herself threw the punch, socking her date in the eye with a knuckle encased in a $30,000 sapphire ring after an old girlfriend kissed him noisily on the mouth. The victim, a small-time singer named Sonny Tufts, seemed almost pleased to be caught mixing it up with such a famous lady and told everyone who would listen that he gave as good as he got. "You ought to see her," he bragged to the *Daily News.* "She's black and blue from head to foot." The whole episode made Peggy so livid she called the paper in a rage to deny the story and demand a retraction. But no one took her complaints terribly seriously, for by now the idea of Peggy's causing a ruckus in a public place was old news.

Increasingly, she was the butt of jokes, with her signature furs an especially tempting target. Cornelia Otis Skinner was one of many unable to resist. In her 1942 memoir *Our Hearts Were Young and Gay* she described the time she and a friend encased themselves in billowy rabbit fur evening wraps for a night on the town, "feeling like the personification of the Queen of Roumania and Peggy Hopkins Joyce." Peggy's coats also made eyes roll in the household where actress Kitty Carlisle Hart grew up. "My mother had an ermine coat that got older and older and began to resemble an ermine coat that Peggy wore to openings," Hart remembers. "My mother used to call it her Peggy Hopkins Joyce coat." It was hardly surprising that her name began appearing in ribald college songs.

Even Peggy's mail began to change. Instead of worshipful letters from adoring young women and heartsick lovers, she started to get abuse. "You have sawdust in your head," charged a correspondent who had tried to interest her in a business proposition and been ignored. "I do not see why six young gentlemen had committed suicide over you, because in my eyes you appear not only an ugly and homely woman but also one of the most rottenest actress I have ever seen." The note was so nasty that only a woman with a desperate need for attention would have refrained from tossing it into the trash.

Peggy moved around a lot in those years, wandering like a gypsy from one hotel to another. For a while she lived at the Savoy-Plaza, one of the city's most exclusive residential establishments. The ambience was typified by the nightly shows in the Café Lounge, where the incomparable Hildegarde, wearing elbow-length white gloves, performed cabaret songs to an audience that might include Katharine Hepburn, Lorenz Hart, Danny and Sylvia Kaye—"anyone who was anyone," according to Anna Sosenko, who worked for a time as Hildegarde's manager. But that category increasingly did not include Peggy. She and her companion—a different one every night, it seemed—usually started with mixed drinks like martinis but quickly moved on to scotch. Long before the set had ended, streams of obscenities were pouring forth from her lipstick-smeared mouth, and guests throughout the room were craning their necks to see who was making such a racket. The commotion ended only when a waiter firmly ushered her and her date out the door.

The Café Lounge was not the only club that ejected Peggy. She was also thrown out of Cerutti, an East Side supper club where black singer Mae Barnes made a name for herself by belting out such rollicking standards as "Sweet Georgia Brown." One evening in the forties, when Barnes was moving from table to table interspersing her songs with snatches of patter, Peggy drifted in with a soldier. Despite his illustrious companion, he was so entranced with Barnes's performance, he couldn't take his eyes off her. Fed up after a few minutes of being ignored, Peggy turned to her date and muttered loudly, "It seems as though you're more interested in that nigger than you are in me!"

After finishing her song, Barnes went over to their table. "You say that word again, and I'll kick you square in your ass!" she announced firmly. Peggy screamed for the owner, but he no sooner heard her story than he promptly ordered her off the premises.

Back in her room, Peggy's behavior was hardly more appetizing. The princes, counts, and snappy tycoons who once peopled her life had been replaced by very different sorts of companions—married, of course, but far coarser than their predecessors. Peggy's maid regaled friends with stories about the long and arduous task of preparing her mistress for her late-night visitors, but by now no one even bothered to pretend the assignations involved anything except quick and impersonal sex. In the opinion of a male acquaintance familiar with her behavior during those years, she had become a woman who did nothing more than spread her legs in anticipation of the parade of men who trooped up to her room each evening.

Perhaps because the world that once welcomed her so warmly was growing colder, Peggy grew closer to her family. Though New York's social circles increasingly regarded her as a figure of mockery and pathos, to her relatives she was still a golden girl, an exotic creature who swooped down from time to time to bring a touch of glamour to their humdrum lives.

The closeness was selective. Peggy had a sporadic relationship with her half sister, Lucille, whom she affectionately called Buttons, and for a time she milked the idea of playing older sibling to a flapper with theatrical aspirations, with reporters happy to play along. But she had never had much to do with her father's family in Farmville. Except for two brief visits, one of them after Sam Upton's death in 1928, there is no record that she ever set foot in the town he called home for most of his adult life.

Toward her mother's family, however, especially her younger cousins back in Norfolk, she felt lingering affection. By the midtwenties, her mother, Dora, who had resettled herself in her hometown, had established a family base that included Dora's sister Evelyn and Evelyn's eight children. Every couple of years, Peggy would breeze into town for a brief stay, to the accompaniment of much media fanfare and expressions of local civic pride—Norfolk hotels were always ready to offer her free lodging—and bask briefly in the glow of the attention.

Maybe the chance to play Lady Bountiful appealed to her, or maybe it was simply that other sources of admiration had dried up. In any case, by the forties her pilgrimages back home became regular events. With fewer activities to occupy her days and nights up north and abroad, the trips were less of an imposition than they had been when she was younger and busier. While jaded New Yorkers and Continentals were losing interest in her, her provincial relatives, especially her impressionable cousins, now in their teens and twenties, found her as thrilling a creature as ever. "In the back of her mind, she had ties at home," says her youngest cousin, Francis Price. Though the sentiment may have been partly wishful thinking, Peggy clearly found herself more comfortable among her own people as the years passed.

She came bearing a motley assortment of gifts—stuffed animals for the children, an ornate liquor cabinet for her mother, and in a rare burst of generosity, a tiny diamond ring set in filigreed platinum for her cousin Hudson Price's wife, Helen. Sometimes Peggy got quite drunk—the time she arrived with a case of champagne, she consumed a good deal of it herself—but her relatives, grateful for any attention, were indulgent about her peccadilloes.

Also indulgent toward Peggy's misbehavior were Madeline Copeland and her husband, Hunter. The Copelands had moved to New York from the Norfolk area in the thirties with their teenage daughter, Jackie, and shortly after meeting the couple, Peggy had decided, in her slightly imperious fashion, that they would be her adopted aunt and uncle. She called Hunter Popsie and Jackie her little cousin. But it was Madeline who had the brunt of the responsibility of fussing over Peggy and catering to her whims. Peggy rarely if ever had a close woman friend, but in Madeline she found someone willing to play that role. "Madeline was a slave to her," recalls Joan Harding, who worked alongside Madeline at the Damon Runyon Memorial Fund, a charity founded in the forties by Walter Winchell. "She was always rushing from the office to the Barclay Hotel, where Peggy was living at the time, to take her somewhere." One afternoon Peggy telephoned Madeline at work to learn that everyone in the office was sitting around eating a cherry cheesecake from Lindy's. It sounded delicious, Peggy said wistfully. "So Madeline just jumped up and rushed over to the Barclay Hotel to bring her some," Harding remembers. "Peggy called Madeline all the time, and Madeline, on the button, just dashed to her apartment." For a time, Peggy and the Copelands were so close they even shared a brownstone at 11 West Eleventh Street in Greenwich Village. But the arrangement fell apart as a result of Peggy's drinking and obstreperous behavior, and finally she had to move out.

In view of Peggy's indifference to the world, it was hardly surprising that the Second World War touched her not at all. The first winter after the fighting ended, she made a brief splash in the news with a fifth marriage. But there was nothing glamorous or impressive about her choice, an obscure thirty-eight-year-old engineer, recently divorced, named Anthony Easton.

Easton, who lived in Westwood, California, told reporters he was a British-born American citizen who had been an instructor at the California Institute of Technology and had tested aircraft equipment as part of the war effort. New York Supreme Court Judge Ferdinand Pecora performed the ceremony on December 3, 1945, in his Manhattan chambers, where the fifty-two-year-old bride, outfitted in mink, diamonds, and a few orchids, gave her age as thirty-nine. Perhaps with her previous matrimonial experiences in mind, she pointedly asked Pecora to omit the word *obey* from the traditional vows.

But the actual language mattered little, for this marriage fared no better than her others, and Easton dropped out of her life as abruptly as he had entered it. Within six months he was back in California living with his mother; reporters caught up with him when police arrested him on a drunk-driving charge near her home in Pasadena. Asked about his wife's whereabouts, he replied with an indifferent shrug: "I don't know. She's somewhere in the East."

For a woman who had been married five times, Peggy had spent remarkably little time actually living with a mate. But in 1951, with the years closing in on her, she stumbled across a man she wanted to hang on to.

Andrew Clifford Meyer, a Brooklyn boy with the reddish-blond good looks of a young Van Johnson, was born in 1915 to Scandinavian immigrants living in the borough's Bay Ridge section. By the time he turned seven, both parents were dead, and he was shipped to a church orphanage in Fort Lee, New Jersey, the only home he knew for most of his childhood. Soon after reaching his teens, he landed a job as a page at Bankers Trust in Manhattan, and he diligently worked his way up to the position of teller. Drafted in 1941, he served in the army for five years, mostly in England. By the time he returned home, he had risen to the rank of lieutenant.

Like countless other Americans who had come through hard times and discovered a life of sorts during the war, Andy Meyer found peacetime existence sadly empty. Back at his old job at the bank, his bosses made it clear he was unlikely to go far in the world of finance. They called him an administrator, but he had no title, and he realized bitterly that he would never get one. A loner by nature, he did not have much of a social life either, and after a while he began stopping off at a bar on Third Avenue after work in search of a little companionship. A customer he knew from the bank, a woman named Lucille who sold women's clothes, used to see him sitting there alone night after night. One evening she suggested that he might like to meet an ex-Ziegfeld girl who could do with the attentions of a presentable younger man.

Andy readily agreed. He knew the name, of course, and he surmised that Peggy had complained to Lucille that she was getting lonesome. He was lonesome himself. His chances of marriage seemed to have evaporated during his years in the army, and the solitary evenings nursing a scotch and his unarticulated dreams were starting to take their toll.

Peggy talked very little about her past the evening that the two of them met for drinks at that same Third Avenue bar. But she didn't have to. For as Andy gazed across the table into her still-luminous blue eyes, he saw not a faded glamour girl more than twenty years his senior but an ageless beauty trailing clouds of remembered glory. "She looked so lovely," he recalled half a century later, his voice softening at the memory. "She was friendly, outgoing, full of life. She had a sense of humor." The day he met her, he told Jackie Olson some years later, was the most wonderful day of his life. To him, perhaps only to him, she was not a has-been but a star.

With his open face, his easy smile, and his kindly manner, Andy possessed a certain low-key appeal. But he had nothing in common with the types Peggy used to go around with, none of the money, power, or Continental sheen she gravitated toward. Yet she herself had changed a great deal. While she still did not look her age and her passport had long since been doctored to chop a decade off her actual birth date—even Andy never suspected the truth—she was nearly sixty years old. Despite the miracles to be worked by the innumerable creams and unguents on her dressing table, despite the expression in Andy's eyes when he stared at her adoringly, she knew better than anyone else how her looks had faded and how her life had been drained of glamour. It had been nearly two decades since she had reigned as a darling of the press, nearly two decades since men treated her like the lovable china doll she always believed herself to be. She desperately wanted someone young and attractive to fuss over her, to baby her and keep an eye on her dwindling fortune. Andy, she sensed, would do exactly that.

Peggy pursued Andy as she had rarely pursued anyone; she was even the one to propose marriage. He, in turn, was more than happy to oblige. He was beguiled not only by her but also by the world of swank restaurants and clubs in which she moved so easily, a world utterly different from anything he had ever known. He was especially impressed by the affability of headwaiters who remembered her from the old days. Though too decent (and perhaps too passive) to be a fortune hunter, he was unsophisticated enough to be overwhelmed by the life she offered him. And the price of admission—a willingness to dance attendance upon a onetime starlet entering her twilight years—seemed a modest one.

Peggy's love life was no longer news, and not until 1954, three years after she and Andy became an item, did the gossipy *Confidential* magazine decide to take an extended look at their relationship. Once the magazine did so, however, it mocked the couple with a vengeance, suggesting that Walter Chrysler's erstwhile paramour had sunk to unimaginable depths by taking up with the man it dubbed

"Handy Andy" and described as a glorified lackey content to play errand boy to an over-the-hill chorine. "Peggy's sophisticated circle of friends couldn't be blamed for thinking they were suffering alcoholic delusions when Andy arrived on the scene," *Confidential* concluded. "He was just about everything that the expensive lady had been avoiding all her life—a nice, quiet chap with little background, no money and a talent for selecting the wrong clothes. Chrysler's ghost probably wept."

But there were few sophisticated friends left; Peggy had gone to seed so badly she refused even to go near her old haunts. In a rare burst of frankness she confided to an acquaintance, "I've got to move to the country, so people won't see me unless I want them to." And so in 1954 she headed with Andy to the small farming community of Woodbury, Connecticut, to a white-shingled, pink-shuttered cottage set in a dense growth of hickory at the end of a winding dead-end road. The house lay deep in the woods, on a tract of land so quiet deer emerged from the shadows at dusk. There Peggy proceeded to make a life for herself amid the few trappings of her former existence. She had sold most of her expensive possessions; one of the last items to go had been the sparkling blue diamond from Chrysler, which the jeweler Harry Winston acquired in 1951 and frequently exhibited at charitable functions around the country in his so-called Court of Jewels. Tellingly, it was identified as the "Portuguese Diamond," a reference to its apocryphal origins, with no mention of the woman whose throat it had graced on so many glamorous occasions. The following year Peggy got rid of her villa on the Riviera; she hadn't been to the house in years.

Peggy was not exactly living in the past, but increasingly it struck her as an appealing place to visit. Occasionally in the evening she curled up next to Andy, her standard black French poodle, Baron, by her feet, to watch an original reel of *International House*. Once in a while the mail contained a card from an actress who remembered her from the old days. She could sit in her bedroom, its wallpaper splashed with enormous pink and red cabbage roses, and trace her name engraved on the gold perfume bottles lined up on the vanity. If she was in a particularly resilient mood, she could wander into the living room and admire an ornately framed portrait of herself painted decades earlier, an image in which she stared dreamily into the distance through large doelike eyes, her off-the-shoulder gown exposing her ivory skin, one hand held to her breast, her diamond ring glowing softly. The portrait, painted in 1926 by an artist named Hugo Figge, had once hung in the Waldorf-Astoria Galleries.

Peggy was considered something of a minor celebrity in Connecticut, and sometimes glimmers of the old magic shone forth. At the dressy candlelit parties to which she occasionally invited a few neighborhood people, she still projected what Grayce Lizauskas, a frequent guest, remembers as "a golden magnetic power of making everyone feel great." Nor had Peggy's ability to make a man's blood tingle deserted her, as Grayce observed when her own husband, a local dairy farmer, walked in the door. "My darling kissable Eddie!" Peggy invariably exclaimed, enfolding her visitor in an affectionate hug.

But such evenings were rare. While she didn't self-destruct as rapidly or as dramatically as some of her Hollywood peers, many of whom ended their days in a haze of pills and debauched living, Peggy was in sorry shape. She had begun drinking ever more heavily, especially as the day wore on. "She became quite a pest," acknowledges Robert Deacon, whose family lived nearby. "She would go out tripping around the neighborhood in the afternoon, then stop off at our house for a little visit and a little drinkie, which led to several drinkies." She and Andy would then invite themselves for dinner. Initially, the Deacons were enchanted by the idea of entertaining an ex-Ziegfeld girl, but as the hours passed and Peggy grew increasingly raucous, the charm of playing host quickly palled.

★ ★ ★

Although Peggy and Andy had been a couple since 1951, they did not make their relationship official until the middle of 1956. A local justice of the peace married them at a private civil ceremony in the town of Brewster, New York, an hour's drive north of New York City. Even at this late date, Peggy was not above tweaking her biography in the interest of a good story. When she informed reporters of the marriage as she and Andy were sailing to Europe that summer, she gave the news extra sizzle by claiming the nuptials had actually taken place three years previously in Switzerland. It was, Jackie Olson thought to herself at the time, just the sort of story Peggy would concoct, even now that few people cared about the much-married Peggy Joyce.

The Meyers' destination was the south of France. But the trip proved brief, for in Cannes they discovered that Peggy was extremely sick. A persistent sore on the roof of her mouth refused to heal, and French doctors feared the worst. Not even bothering to pack up all their clothes, the couple quickly turned around and headed for home.

For a few months after their return, Peggy was in and out of Memorial Hospital in Manhattan, the doctors not quite sure what was wrong, or at least that was what they initially told her husband. Finally, however, the diagnosis was inescapable. Years of smoking had caught up with her. She was dying of throat cancer.

On June 1, 1957, Peggy entered Memorial Hospital for the last time. Yet unlike in the old days, when every sore throat and sniffle made headlines, only near the very end did the papers take notice of her condition. On June 12 the *New York Times* reported in a brief article that "Peggy Hopkins Joyce, theatrical beauty of the 1920's and 30's, is critically ill with cancer of the throat." By that point she had sunk into a coma, and at 10:25 that night, with Andy by her bedside, she died. That same day brought the death of bandleader Jimmy

Dorsey. Taken together, the two deaths seemed to mark the end of an extraordinary era.

The death certificate identified Peggy as a retired actress, married, age fifty-four. She was married, it was true, but her age was sixty-four, and "retired actress" didn't begin to tell the real story. That was left to the newspapers and magazines.

"Peggy Hopkins Joyce, whose name became a synonym for the much-married some thirty years ago, died last night of throat cancer," began the obituary in the *New York Times*. "Miss Joyce was a Virginia-born beauty whose blonde charms and financially astute matrimonial ventures brought her international renown during the Nineteen Twenties and Thirties." The *New York Journal-American* called her "the toast of two continents," and the *New York Herald Tribune* described her as "one of the most celebrated showgirls Broadway ever boasted . . . a Jazz Age legend, an It girl whose beauty was debated but whose glamour was unquestioned."

Although *Time* magazine mentioned her death only briefly, it characterized the event as a milestone and jogged readers' memories by reminding them that her passion for Rolls-Royces, furs, jewels, champagne, and swimming pools had helped her "symbolize the high-living, big-spending Twenties." Louis Sobol rhapsodized in his column, "New York Cavalcade": "There has never been a more colorful or joyous figure to invade the Broadway scene. Her collection of jewels and husbands, her gay, uninhibited viewpoint on life, her unrestrained, often provocative comments on folks and manners, made her dominate paragraphs and feature stories for years. In her day she tugged as much newspaper space as Marilyn, Grace and even Frankie."

Peggy had not been born or raised in the Roman Catholic faith, but she had always had a taste for the pomp of Catholicism, and a priest had visited her hospital room shortly before she died. A Catholic funeral seemed in order.

No one was particularly surprised when Peggy's hoped-for grand ceremony in Saint Patrick's could not be arranged. Perhaps it was just as well: the group of friends who gathered the morning of June 14 for her funeral mass at Saint Catherine of Siena a few blocks to the north would have seemed pitifully small in the vast cathedral. But it was Gate of Heaven Cemetery in Mount Pleasant, New York, where her simple white marble mausoleum was marked only with the words *Peggy Joyce Meyer* and a small cross, that was particularly appropriate.

For a woman who had always liked mingling with the rich and famous of her day, Gate of Heaven represented an ideal final resting place. She joined the company of others who had enjoyed celebrity during her era—Babe Ruth, Mayor Jimmy Walker, newspaper columnist Westbrook Pegler, Flo Ziegfeld's first wife, Anna Held. Amid this star-studded community, on a sun-dappled hilltop, Peggy Hopkins Joyce could feel right at home.

Epilogue

In 1950, when *Life* magazine observed the half-century mark with a special issue on the state of American life, the publication included Peggy Hopkins Joyce in the company of actresses Mary Pickford and Ethel Barrymore, birth-control pioneer Margaret Sanger, opera star Geraldine Farrar, and author Anita Loos on a list of women said to have left a lasting imprint on the modern era. While many on the list were enshrined because of their accomplishments or social impact, the magazine concluded that the prototypical Jazz Age woman resembled "nothing so much as an unabashed slut." And it described Peggy as one of the decade's "most typical female figures, an ostentatious Ziegfeld Girl who became famous mainly for marrying millionaires." Although it did not suggest that her achievements ranked with those of Barrymore or Sanger, by placing her in such illustrious company the influential weekly did a great deal to establish her official niche in the annals of her country.

But this imprimatur, too, quickly passed into history. Telegenic newcomers, beaming out of now-ubiquitous television screens, had long since taken the place of 1920s golden girls. The swelling baby boom generation was flexing its muscles, a man-made creature called

Sputnik was whizzing around the globe, and the cold war was commanding the nation's attention.

Hardly anyone was around to tend to Peggy's legacy. She had left no body of work, her parents had long since passed away—her father in 1928, her mother in 1940—and there were no offspring to carry the torch. Her half sister, Lucille, had died an alcoholic after a series of troubled marriages; to her other half siblings she was a virtual stranger. Andy Meyer, her last husband, had married Peggy's friend Madeline Copeland and moved to California, surrounding himself with many of his first wife's treasures and contemplating the day he would be buried by her side at Gate of Heaven Cemetery, as he was after his death in 1998. Nearly all her other husbands had drifted into oblivion, generally after coming to bad ends. The only notable exception was Count Morner, who went on to a successful business career and was married until his death in 1947 to Geraldine Fitch, a New York journalist. Except to those cousins back in Norfolk to whom she had grown closer in the last decades of her life, Peggy was a shadowy figure.

Her luxurious possessions were scattered. The winking blue diamond from Chrysler had been acquired by the Smithsonian Institution. Her tiny pink villa on the Riviera had passed into other hands. Although she left an estate of a half million dollars, bequeathed primarily to Andy Meyer, nearly all her jewels had long ago been sold to cover day-to-day expenses, and almost nothing remained of her once-glorious wardrobe. Her personal papers languished in Poughkeepsie, New York, in a Victorian house whose current occupants had no idea what a treasure trove lay in their dusty attic.

Her imprint lingered only in a few cultural artifacts, and even there just barely. The movie *International House* had long since become identified with W. C. Fields, a figure whose fame far outstripped hers. The number of elderly listeners whose memory was stirred by the mention of her name in such haunting Cole Porter classics as "Why Shouldn't I?" dwindled sharply over the years, as a generation with vivid recollections of his era and its icons gradually began to die out. Only show-biz buffs and film historians recalled a glamorous blonde named Peggy Hopkins Joyce who had once donned gold lace and purple chiffon to stride across the New Amsterdam stage in Ziegfeld's celebrated *Follies* and enjoyed a steamy affair with the great Chaplin. And few of the countless girls who had been christened Peggy Joyce had any idea where the name came from.

Official histories gave her short shrift. Frederick Lewis Allen, the classic popular chronicler of the age, awarded her little more than a passing mention in *Only Yesterday,* his gossipy anecdotal account of the individuals and events that made the Jazz Age hum. Elsewhere, she survived, if at all, as a footnote to other, more compelling lives.

Although the twenties had proved to be an age in which a person could make headlines for such dubious achievements as perching atop a flagpole, Peggy's accomplishments, however colorful, would have struck traditional analysts as thin, especially in a century noted for so many transforming milestones. Unlike that of a Chaplin or a Lindbergh, her fame was buttressed by little of real consequence. Nor by any yardstick could she be considered an exemplary character. And what could be the lasting significance of a woman whose primary claim to fame was the number of times she had been a bride?

Yet despite the obscurity into which she slipped so inexorably, Peggy Hopkins Joyce should be remembered. She was important not in what she accomplished but for what she represented. Quite simply, she stood as a harbinger of a new age. Her life illustrates what has emerged as one of the most significant phenomena of twentieth-century America—the rise and triumph of the modern celebrity in an image-driven culture and the transcendent role of the media in creating, anointing, and ultimately destroying these creatures. Peggy was, albeit inadvertently, a precursor of a breed that would become commonplace in the years and decades after her death.

She was the ultimate celebrity, a person "known for his well-knownness," as Daniel Boorstin memorably expressed it. Very possibly the first American celebrity to be created solely by the mass media, the first to become famous simply for being famous, Peggy was also the paradigm, the prototype for the seemingly endless parade of people who savor their fifteen minutes of fame, often for the most dubious of reasons, and then fall off the cultural radar screen, disappearing as swiftly as they arrived.

As the century progressed, her kind of fame became increasingly commonplace. Men and women—it was often women—made news simply by marrying, or, more commonly, by divorcing. Movie stars who had not appeared in a film for decades became fixtures on television talk shows. It was no accident that *People,* a publication devoted entirely to the creation and glorification of celebrities, was the most successful magazine launched in modern publishing history, for the appetite for such figures proved insatiable. By the century's end, Americans and much of the rest of the world had become mind-numbingly familiar with the power of the media to fashion instant celebrities; every spin of the news cycle brought fresh examples. Whether she created a wave or simply rode one, Peggy Hopkins Joyce was a brilliant trailblazer in winning this kind of acclaim.

The story of how America evolved into a celebrity-obsessed nation intent on "amusing ourselves to death," in the words of Neil Postman, is by now a familiar tale. A small army of historians has analyzed the extraordinary changes wrought by the twentieth-century revolution in communications, demonstrating how the mechanical reproduction of images and mass distribution of information combined with sweeping social, political, and economic shifts to produce a country whose main goal is its own entertainment. We have learned much about the star-making apparatus that, fueled by mass-circulation newspapers and especially movies, took a giant leap forward with the advent of television, then via vast cable networks, and finally through the Internet, penetrating every corner of the globe.

Modern American celebrity, however, follows its own logic: renown results not from any particular accomplishment but from living a life that for one reason or another touches deep chords among a broad audience. From Zsa Zsa Gabor, the Hungarian beauty whose talent for media exposure made her a television and film personality, to Elizabeth Taylor, whose melodramatic life proved more gripping than any screenplay; from Amy Fisher, the "Long Island Lolita," to O. J. Simpson and his interminable murder trial, the media industries have been extraordinarily adept at finding and promoting such individuals, people who, like Peggy, have parlayed their lives into a career.

The hold of celebrities on our imagination seems on the face of it easy to explain. Simple envy is part of it, along with the desire to partake, if only voyeuristically and vicariously, of a world more enticing or at least more dramatic than one's own. But there are also darker and more complex factors at work. An international audience was transfixed by the Simpson murder trial because the proceedings laid bare secrets about love, hate, jealousy, and revenge that usually remain hidden behind closed doors, far from public scrutiny. The world mourned the death of Princess Diana in unprecedented fashion because her life, which began as a fairy-tale cliché and disintegrated into a series of personal tragedies, spoke eloquently to the fantasies and private pain of a global audience. A nation was mesmerized by Bill Clinton's relationship with Monica Lewinsky because the account of their trysts revealed that the high and mighty were as much prey to shameful and embarrassing impulses as ordinary folk.

Peggy, too, engaged a nation's desires, secret and admitted. As in the best tabloid tales, the most irresistible elements of her story were sex and money. It was no accident that from the time of her divorce from

Stanley Joyce in 1921 until her death in 1957 she was invariably known as the much-married Peggy Joyce, collector extraordinaire of millionaire spouses. Despite the discrepancies between image and fact—her last two husbands made their appearances long after the myth had been established, and only one of her six spouses was a truly wealthy man—the label endured, for it underscored the elements of her story that so powerfully struck a public nerve.

Most tantalizing was the idea of multiple marriages. Indeed, even decades later, Zsa Zsa Gabor, Tommy Manville, Artie Shaw, Mickey Rooney, and Elizabeth Taylor managed to generate headlines for their frequent trips to the altar. Today, when divorce and remarriage barely excite a murmur, collecting four husbands, let alone six, retains the power to surprise. In Peggy's day, when women were just beginning to enjoy a taste of sexual freedom and the new, more flexible morality had as many detractors as supporters, her actions blasted a hole in society's carefully constructed wall of decorum. They suggested thrillingly lascivious details about every aspect of the sexual act and offered indisputable proof of a richly textured erotic life teeming with an impressive assortment of partners. The endless gossip and speculation about the stream of lovers who paraded through her bedroom between nuptials only added spice to an already exciting narrative.

What provided the guiltiest pleasure to her audience, however, was the extent to which she reveled in her role. While portions of the population envied the abandon with which she lived her life, equal numbers found themselves appalled by her loose behavior. She never even had children, an almost un-American failure back in her day. Yet she cared not a whit how other people viewed her conduct, and she made no apology for how she lived her life. If her fellow Americans chose to label her a fallen woman, so be it. She glided through life with no pretense, no shame, and most of all no regrets. She was the ultimate risk taker, and she never looked back.

The carefully constructed myth that all her husbands were millionaires underscored another aspect of her story that had considerable resonance for an early-twentieth-century audience. At the time Peggy was beginning to compile her matrimonial record, the once rigid boundaries between social classes had started to blur, and the idea that a woman without money or social standing could take advantage of this flux and ascend to lofty heights by means of a wedding ring proved enormously appealing. A trajectory such as Peggy's showed that the fantasy of striding boldly across social boundaries could become a reality, even for a girl of modest origins. Like Undine Spragg, the chillingly calculating heroine of Edith Wharton's novel *The Custom of the Country,* who marches up the social and economic ladder on the backs of a series of successively more affluent mates, or Theodore Dreiser's eminently practical Sister Carrie, who has scant compunction about shedding old protectors in favor of new and improved models, Peggy demonstrated that the repeated act of marrying the right sort of man could, even in the absence of qualities normally associated with "good" women, serve as a powerful catapult.

In numbering among her husbands an authentic millionaire, a socially prominent attorney, and a member of one of Europe's royal families, she was the prototype of the modern version of marrying well; she democratized the act of marrying glamorously. Vanderbilt girls were routinely "bought" rich or titled husbands, and a raft of American heiresses traded money for class, but Peggy was the first real indication that the components of "marrying up" might be reshuffled so even a girl from humble circumstances could reap its rewards. Like the financiers who were speculating wildly on Wall Street during the very years she made her own meteoric rise, Peggy was the ultimate speculator—her capital being her looks, her personality, and her passionate drive for money, attention, and glamour.

Although the various elements of her persona—rich husbands, passionate sex, and a breathtaking indifference to public opinion—went a long way to helping Peggy forge her image, most important was her timing. Others before her had led colorful lives, but the means to broadcast the details with considerable force and clarity did not yet exist. Peggy burst onto the scene at exactly the right moment, when the mass media were transforming the country into a celebrity-based culture in which image and personality were paramount. What made her ideally suited for their purposes was the fact that she was the quintessential example of a certain point in time; few lives more perfectly mirrored their eras. In her appearance, her bearing, and her behavior, she encapsulated the very spirit of her age—its sheen, its staccato pace, its evanescent glamour. Her remarkable grasp of the technological advances at her disposal and her ability to manipulate them to serve her own purposes helped ensure that her tale would not be ignored. For all these reasons, it was inevitable that she be swept up and blasted into public prominence relentlessly and dramatically.

At the tail end of the twentieth century, when women have come so far after struggling so hard to establish a place for themselves in the world, it is tempting to dismiss Peggy Hopkins Joyce as nothing more than a mercenary husband hunter, to argue that her accomplishments were not only paltry but politically incorrect. Long before she stepped on stage in Ziegfeld's *Follies* she had molded herself into what feminist theorists of a subsequent generation would describe as an object to be devoured by the male gaze, one whose sole purpose was to satisfy men's desires, needs, and curiosity—in other words, their lust.

But that ability to satisfy was all she had to work with. In every other way, the odds were against her. She was blessed with neither a fierce intellect, nor a particularly selfless nature, nor a family that might have guided her along more socially useful paths. Yet despite these limitations, Peggy used her energy and resourcefulness to live the sort of life she wanted to live. Having acquired a taste of the glamour to be found outside the world of her birth, she pursued it purposefully and successfully. Yes, she was superficial and shallow, but she was also high-spirited, life-embracing, and unafraid. "When a girl has good looks, she might as well make the best of them," she wrote in her memoirs, and she brilliantly exploited her God-given gifts in chasing her desires. Offscreen as much as on-screen, she had mastered the art of the close-up. She was created for the camera's lens, not to mention the full-length mirror.

If her eye was on the main chance, if she made a career out of applying business methods to sex, she also understood the rules of the game and played it with considerable gutsiness and flair. If she displayed a shameless willingness to use men to her own advantage, they certainly knocked themselves out vying for a chance to be so used.

Perhaps the individuals who best understood Peggy and her legacy were those kindred spirits who identified with her and regarded her not with scorn but with admiration, even affection. Pamela Harriman, who knew a thing or two about men but who performed in higher, more reputable venues, wrote almost wistfully: "Peggy Joyce had made her life for herself. She had had lucky breaks, but she had known what she wanted." Fellow Jazz Age icon Texas Guinan offered the most fitting epitaph: "Peggy should not be buried like ordinary folk, or cremated, or anything like that, but just be put into Tiffany's window to sparkle forever."

Notes

The following sources of information about Peggy Hopkins Joyce are abbreviated in the notes:

Her collection of personal papers, owned by the author (PHJ papers)

Her memoirs, *Men, Marriage and Me,* published in 1930 (*MMM*)

James Stanley Joyce's collection of personal papers, owned by the Joyce Foundation of Chicago (JSJ papers)

The court records of the Joyce divorce proceedings, including documents filed in connection with the case and transcripts of the testimony (J.vs.J.)

A series of biographical articles published in 1921 by the Hearst organization (Hearst series)

A series of autobiographical articles distributed in 1922 by Hearst's International Feature Service (PHJ/Hearst series)

An unpublished manuscript by Beatrice Morosco, sister-in-law of producer Oliver Morosco (Morosco ms.)

The Robinson Locke Collection at the Billy Rose Theatre Collection of the New York Public Library for the Performing Arts at Lincoln Center (Locke Collection, NYPL)

The Margaret Herrick Library of the Academy of Motion Picture Arts and Sciences in Los Angeles (AMPAS)

The Film Study Center of the Museum of Modern Art, New York (MOMA)

Introduction

5. "He must be rich": *Seattle Star,* Mar. 13, no year, PHJ papers.
8. "No! She was a flamboyant": Interview, Celeste Holm, Jan. 1997.

Chapter 1: "I Am Not Going to Have a Dull & Dreary Life"

11. "Emma Jane used to say": Interview, Francis Price, June 1997.
12. "a large crowd present": *Norfolk Virginian,* Apr. 20, 1892.
13. She entered the world: The discussion here and elsewhere of the changes that transformed life in twentieth-century America are drawn largely from Daniel J. Boorstin's *The Image,* Leo Braudy's *The Frenzy of Renown,* Neal Gabler's *Life the Movie,* Neil Postman's *Amusing Ourselves to Death,* Richard Schickel's *Intimate Strangers,* and Warren Susman's *Culture as History.*
    "culture of personality": Susman, *Culture as History,* p. 277.
14. "She was a smashingly": *Virginian-Pilot,* Feb. 2, 1986.
15. "She had nice manners": *Virginian-Pilot,* June 9, 1921.
    "The men getting haircuts": Interview, Elizabeth Nixon, June 1977.
    "Every Friday": *Virginian-Pilot,* June 9, 1921.
16. "Deep inside me": *MMM,* p. 89.
18. "the Coney Island of the South": Amy Waters Yarsinske, *Norfolk, Virginia,* p. 90.
21. "My life really began": *MMM,* pp. 11–31.
24. "Sheer strength of determination": Hearst series.
    "the sensation": *San Francisco Chronicle,* Aug. 28, 1930.
    And among those: There was, in fact, a man known as the Borox King; a Westerner named Francis Marion Smith claimed the unofficial title around the turn of the century. But any connection with his offspring and Peggy would have been impossible. His family with his first wife consisted entirely, and famously, of foster daughters. And his only son, the product of his second marriage, was not born until 1913.
    on May 18, 1910: Marriage license, County of Salt Lake, State of Utah.
25. "I had one or two discussions": J.vs.J.
    "Peggy is the only woman": *San Francisco Chronicle,* Aug. 28, 1930.
26. When he was four months old: Burial records, Magnolia Cemetery; funeral records, Williams Funeral Home; *Norfolk Ledger Dispatch,* Aug. 4, 1911.

PAGE

26. "There were little snatches": Interview, Hudson Price, June 1997.
    "no chick or child": PHJ/Hearst series.
    "All I want": Charles Chaplin, *My Autobiography,* p. 294.

Chapter 2: "I Would Do Anything for a Real Silk Chemise"

28. "most exclusive": Advertisement, Chevy Chase College, Martin Luther
    King Jr. Library, Washington, D.C.
    "the better classes": Andrea Price Stevens, "Suburban Summer Resorts
    of Montgomery County, Md., 1870–1910," submitted to George
    Washington University, 1980; at Montgomery County Historical
    Society Library.
    "There are hundreds of girls": *MMM,* pp. 36–38.
29. "a live wire": J.vs.J.
    "her taste for speed": Hearst series.
31. "You are Miss Upton": *MMM,* p. 40.
    "Each generation": John Clagett Proctor, ed. in chief, *Washington Past
    and Present,* vol. 4, p. 737.
32. "I had never even": *MMM,* p. 45.
33. On September 1, 1913: Marriage license, County of Harford, State of
    Maryland.
    "Beyond telling their secret": *Washington Star,* Nov. 15, 1913.
    "After all": *MMM,* p. 51.
34. "She is very charming": Ibid., p. 53.
    "silly little brat": PHJ/Hearst series.
35. "When a girl is not riding": *MMM,* pp. 55–59.
36. "the prettiest and best-dressed": *Philadelphia Record,* Apr. 25, 1915,
    Locke Collection, NYPL.
37. "Had a wonderful time": *MMM,* p. 57.
    "In the brilliant social circles": *Philadelphia Record,* Apr. 25, 1915.
38. "Sherby asked me today": *MMM,* pp. 59–68.
39. "His mother watched over me": Undated article, Locke Collection,
    NYPL.

Chapter 3: "I Am a Celebrety"

43. "I have been": *MMM,* pp. 72–79.
44. "a sort of female Robin Hood": Anita Loos, *The Talmadge Girls,* p. 59.

PAGE

44. "You are a beautiful little thing": *MMM,* p. 80.

46. "I knew I could find something": *New York Times,* Apr. 8, 1915.

 "The Palace gave vaudeville": Abel Green and Joe Laurie Jr., *Show Biz,* p. 156.

47. "the psychic eighth wonder": PHJ papers.

 "chiffon, silver-threaded net": *Chicago Herald,* May 23, 1915, Locke Collection, NYPL.

 "Someone has said": *Philadelphia Record,* Apr. 25, 1915, Locke Collection, NYPL.

 "wife of two millionaires": *Grand Rapids Press,* May 26, 1915, Locke Collection, NYPL.

48. "Of course, Washington": Undated article, Locke Collection, NYPL.

49. The first time the name: Although none of Peggy's early films with Metro appears to have survived, her career with the company is documented by film synopses, newspaper articles, and publicity material at the Library of Congress and the Film Study Center of the Museum of Modern Art, New York.

50. "Rome had its Vestal Virgins": *Vanity Fair,* Feb. 1933.

52. "Broadway producers": Marian Spitzer, *The Palace,* p. 26.

53. "He won't eat you": *MMM,* pp. 81–87.

54. "It was hard": Interview, Muriel Merrill, Jan. 1997.

 "Mr. Ziegfeld said publicly": *MMM,* pp. 85–87.

56. "a glance into fairyland": Unidentified publication, Nov. 1, 1903, Locke Collection, NYPL.

 When the curtain rose: Details about the 1917 *Follies* are drawn from the script, which is part of the Ole Olsen Collection (Ned Wayburn material) at the University of Southern California Cinema-Television Library, Los Angeles.

58. "English type of beauty": *Green Book,* Sept. 17, 1917, Locke Collection, NYPL.

 "so overwhelmingly glittering": *Morning Telegraph,* June 13, 1917.

 "Not since Florenz Ziegfeld": *New York Herald,* June 13, 1917.

 "Spent a hundred dollars": *MMM,* pp. 92–95.

60. "Have you seen": *Town Topics,* Mar. 1, 1917, Locke Collection, NYPL.

 "My God, child": *MMM,* pp. 94–95.

 "The era [abounded]": Loos, *Talmadge Girls,* p. 39.

61. "He was an outstanding example": Ibid., p. 28.

PAGE

61. "I am sorry": *MMM,* pp. 96–97.

The dizzyingly eclectic program: The script for *Miss 1917* is part of the Ole Olsen Collection, University of Southern California Cinema-Television Library, Los Angeles.

62. "not one cheap moment": *New York Tribune,* Nov. 6, 1917.

"noted for their pictorial": New York *Evening Mail,* Nov. 24, 1917, Marion Davies scrapbook, Billy Rose Theatre Collection, New York Public Library for the Performing Arts at Lincoln Center.

"historic floperoo": P. G. Wodehouse and Guy Bolton, *Bring On the Girls!,* p. 84.

"When I came to the theater": *MMM,* pp. 98–100.

64. "gone and made a peacock feather": *Vanity Fair,* Jan. 1918, Locke Collection, NYPL.

"beautiful young blonde": James Montgomery Flagg, *Roses and Buckshot,* pp. 164–65.

"Will you be our bride?": The film, a copy of which still exists, is part of the George Kleine Collection, which is owned by the Library of Congress and can be viewed there.

65. "most widely famed beauties": *New York Star,* n.d., Locke Collection, NYPL.

"selected eight": New York *Morning Telegraph,* Mar. 10, 1918, PHJ papers.

66. "internationally sensational": Fox Film Corporation Guide for Exhibitors, MOMA. Although the film no longer appears to exist, the museum has a description of the titles.

"Are there provocations": Program, Lyric Theatre, MOMA.

"a high-class tramp": Miriam Cooper, *Dark Lady of the Silents,* p. 146.

67. "Where's that son of a bitch?": Ibid., p. 147.

"Peggy Hopkins as the adventuress": *Variety,* March 15, 1918.

"The Shuberts called up": *MMM,* p. 101.

69. "At least two shockingly bad": *New York Tribune,* Nov. 29, 1918.

" 'A Place in the Sun' is about the worst": Undated article, Shubert Archive, New York.

"She is about as convincing": New York *Evening World,* Nov. 29, 1918.

"One of the papers": *MMM,* pp. 97–110.

70. "charming": *Journal of Commerce,* Feb. 18, 1919.

71. "To this extent": New York *World,* Feb. 18, 1919.

PAGE

71. "highly suspect reputation": Cleveland Amory, *Who Killed Society?*, p. 523.

"When someone tells us": Neal Gabler, *Winchell*, p. 77.

72. "Can you design": PHJ papers.

"What a blow": *Town Topics,* Jan. 24, 1918, Locke Collection, NYPL.

"Dearest sweetheart": PHJ papers.

73. "Although it came about": *Town Topics,* Nov. 15, 1917, Locke Collection, NYPL.

74. "Wall Street financiers": Lloyd Morris, *Incredible New York*, p. 259.

"The supreme shrine": Ibid., p. 262.

"Miss Peggy Hopkins is wearing": *Town and Country,* Jan. 20, 1919, Locke Collection, NYPL.

Chapter 4: "It Is Marvelous to Be Rich"

76. "home of thirteen millionaires": Clinton County Historical Society, *History of Clinton County,* p. 94.

"breathed a different air": Katherine Long and Melvin Erickson, *Clinton: A Pictorial History,* p. 46.

77. "had been engaged": Decennial Record, Class of 1910S, Yale University.

"Eight telephone calls": *MMM,* pp. 113–16.

78. "Who's the boob?": *Chicago Daily Journal,* Nov. 8, 1921.

"Personally," Peggy confessed: *MMM,* pp. 117–25.

80. "best fiction in New York": Simon Michael Bessie, *Jazz Journalism,* p. 100.

82. "city editor's dream girl": Ibid., p. 141.

"You have no idea": J.vs.J.

"The photographers are always": *MMM,* p. 127.

83. Two days later: Marriage license, County of Dade, State of Florida.

"I cashed it": Charles Chaplin, *My Autobiography,* p. 294.

85. "I think a home": *MMM,* p. 131.

86. "Florida [has] long been": *Town Topics,* Feb. 19, 1920, Locke Collection, NYPL.

"It is marvelous": *MMM,* pp. 132–43.

89. "Stanley was a man": Interviews with Joyce Company employees, JSJ papers.

PAGE

90. "not so much after all": *MMM*, pp. 146–49.
91. But the detailed records: JSJ papers.
   "My God": *MMM*, pp. 148–49.
92. "the land where dalliance": Quoted in Cornelia Otis Skinner, *Elegant Wits and Grand Horizontals*, p. 23.
   "I wonder which one": *MMM*, pp. 152–56.
94. "everything that can be said": Helen Josephy and Mary Margaret McBride, *Paris Is a Woman's Town*, p. 24.
95. "We had a terrible fight": *MMM*, p. 157.
96. "Beer, Lapland": The account of the French affair is in J.vs.J.
98. "the uncrowned king": *New York American*, May 5, 1925.
   "without a soft bundle": *New York American*, Apr. 13, 1924.
   "Do you mean that man": J.vs.J.
   "Nearly everyone I know": *MMM*, pp. 159–63.
99. "the high priest": Lloyd Morris, *Incredible New York*, p. 320.
   "Sit down!": *MMM*, pp. 165–78.
101. "gilded butterfly": *Chicago Herald-Examiner*, June 9, 1921.
102. "She told me to save": J.vs.J.
   "if his pretensions": *Chicago American*, June 3, 1921.
   "not full of love": *MMM*, pp. 173–76.
103. "I have a $2,000,000 home": *New York Times*, Oct. 31, 1921.

Chapter 5: "A Vampire with the Sting of Death"

104. "amorous pilgrimage": *Chicago Herald-Examiner*, May 17, 1921.
106. "I'll Be Your Peggy Hopkins": *New York Review*, June 11, 1921.
   "a vampire with the sting": *Chicago Herald-Examiner*, June 12, 1921.
107. "extreme and repeated": J.vs.J.
   "Absurdly untrue": *Chicago Daily Journal*, Nov. 8, 1921.
   "violent sallies": The quotations from Peggy's rebuttal are from J.vs.J.
108. "Joyce Dubs Peggy": *Chicago Daily News*, May 31, 1921; *Chicago Evening Post*, June 7, 1921; *Chicago American*, June 9, 1921; Ibid., Nov. 8, 1921; *Chicago Daily Journal*, Nov. 8, 1921.
   "the biggest case": *Chicago Evening American*, n.d., JSJ papers.
   "one of the most sensational": *Denver Post*, Apr. 12, 1921.
   "dark star of destiny": *New York Times*, June 16, 1921.
   "the instrument": *Chicago American*, May 31, 1921.
109. "Peggy is at this hotel": The letters are among the JSJ papers.

PAGE

109. "Out of what childhood": Hearst series.
110. "The story of Peggy's early life": New York *Morning Telegraph,* June 7, 1921.

    "Is Peggy a smuggler?": *Chicago American,* June 3, 1921.
111. "the finest luster": JSJ papers.

    "all this mean publicity": *Chicago Evening American,* Apr. 29, 1921.
112. "a rich black velvet": *Chicago Daily Tribune,* Apr. 29, 1921.
113. "the central figure": *Chicago American,* Apr. 12, 1921.

    "prince without a principality": The two women's testimony is in J.vs.J.
114. "It was wilting me": Unidentified publication, Nov. 10, 1921, JSJ papers.
115. "theater tickets": *New York Times,* July 9, 1921.

    "I get something like": *Chicago Herald-Examiner,* Nov. 9, 1921.
116. "If he is ever free": New York *Morning Telegraph,* June 12, 1921.
118. "M. Letellier has been pleading": *New York Times,* May 12, 1922.

    "I feel that he would": *MMM,* p. 194.

    "I know that I love Billy": Ibid., p. 196.

    "I was tired out": *New York Times,* May 13, 1922.
119. "Am in terrible trouble": *San Francisco Chronicle,* May 2, 1922.

    "If I had received": *Toledo Blade,* May 5, 1922, Locke Collection, NYPL.

    "Jack is a peach": *New York Times,* May 13, 1922.

    "I have seen Peggy Joyce": Quoted in Carlos Baker, *Ernest Hemingway,* p. 91.
120. "Peggy Joyce will not be permitted": Unidentified publication, May 12, 1922, Locke Collection, NYPL.

Chapter 6: "The Most Famous Woman in the U.S."

122. "Charlie's nymphs": Kenneth Anger, *Hollywood Babylon,* p. 79.

    "bizarre, though brief": Charles Chaplin, *My Autobiography,* p. 294.
123. "the greatest beau": Colleen Moore, *Silent Star,* p. 100.

    "Though Peggy photographed": Ibid., pp. 102–03.
124. "In Peggy, Charlie found": *Photoplay,* Feb. 1923.

    "Her opener": Anger, *Hollywood Babylon,* p. 74.
125. "It was in the evening": Chaplin, *Autobiography,* p. 294.

    "Mickey hadn't lied": Moore, *Silent Star,* p. 103.

    "Peggy, After All, Not to Wed": *San Francisco Examiner,* Sept. 6, 1922.

125. at a party: This incident is described in the Morosco ms.

126. "Instead of being called": New York *Daily News,* Apr. 8, 1924.

"Peggy told me several anecdotes": Chaplin, *Autobiography,* p. 294.

127. "In the earliest stages": David Robinson, *Chaplin,* p. 304.

"There is more real genius": Kenneth Lynn, *Charlie Chaplin and His Times,* p. 274.

"She didn't need": Interview, Sol Jacobson, Jan. 1997.

128. "New husband?": *Los Angeles Times,* Mar. 23, 1926.

"a Vanderbilt": New York *Sun,* Nov. 12, 1931.

"Peggy Joyce to Marry?": *Los Angeles Examiner,* Mar. 25, Apr. 18, Apr. 25, May 2, May 15, May 26, June 4, 1928.

129. "easily the most famous woman": *Time,* Feb. 17, 1930.

"Comes the revolution": Joyce Milton, *Tramp,* p. 207.

130. "Peggy Joyce Tells": *New York Times,* July 30, 1924.

sucker's list: New York *Daily News,* July 14, 1928.

"Peggy Joyce, who is capitalizing": *Chicago Daily Tribune,* May 8, 1922, Shubert Archive, New York.

131. "Italian of the fifteenth period": *Hollywood Citizen,* June 1922.

"I can never face": Morosco ms.

"endowed with talent": Ken Murray, *The Body Merchant,* p. 18.

132. "preacher with an erection": Ibid., p. ix.

"We dock tomorrow": *MMM,* p. 201.

"Come on, Peggy": Murray, *Body Merchant,* pp. 29–30.

133. "He might think": *MMM,* pp. 201–02.

"the most elaborate": Murray, *Body Merchant,* p. 35.

134. "What your weary businessman": *Theater Magazine,* Sept. 1921.

"living curtains": Abel Green and Joe Laurie Jr., *Show Biz,* p. 287.

135. "from behind the bars": Undated photograph, Wide World Photos.

"large and supposedly wicked": *Detroit News,* Sept. 2, 1923.

"$500 was all": *Boston Post,* Sept. 21, 1923.

136. "I would suggest": PHJ papers.

"She is delicately formed": New York *World,* July 6, 1923.

"Just what qualifies her": *New York Evening Post,* July 6, 1923.

"Her greatest talent": *New York Herald,* July 6, 1923.

137. "Peggy, open the door": Murray, *Body Merchant,* p. 36.

138. "The count is more than": *New York Times,* June 4, 1924.

139. "practically engaged": *MMM,* p. 205.

139. "The baron was a dear": *MMM,* p. 208.

on June 2, 1924: Bureau of Vital Statistics, State of New Jersey.

141. "It's none of your business!": *New York Times,* July 31, 1924.

he was "through": *New York Times,* July 30, 1924.

"raven-haired beauty": New York *Daily News,* Aug. 24, 1924.

"There was no honeymoon": *New York Times,* July 30, 1924.

142. "Titles are the easiest thing": *New York Times,* July 31, 1924.

"I made a mistake": *MMM,* p. 209.

"I am as much in love": *New York Times,* Nov. 22, 1925.

143. "was not faithful": *New York Times,* Feb. 21, 1926.

"She is what newspaper men": Associated Exhibitors press book, Billy Rose Theatre Collection, New York Public Library for the Performing Arts at Lincoln Center.

"If it were announced": Ibid.

144. "the notoriety she had achieved": *Variety,* Mar. 18, 1924.

145. "Oh, no": Bob Thomas, *Thalberg,* p. 118.

146. "a screen diamond": Associated Exhibitors press book.

"Directors are funny people": *MMM,* pp. 214–15.

147. "everything that Mary Pickford has": Jack Spears, *Hollywood,* p. 302.

"Take her down": Anthony Slide, oral history interview with Harold Grieve, Feb. 27, 1980, AMPAS.

148. "forging ahead": *Moving Picture World,* Nov. 7, 1925.

"It's big!": *Moving Picture World,* Oct. 31, 1925.

"No matter how much": Associated Exhibitors press book.

"Peggy Hopkins Joyce sundae": *Film Daily,* Feb. 11, 1926.

149. "you can't get": Associated Exhibitors press book.

"The truth about this Joyce girl": *Moving Picture World,* Nov. 28, 1925.

"the Circe of this age": *Photoplay,* Nov. 1925.

150. "one of the most novel": *Moving Picture World,* Jan. 2, 1926.

151. "one of the very best": Spears, *Hollywood,* p. 301.

"not unknown": *New York Times,* Jan. 26, 1926.

"This girl has obtained": *Variety,* Jan. 27, 1926.

"Every woman in America": *Photoplay,* Jan. 1926.

"the biggest disappointment": *Exhibitors Herald,* Mar. 13, 1926.

152. "She didn't create": Interview, Elaine St. Johns, Mar. 1997.

153. "overfed Buddha": Anita Loos, *Kiss Hollywood Goodbye,* p. 100.

153. "When he walks into a room": Lester Sweyd Collection, Billy Rose Theatre Collection, New York Public Library for the Performing Arts at Lincoln Center.

"bosh" and "drivel": Wilfred J. Riley, Dec. 14, 1928, unidentified publication, Billy Rose Theatre Collection, New York Public Library for the Performing Arts at Lincoln Center.

154. "I can always say": Robert Garland, Dec. 14, 1928, unidentified publication, Billy Rose Theatre Collection, New York Public Library for the Performing Arts at Lincoln Center.

"orchidacious Peggy Joyce": unidentified publication, n.d., PHJ papers.

Chapter 7: "Life after the Sun Went Down"

155. "the dumbest blonde": Anita Loos, *Gentlemen Prefer Blondes,* p. 12.

"I know that Anita": Interview, Mary Anita Loos von Saltza, Mar. 1997.

156. "the original blonde": *New York Evening Graphic,* Jan. 7, 1932.

"Mr. Spoffard": Loos, *Gentlemen,* p. 104.

"Loos made no secret": Eve Golden, "Peggy Hopkins Joyce, the Gentlemen-Preferred Blonde," *Films of the Golden Age,* summer 1999.

"Kissing your hand": *Gentlemen,* p. 80.

157. "Rare inlaid pieces": *Movie Weekly,* Oct. 18, 1924.

158. "barricaded worse": NEA Service, Feb. 4, 1933, PHJ papers.

"presumably kept": Scott Meredith, *George S. Kaufman and His Friends,* p. 426. The interior of the house is described in detail in Moss Hart's *Act One.* Hart visited No. 158 regularly during the months he was collaborating with Kaufman on their comedy *Once in a Lifetime.*

"It would be a cinch": PHJ papers.

159. "Peggy Hopkins Joyce and Her Orchid": Unidentified publication, May 24, 1934, Billy Rose Theatre Collection, New York Public Library for the Performing Arts at Lincoln Center.

"That's my business!": *New York Herald Tribune,* May 24, 1934.

"terrible rumpus": New York *Daily News,* May 13, 1926.

"Please," she begged: Morosco ms.

160. "Peggy Hopkins Joyce says": *Los Angeles Times,* Feb. 14, 1933.

"the best-dressed woman": Paramount press sheets for *International House,* AMPAS.

"the most perfectly matched": Photograph, 1925, MOMA.

PAGE

160. "the finest in the world": New York *Daily News,* Apr. 28, 1930.

"She was famous": Diana Vreeland, *D.V.,* p. 55.

161. "Money flows like glue": Quoted in *New York Times,* Jan. 27, 1925.

"If any man": *Confidential,* Mar. 1954.

"The wrap which we sent": PHJ papers.

"Unless we receive": Ibid.

162. "Peggy sent her mother": Interview, Francis Price, June 1997.

"Her bath salts": New York *Daily News,* Apr. 28, 1930.

163. "The glory of old Versailles": The invitation and other documents are among the PHJ papers.

165. "a society a little livelier": F. Scott Fitzgerald, "My Lost City," *The Crack-Up,* p. 27.

166. "Jimmy Walker rules": Stephen Graham, *New York Nights,* p. 87.

"a gorgeous tamer": Ibid., p. 92.

167. "She personified life": Interview, Gary Stevens, Jan. 1997.

"Texas Guinan desires": PHJ papers.

"Peggy Joyce is a vegetarian": Texas Guinan file, Billy Rose Theatre Collection, New York Public Library for the Performing Arts at Lincoln Center.

168. "That's Jean Acker!": Berliner, *Texas Guinan,* pp. 94–95.

169. "Peggy Joyce became": London *Evening Standard,* Sept. 3, 1946.

"Miss Joyce, who had arrived": Margaret Case Harriman, *Take Them Up Tenderly,* p. 138.

170. "unique charm": London *Evening Standard*, Sept. 3, 1946.

171. "Well I said some things": *MMM,* pp. 250–54.

172. "easily the most popular": Harpo Marx, *Harpo Speaks!,* pp. 255–58.

Chapter 8: "That Strange Art of Being a Woman"

174. "the national symbol": Emile Gauvreau, *My Last Million Readers,* p. 141.

"the seating arrangement": New York *Morning Telegraph,* Feb. 11, 1926.

"a certain muscle": Interview, Miles White, Jan. 1997.

175. "And she was just gorgeous!": Interview, Robert Deacon, July 1997.

176. "She understands that strange art": *Photoplay,* Nov. 1925.

"She knew how to handle them": Interview, Herman Klurfeld, Apr. 1997.

"She has the art": *Brooklyn Eagle,* Aug. 3, 1924.

PAGE

176. "She had a terrific sense": Interview, Jackie Olson, June 1997.
177. "Using obscene words": Interview, Herman Klurfeld.
     "She genuinely liked": Diana Vreeland, *D.V.*, p. 55.
     "I know this is terribly": Ken Murray, *The Body Merchant*, p. 38.
     "She knew her way": Interview, John Kenly, Oct. 1997.
178. "The leading cocottes": Cornelia Otis Skinner, *Elegant Wits and Grand Horizontals*, pp. 218–19.
179. "a member in good standing": The various speculations are enumerated in David Grafton, "Peggy Hopkins Joyce Inc.," *Forbes 400*, Oct. 23, 1989.
180. "the best screen kiss": William Mann, *Wisecracker*, p. 70.
     "as big as large marbles": New York *Daily Mirror*, Apr. 13, 1926.
     "sour grapes": *New York Times*, Apr. 18, 1926.
     "Changed my mind": *New York Times*, July 26, 1926.
     "last season's fiancé": New York *Daily News*, Jan. 18, 1927.
181. "I have just met": *MMM*, pp. 220–22.
     "The thin-worn standing headline": *Brooklyn Eagle*, July 29, 1928.
182. "Northesk Free for Peggy!": *New York Journal,* Oct. 26, 1928.
     "I can't marry everybody!": *New York Evening Graphic,* Oct. 30, 1928.
     "Miss Joyce is not to marry": *New York American,* Oct. 28, 1928.
     "I didn't see": New York *Daily News,* Nov. 2, 1928.
183. "all-powerful society dowager": New York *Daily News,* Jan. 8, 1932.
     "New York society sat back": Ibid.
     "You can't eat": New York *Daily News,* Jan. 21, 1932.
184. "Take me out of here!": Frank Mallen, *Sauce for the Gander,* p. 239.
     "I have a very ardent": *MMM*, p. 238.
185. "he didn't even think": *Confidential,* Mar. 1954.
     "someone said to be prominent": *Time,* Feb. 17, 1930.
186. "the largest and finest": *New York Times,* Mar. 13, 1928. The stone, which is on permanent view as part of the National Gem Collection in the Smithsonian Institution's Museum of Natural History in Washington, DC, is described in Jeffrey Post's *The National Gem Collection* and Penny Proddow and Marion Fasel's *Diamonds.*
     "the largest blue diamond": *Vogue,* Feb. 1924.
     "Cleopatra, the Serpent": *Brooklyn Eagle,* Mar. 12, 1928.
     "Peggy's skating rink": *Confidential,* Mar. 1954.
     "The largest perfect diamond": *Time,* Feb. 17, 1930.

PAGE

186. "I sometimes think": *London Daily News,* Apr. 2, 1928.

187. "I knew that nothing": *Photoplay,* Oct. 1928.

"How many times": The letters are among the PHJ papers.

189. *Eternal Springtime:* A photograph of this work appears in Tellegen's *Women Have Been Kind.*

"the perfect lover": Dorothy Parker, *Constant Reader,* p. 123.

"our little home": PHJ papers.

190. "Peggy darling": Ibid.

"never, apparently": *New York Evening Graphic,* Jan. 7, 1932.

"I've been fond": *New York Evening Graphic,* Jan. 8, 1932.

"I haven't been in love": *Photoplay,* Aug. 1935.

191. "I'm in love": New York *Daily News,* June 4, 1924.

Chapter 9: "The Most Preferred Blonde"

193. "Mrs. Nash": The lyrics are from Robert Kimball, ed., *The Complete Lyrics of Cole Porter,* pp. 73–74, 89, 130, 217, 290.

194. "Peggy Joyce has a bus'ness": Robert Kimball and Dorothy Hart, eds., *The Complete Lyrics of Lorenz Hart,* p. 167.

"Take Peggy Joyce": Eddie Cantor, *Take My Life,* p. 192.

195. "takes two men": *Louisiana Purchase* script, Billy Rose Theatre Collection, New York Public Library for the Performing Arts at Lincoln Center.

"Why don't you": Music by Spivvy, lyrics by Everett Marcy, c. 1940.

"If Peggy Joyce calls": Quoted in Ellen Schiff, ed., *Awake and Sing,* p. 205.

"calls up Mindy's": Damon Runyon, *The Bloodhounds of Broadway and Other Stories,* p. 248.

"young brothers quarreling": Dawn Powell, *The Diaries of Dawn Powell,* p. 119.

"too much notoriety": Louis Sheaffer, *O'Neill, vol. 2, Son and Artist,* p. 362.

"We want Scandal": Will Rogers, *The Weekly Articles of Will Rogers,* p. 61.

196. "Like Jimmy Walker": Polly Adler, *A House Is Not a Home,* p. 4.

"At certain times": Zora Neale Hurston, *I Love Myself When I Am Laughing,* pp. 154–55.

197. "just a couple of little girls": Cited in Wendy Wick Reaves, *Celebrity Caricatures,* p. 22.

PAGE

198. "Dear Dorothy Dix": *Vanity Fair,* June 1935.
"Think of the fun": *Vanity Fair,* July 1933.
"Those Peggy Joyce revelations": *New Yorker,* Sept. 12, 1931.
199. "Peggy Hopkins Joyce, the most preferred": New York *Daily Mirror,* Apr. 21, 1927.
200. "Peggy Hopkins Countess Morner": *New York American,* Apr. 29, 1927.
201. "I will begin": *New York Evening Graphic,* Jan. 18, 1925.
"Ten Commandments": Wheeler Syndicate, 1923, PHJ papers.
"The Famous Beauty": PHJ/Hearst series.
203. "Dear Mrs. Peggy Hopkins Joyce": The letters are among the PHJ papers.
206. "trunkloads of letters": PHJ/Hearst series.
"It's my diary": *Brooklyn Eagle,* Jan. 30, 1930.
207. "A woman should never": *MMM,* pp. 234–48.
"I am fond": Ibid., pp. 191–92.
208. "My Husbands I Have Met": Unidentified publication, Feb. 24, 1930, PHJ papers.
"I have decided hereafter": *Vanity Fair,* Apr. 1930.
209. "Peggy Hopkins Joyce, the famed blonde": New York *Sun,* Jan. 30, 1930.
"I hardly know what": Ibid.
"I danced and danced": "The Reminiscences of Samuel Loveman," Aug. 4, 1962, pp. 33–34, in the Oral History Research Office Collection of Columbia University, New York.
"Though cancellation": *Time,* Feb. 17, 1930.
210. "the babblings": *London Daily Mail,* Oct. 2, 1930.
"I hope": *New York Evening Graphic,* Sept. 26, 1931.
"She had happiness": *New York Evening Graphic,* Sept. 12, 1931.
"no matter how fascinating": *New York Evening Graphic,* Oct. 3, 1931.
"All these unexplained suicides": *New York Evening Graphic,* Sept. 5, 1931.
211. "The Peggy Joyce Love Chart": *New York Evening Graphic,* May 21, 1931.
"one of the best sellers": Associated Press, Oct. 18, 1932.
"quiver with passion": Peggy Hopkins Joyce, *Transatlantic Wife,* p. 71.
212. "Take me back": Ibid., p. 316.
"Whatever she does": Undated advertisement, PHJ papers.

212. "Of course, she's a charming lady": *Los Angeles Times,* n.d., PHJ papers.
"Millionaires may be": *Herald Tribune,* European ed., Sept. 11, 1932.

213. "I've been so busy": *New York World-Telegram,* Jan. 18, 1933.
"Mario quivered": Joyce, *Transatlantic Wife,* pp. 99–102.
"Naturally in a Joyce book": *New York Evening Post,* May 5, 1933.

214. "There are parts": *New York Times,* Nov. 25, 1933. The Woon book
was *Incredible Land: A Jaunty Baedeker to Hollywood and the Great Southwest.*
"lovely menace": *New York Herald Tribune,* Jan. 8, 1925.

216. "More stars than you saw": Paramount press sheets for *International
House,* AMPAS.

218. "As you are doubtless aware": MPAA/PCA Collection, AMPAS.
"wild fun": *New York Times,* May 27, 1933.
"wears a whole fox farm": *Variety,* May 30, 1933.
"suitable for children": *Harrison Reports,* June 3, 1933.
"It seems apparent": MPAA/PCA Collection, AMPAS.
"The whole picture": Ibid.

219. "Considered unsuitable": Ibid.
"the most alluring": Unidentified publication, PHJ papers.

220. "He is the most charming": Unidentified publication, PHJ papers.
"Jack Oakie's sense of humor": Paramount press sheets for *International
House,* AMPAS.
"How's my girl?": Jack Oakie, *Jack Oakie's Double Takes,* p. 113.
"a fading blonde": Serialization of *Broadway thru a Keyhole,* Twentieth
Century–Fox Collection, University of Southern California Cinema-
Television Library, Los Angeles.

Chapter 10: "The Last Generation's Celebrity"

222. "Fifteen years from now": Serialization of *Broadway thru a Keyhole,*
Twentieth Century–Fox Collection, University of Southern California
Cinema-Television Library, Los Angeles.

223. "No one is more forgotten": Daniel J. Boorstin, *The Image,* p. 63.
By the midthirties: While it is impossible to prove that Peggy gave her
papers to Frank Williamson, letters in the possession of Peggy's relatives
in Norfolk strongly suggest that she did so. These letters show that
Williamson, a naval engineer who subsequently married Myrtie Price,
lived in Poughkeepsie in the midthirties. Peggy knew Williamson, and

the three of them occasionally met in New York City. His house in up-state New York would have seemed a logical place for her to stow her papers for safekeeping. But the collection, which includes thousands of documents—letters, newspaper clippings, telegrams, photographs, and memorabilia—was never claimed, and the papers remained there for nearly fifty years as the house went through a series of owners. In the early 1980s, they were purchased by the author's mother, Beatrice Rosenblum.

224. "instinct of Peggy Joyce": Fitzgerald, *The Crack-Up,* p. 168.
"if somebody'll donate": *New York Telegram,* Nov. 20, 1930.
"The famous Peggy Hopkins Joyce jewels": *Los Angeles Times,* Apr. 17, 1933.

225. "I don't think it is wise": Unidentified publication, Sept. 11, 1933, PHJ papers.
"I think it was for a chair": *Brooklyn Eagle,* June 10, 1934.

226. "Auctioneer Dan Greenwald": *New York Sun,* Nov. 23, 1932.
"She had a gold lamé jumpsuit": Interview, Billy Livingstone, Feb. 1997.

227. "Well, Mr. Sarong": Louis Sobol, *The Longest Street,* p. 248.
"Ah, Peggy!": *Washington Herald,* Feb. 1, 1934.
"it is not enough": International News Service, Dec. 24, 1946.
"She was like a marvelous drawing": Interview, Miles White, Jan. 1997.

228. "We both love horses": Associated Press, Nov. 10, 1936.

229. "She used to be": Interview, Anna Sosenko, Jan. 1997.

230. "By the end": Interview, Billy Livingstone.
"It was all terribly sad": Interview, Jackie Olson, June 1997.
"implied it had been": New York *Daily News,* Nov. 23, 1940.

231. "Our hearts will rhyme": *New York World-Telegram,* Sept. 25, 1940.
"I'm not speaking to you": Interview, Billy Livingstone.
"most jeweled woman": Sobol, *Longest Street,* p. 35.

232. "I refuse": Gioia Diliberto, *Debutante,* p. 149.
"She just said": Interview, Jackie Olson.
"Hey, babe": New York *Daily News,* Dec. 10, 1946.
"You ought to see her": New York *Daily News,* June 17, 1941.

233. "feeling like the personification": Cornelia Otis Skinner and Emily Kimbrough, *Our Hearts Were Young and Gay,* p. 76.
"My mother had": Interview, Kitty Carlisle Hart, Nov. 1996.

PAGE

233. "You have sawdust": PHJ papers.
    "anyone who was anyone": Interview, Anna Sosenko.
234. "It seems as though": James Gavin, *Intimate Nights,* p. 89.
235. "In the back": Interview, Francis Price, June 1997.
236. "Madeline was a slave": Interview, Joan Harding, Apr. 1997.
237. omit the word *obey: New York Times,* Dec. 4, 1945.
    "I don't know": *Los Angeles Times,* June 28, 1946.
238. "She looked so lovely": Interview, Andrew Meyer, June 1997.
    The day he met her: Interview, Jackie Olson.
240. "Handy Andy": *Confidential,* Mar. 1954.
    "I've got to move": Interview, Joan Harding.
241. "a golden magnetic power": Interview, Grayce Lizauskas, July 1997.
    "She became quite a pest": Interview, Robert Deacon, July 1997.
242. A local justice of the peace: Southeast Registrar of Vital Statistics, County of Westchester, State of New York.
243. "Peggy Hopkins Joyce, whose name": *New York Times,* June 13, 1957.
    "the toast of two continents": *New York Journal-American,* June 13, 1957.
    "one of the most celebrated": *New York Herald Tribune,* June 13, 1957.
    "symbolize the high-living": *Time,* June 24, 1957.
    "There has never been": *New York Journal-American,* June 13, 1957.

Epilogue

245. "nothing so much": Winthrop Sargeant, "Fifty Years of American Women: A Prejudiced Survey of Their Role in the First Half of Our Century," *Life,* Jan. 2, 1950.
253. "When a girl has good looks": *MMM,* p. 168.
    "Peggy Joyce had made": London *Evening Standard,* Sept. 3, 1946.
    "Peggy should not be buried": PHJ papers.

Bibliography

Adler, Polly. *A House Is Not a Home*. New York: Rinehart, 1953.

Allen, Frederick Lewis. *The Big Change: America Transforms Itself, 1900–1950*. New York: Harper and Row, 1952.

————. *Only Yesterday: An Informal History of the Nineteen-Twenties*. New York: Perennial Library, 1964.

————. *Since Yesterday: The Nineteen-Thirties in America*. New York: Harper and Brothers, 1940.

Allen, Irving. *The City in Slang: New York Life and Popular Speech*. New York: Oxford University Press, 1995.

Amory, Cleveland. *The Last Resorts*. New York: Harper and Brothers, 1948.

————. *Who Killed Society?* New York: Pocket Books, 1962.

Anger, Kenneth. *Hollywood Babylon*. San Francisco: Straight Arrow, 1975.

Atkinson, Brooks. *Broadway*. New York: Macmillan, 1970.

Baker, Carlos. *Ernest Hemingway: A Life Story*. New York: Charles Scribner's Sons, 1969.

Banner, Lois W. *American Beauty*. New York: Alfred A. Knopf, 1983.

Beauchamp, Cari. *Without Lying Down: Frances Marion and the Powerful Women of Early Hollywood*. New York: Lisa Drew/Scribner, 1997.

Berle, Milton, with Haskel Frankel. *Milton Berle: An Autobiography*. New York: Delacorte Press, 1974.

Berliner, Louise. *Texas Guinan, Queen of the Nightclubs*. Austin: University of Texas Press, 1993.

Bessie, Simon Michael. *Jazz Journalism: The Story of the Tabloid Newspapers*. New York: E. P. Dutton, 1938.

Bogdanovich, Peter. *Who the Devil Made It*. New York: Alfred A. Knopf, 1997.

Boorstin, Daniel J. *The Image: A Guide to Pseudo-Events in America*. Rev. ed. New York: Vintage, 1992.

Braudy, Leo. *The Frenzy of Renown: Fame and Its History*. New York: Vintage, 1997.

Brown, Eve [Mary Eudora Nichols]. *Champagne Cholly: The Life and Times of Maury Paul*. New York: E. P. Dutton, 1947.

Brownlow, Kevin. *Behind the Mask of Innocence*. New York: Alfred A. Knopf, 1990.

Cantor, Eddie, with Jane Kesner Ardmore. *Take My Life*. Garden City, NY: Doubleday, 1957.

Card, James. *Seductive Cinema: The Art of the Silent Film*. New York: Alfred A. Knopf, 1994.

Carey, Gary. *Anita Loos: A Biography*. New York: Alfred A. Knopf, 1988.

Chaplin, Charles. *My Autobiography*. New York: Plume/Penguin, 1992.

Chaplin, Lita Grey, with Morton Cooper. *My Life with Chaplin: An Intimate Memoir*. New York: Bernard Geis, 1966.

Chrysler, Walter Percy, with Boyden Sparkes. *Life of an American Workman*. New York: Dodd, Mead, 1950.

Churchill, Allen. *The Great White Way: A Re-Creation of Broadway's Golden Era of Theatrical Entertainment*. New York: E. P. Dutton, 1962.

Clinton County Historical Society. *History of Clinton County, Iowa, 1976*. Clinton: Clinton County American Revolution Bicentennial Commission, 1978.

Cooper, Miriam, with Bonnie Herndon. *Dark Lady of the Silents*. New York: Bobbs-Merrill, 1973.

Curl, Donald W. *Palm Beach County: An Illustrated History*. Northridge, CA: Windsor Publications, 1986.

Custen, George F. *Twentieth Century's Fox: Darryl F. Zanuck and the Culture of Hollywood*. New York: Basic Books, 1997.

Davies, Marion. *The Times We Had: Life with William Randolph Hearst*. New York: Bobbs-Merrill, 1975.

Davis, Lee. *Bolton and Wodehouse and Kern: The Men Who Made Musical Comedy*. New York: James H. Heineman, 1993.

Dempsey, Jack, with Barbara Piattelli Dempsey. *Dempsey*. New York: Harper and Row, 1977.

Diliberto, Gioia. *Debutante: The Story of Brenda Frazier*. New York: Alfred A. Knopf, 1987.

Douglas, Ann. *Terrible Honesty: Mongrel Manhattan in the 1920s.* New York: Farrar, Straus and Giroux, 1995.

Duff–Gordon, Lady. *Discretions and Indiscretions.* New York: Frederick A. Stokes, 1932.

Dyer, Richard. *Heavenly Bodies: Film Stars and Society.* Houndmills, Eng.: Macmillan Education, 1986.

Erenberg, Lewis A. *Steppin' Out: New York Nightlife and the Transformation of American Culture, 1890–1930.* Westport, CT: Greenwood Press, 1981.

Farnsworth, Marjorie. *The Ziegfeld Follies.* New York: Putnam, 1956.

Farrar, Geraldine. *Such Sweet Compulsion.* New York: Greystone Press, 1938.

Fass, Paula. *The Damned and the Beautiful: American Youth in the Nineteen-Twenties.* New York: Oxford University Press, 1977.

Fields, Armond, and L. Marc Fields. *From the Bowery to Broadway: Lew Fields and the Roots of America Popular Theater.* New York: Oxford University Press, 1993.

Fitzgerald, F. Scott. *The Crack-Up.* Ed. Edmund Wilson. New York: New Directions, 1993.

Flagg, James Montgomery. *Roses and Buckshot.* New York: G. P. Putnam, 1946.

Flamini, Roland. *Thalberg: The Last Tycoon and the World of M-G-M.* New York: Crown, 1994.

Fowler, Gene. *The Great Mouthpiece: A Life Story of William J. Fallon.* New York: Covici, Friede, 1931.

Gabler, Neal. *An Empire of Their Own: How the Jews Invented Hollywood.* New York: Crown, 1988.

———. *Life the Movie: How Entertainment Conquered Reality.* New York: Alfred A. Knopf, 1998.

———. *Winchell: Gossip, Power, and the Culture of Celebrity.* New York: Vintage, 1995.

Gauvreau, Emil. *My Last Million Readers.* New York: E. P. Dutton, 1941.

Gavin, James. *Intimate Nights: The Golden Age of New York Cabaret.* New York: Limelight Editions, 1992.

Gilbert, Douglas. *American Vaudeville, Its Life and Times.* New York: McGraw-Hill, 1940.

Goldman, Herbert G. *Banjo Eyes: Eddie Cantor and the Birth of Modern Stardom.* New York: Oxford University Press, 1997.

———. *Fanny Brice: The Original Funny Girl.* New York: Oxford University Press, 1992.

Graham, Stephen. *New York Nights.* New York: George H. Doran, 1927.

Green, Abel, and Joe Laurie Jr. *Show Biz: From Vaude to Video.* New York: Holt, 1951.

Green, Stanley. *The Great Clowns of Broadway.* New York: Oxford University Press, 1984.

Grossman, Barbara. *Funny Woman: The Life and Times of Fanny Brice.* Bloomington: Indiana University Press, 1991.

Guiles, Fred Lawrence. *Marion Davies, a Biography.* New York: McGraw-Hill, 1972.

Hansen, Arlen J. *Expatriate Paris: A Cultural History of Paris in the Twenties.* New York: Arcade, 1990.

Harriman, Margaret Case. *Take Them Up Tenderly: A Collection of Profiles.* New York: Alfred A. Knopf, 1944.

Hart, Moss. *Act One: An Autobiography.* New York: St. Martin's Press, 1989.

Hecht, Ben. *Charlie: The Improbable Life and Times of Charles MacArthur.* New York: Harper and Brothers, 1957.

Henderson, Mary. *The New Amsterdam: The Biography of a Broadway Theater.* New York: Hyperion, 1997.

Herr, Michael. *Walter Winchell, a Novel.* New York: Alfred A. Knopf, 1990.

Hildebrand, George. *Borax Pioneer: Francis Marion Smith.* San Diego: Howell-North Books, 1982.

Hurston, Zora Neale. *I Love Myself When I Am Laughing.* Ed. Alice Walker. New York: Feminist Press, 1979.

Israel, Lee. *Kilgallen.* New York: Delacorte, 1979.

Josephy, Helen, and Mary Margaret McBride. *Paris Is a Woman's Town.* New York: Coward-McCann, 1929.

Joyce, Peggy Hopkins. *Men, Marriage and Me.* New York: Macaulay, 1930.

———. *Transatlantic Wife.* New York: Macaulay, 1933.

Kimball, Robert, ed. *The Complete Lyrics of Cole Porter.* New York: Alfred A. Knopf, 1983.

Kimball, Robert, and Dorothy Hart, eds. *The Complete Lyrics of Lorenz Hart.* New York: Alfred A. Knopf, 1986.

Kobol, John. *People Will Talk.* New York: Alfred A. Knopf, 1986.

Koszarski, Richard. *The Man You Love to Hate: Erich von Stroheim and Hollywood.* New York: Oxford University Press, 1983.

Lanouz, Armand. *Paris in the Twenties.* New York: Golden Griffin Books/Essential Encyclopedia Arts, 1960.

Laurie, Joe Jr. *Vaudeville: From the Honky-Tonks to the Palace.* New York: Henry Holt, 1953.

Leider, Emily Wortis. *Becoming Mae West*. New York: Farrar, Straus and Giroux, 1997.

Long, Katherine, and Melvin Erickson. *Clinton: A Pictorial History*. Rock Island, IL: Quest, 1983.

Loos, Anita. *Cast of Thousands*. New York: Grosset and Dunlap, 1977.

———. *Gentlemen Prefer Blondes: The Illuminating Diary of a Professional Lady*. London: Penguin, 1992.

———. *A Girl Like I*. New York: Viking, 1966.

———. *Kiss Hollywood Good-By*. New York: Viking, 1974.

———. *The Talmadge Girls: A Memoir*. New York: Viking, 1978.

Louvish, Simon. *Man on the Flying Trapeze: The Life and Times of W. C. Fields*. New York: W. W. Norton, 1997.

Lowe, David. *Lost Chicago*. Boston: Houghton Mifflin, 1975.

Lynn, Kenneth. *Charlie Chaplin and His Times*. New York: Simon and Schuster, 1997.

McBrien, William. *Cole Porter, a Biography*. New York: Alfred A. Knopf, 1998.

McCabe, John. *Charlie Chaplin*. New York: Doubleday, 1978.

McIver, Stuart B. *Yesterday's Palm Beach*. Miami: E. A. Seemann, 1976.

McNamara, Brooks. *The Shuberts of Broadway*. New York: Oxford University Press, 1990.

Maland, Charles. *Chaplin and American Culture: The Evolution of a Star Image*. Princeton: Princeton University Press, 1989.

Mallen, Frank. *Sauce for the Gander*. White Plains, NY: Baldwin Books, 1954.

Mann, William. *Wisecracker: The Life and Times of William Haines, Hollywood's First Openly Gay Star*. New York: Viking, 1997.

Marchand, Roland. *Advertising the American Dream: Making Way for Modernity, 1920–1940*. Berkeley: University of California Press, 1985.

Marx, Harpo, with Rowland Barber. *Harpo Speaks!* New York: Bernard Geis, 1961.

Marx, Samuel. *Mayer and Thalberg: The Make-Believe Saints*. New York: Random House, 1975.

Maxwell, Elsa. *R.S.V.P.: Elsa Maxwell's Own Story*. Boston: Little, Brown, 1954.

Meredith, Scott. *George S. Kaufman and His Friends*. Garden City, NY: Doubleday, 1974.

Meyer, Susan E. *America's Great Illustrators*. New York: Harry N. Abrams, 1978.

Milton, Joyce. *Tramp: The Life of Charlie Chaplin*. New York: HarperCollins, 1996.

Moore, Colleen. *Silent Star*. Garden City, NY: Doubleday, 1968.

Mordden, Ethan. *Broadway Babies: The People Who Made the American Musical*. New York: Oxford University Press, 1988.

Morris, Jan. *Manhattan '45*. Baltimore: Johns Hopkins University Press, 1988.

Morris, Lloyd. *Incredible New York: High Life and Low Life of the Last Hundred Years*. New York: Random House, 1951.

Morris, Sylvia Jukes. *Rage for Fame: The Ascent of Clare Boothe Luce*. New York: Random House, 1997.

Mosedale, John. *The Men Who Invented Broadway: Damon Runyon, Walter Winchell, and Their World*. New York: Richard Marek, 1981.

Mott, Frank Luther. *American Journalism: A History of Newspapers in the United States through 250 Years, 1690–1940*. New York: Macmillan, 1941.

Muir, Helen. *Miami, U.S.A.* Coconut Grove, FL: Hurricane House, 1953.

Murray, Ken. *The Body Merchant: The Story of Earl Carroll*. Pasadena: Ward Richie Press, 1976.

Nasaw, David. *Going Out: The Rise and Fall of Public Amusements*. New York: Basic Books, 1993.

Oakie, Jack. *Jack Oakie's Double Takes*. San Francisco: Strawberry Hill Press, 1980.

Paris, Barry. *Louise Brooks*. New York: Alfred A. Knopf, 1989.

Parker, Dorothy. *Constant Reader*. New York: Viking, 1970.

Post, Jeffrey E. *The National Gem Collection*. New York: Harry N. Abrams, 1997.

Postman, Neil. *Amusing Ourselves to Death: Public Discourse in the Age of Show Business*. New York: Penguin, 1986.

Powell, Dawn. *The Diaries of Dawn Powell, 1931–1965*. Ed. Tim Page. South Royalton, VT: Steerforth Press, 1995.

Proctor, John Clagett, ed. in chief. *Washington Past and Present: A History*. Vol. 4. New York: Lewis Publishing, 1930.

Proddow, Penny, and Marion Fasel. *Diamonds: A Century of Spectacular Jewels*. New York: Harry N. Abrams, 1996.

Proddow, Penny, Debra Healy, and Marion Fasel. *Hollywood Jewels: Movies, Jewelry, Stars*. New York: Harry N. Abrams, 1992.

Reaves, Wendy Wick. *Celebrity Caricature in America*. New Haven: Yale University Press and National Portrait Gallery, Smithsonian Institution, 1998.

Robinson, David. *Chaplin: His Life and Art*. New York: Da Capo, 1994.

Rogers, Will. *The Weekly Articles of Will Rogers*, Vol. 2 of *Works: The Writings of Will Rogers*. Stillwater: Oklahoma State University Press, 1973–83.

Runyon, Damon. *The Bloodhounds of Broadway and Other Stories*. New York: William Morrow, 1981.

St. Johns, Adela Rogers. *The Honeycomb*. Garden City, NY: Doubleday, 1969.

———. *Love, Laughter and Tears: My Hollywood Story*. Garden City, NY: Doubleday, 1978.

Schickel, Richard. *His Picture in the Papers: A Speculation on Celebrity in America, Based on the Life of Douglas Fairbanks, Sr.* New York: Charterhouse, 1973.

———. *Intimate Strangers: The Culture of Celebrity*. Garden City, NY: Doubleday, 1985.

Schiff, Ellen, ed. *Awake and Sing: Seven Classic Plays from the American Jewish Repertoire*. New York: Mentor, 1995.

Schumach, Murray. *The Face on the Cutting Room Floor: The Story of Movie and Television Censorship*. New York: William Morrow, 1964.

Sheaffer, Louis. *O'Neill, Son and Artist*. Vol. 2. Boston: Little, Brown, 1973.

Simon, Kate. *Fifth Avenue: A Very Social History*. New York: Harcourt Brace Jovanovich, 1978.

Skinner, Cornelia Otis. *Elegant Wits and Grand Horizontals*. Boston: Houghton Mifflin, 1962.

———, and Emily Kimbrough. *Our Hearts Were Young and Gay*. New York: Bantam, 1963.

Sklar, Robert. *Movie-Made America: A Cultural History of American Movies*. New York: Vintage, 1994.

Slayden, Ellen Maury. *Washington Wife: Journal of Ellen Maury Slayden from 1897–1919*. New York: Harper and Row, 1962.

Smith, Sally Bedell. *Reflected Glory: The Life of Pamela Churchill Harriman*. New York: Simon and Schuster, 1996.

Sobol, Louis. *The Longest Street: A Memoir*. New York: Crown, 1968.

Spears, Jack. *Hollywood, the Golden Era*. New York: Castle Books, 1971.

Spitzer, Marian. *The Palace*. New York: Atheneum, 1969.

Stagg, Jerry. *The Brothers Shubert*. New York: Random House, 1968.

Stenn, David. *Bombshell: The Life and Death of Jean Harlow*. New York: Doubleday, 1993.

———. *Clara Bow: Runnin' Wild*. New York: Random House, 1988.

Susman, Warren I. *Culture as History: The Transformation of American Society in the Twentieth Century*. New York: Pantheon, 1984.

Swanberg, W. A. *Citizen Hearst: A Biography of William Randolph Hearst*. New York: Bantam, 1971.

Taylor, William R., ed. *Inventing Times Square: Commerce and Culture at the Crossroads of the World*. Baltimore: Johns Hopkins University Press, 1996.

Tebbel, John. *A History of Book Publishing in the United States*. Vol. 3. New York: R. R. Bowker, 1978.

Tellegen, Lou. *Women Have Been Kind: The Memoirs of Lou Tellegen*. New York: Vanguard, 1931.

Thomas, Bob. *Thalberg, Life and Legend*. New York: Garland, 1985.

Tucker, George Holbert. *Norfolk Highlights, 1584–1881*. Norfolk, VA: Norfolk Historical Society, 1972.

Vaill, Amanda. *Everybody Was So Young: Gerald and Sara Murphy, a Lost Generation Love Story*. New York: Houghton Mifflin, 1998.

Vreeland, Diana. *D. V.* New York: Alfred A. Knopf, 1984.

Walker, Stanley. *The Night Club Era*. New York: Frederick A. Stokes, 1933.

Walsh, Raoul. *Each Man in His Time*. New York: Farrar, Straus and Giroux, 1974.

Whitfield, Eileen. *Pickford: The Woman Who Made Hollywood*. Lexington: University Press of Kentucky, 1997.

Wodehouse, P. G., and Guy Bolton. *Bring On the Girls!* New York: Simon and Schuster, 1953.

Yagoda, Ben. *Will Rogers: A Biography*. New York: Alfred A. Knopf, 1993.

Yarsinske, Amy Waters. *Norfolk, Virginia: The Sunrise City by the Sea*. Virginia Beach: Donning, 1994.

Ziegfeld, Richard, and Paulette Ziegfeld. *The Ziegfeld Touch: The Life and Times of Florenz Ziegfeld, Jr.* New York: Harry N. Abrams, 1993.

Acknowledgments

All biographers owe an enormous debt of gratitude to other people, and in tracking down the life of an elusive woman like Peggy Hopkins Joyce, I was especially lucky to have had the help of so many knowledgeable and generous individuals.

My deepest thanks go to Neal Gabler, who helped me crystallize the concept of this book and who provided a priceless road map for pursuing it, and to George Custen and Ellen Pall, who were kind enough to read every word of the manuscript and critique it in ways that strengthened it immeasurably. Dwight Blocker Bowers, Holland Cotter, Caryn James, Herbert Muschamp, and Richard Ziegfeld also read portions of the manuscript and offered invaluable suggestions. Others who went out of their way to provide information, insights, and moral support were David Leopold, Robert Marx, Arthur Gelb, Kevin Brownlow, Amy Henderson, Barbara Cohen, Joe Yranski, and Cari Beauchamp.

This book could not have been written without the cooperation of Peggy's family: on her mother's side, Sue Piper, Francis Price, Hudson Price, Norman Price, Jane Sawyer, and Mary Lois Jones; and on her father's side, Elizabeth Nixon, Margaret Jackson, Sarah Walston, Robert Bloxton, Bertha Bloxton, Karen Perkins, Margaret Tierney, and, especially, Keith Nixon, whose passion for tracing his family's history went a long way toward helping me unravel Peggy's past. Jackie Olson, the daughter of Madeline Copeland, Peggy's oldest friend, was as close to Peggy as family; I wish she had lived to see this book. Peggy's sixth and final husband, Andrew Meyer, was also helpful prior to his death in 1998.

Thanks to John Anderson, chairman of the board of directors of the Joyce Foundation in Chicago, along with Deborah Leff, then the foundation's president, and Linda Schelinski, its vice president, I was given access to a priceless collection of the personal papers of James Stanley Joyce, including legal documents and blow-by-blow newspaper accounts of the sensational Joyce divorce trial.

Robert Taylor and his staff at the New York Public Library for the Performing Arts were unfailingly helpful, as were Mary Ann Chach at the Shubert Archives in New York; Madeline Matz, David Parker, and Rosemary Hanes at the Library of Congress; Charles Silver, Terry Geesken, and Mary Corliss at the Museum of Modern Art; Marty Jacobs at the Museum of the City of New York; Ned Comstock at the University of Southern California; Geraldine Duclow at the Free Library of Philadelphia; Sandra Archer, Scott Curtis, Robert Cushman, Kristine Krueger, and Fay Thompson at the Margaret Herrick Library of the Academy of Motion Picture Arts and Sciences; Mary Marshall Clark at the Columbia University Oral History Research Office; Jeffrey Post at the Smithsonian Institution; Wendy Wick Reaves at the National Portrait Gallery; Mary Ann Jensen at the Princeton University Library; Tom Bourke at the New York Public Library; Joy Holland at the Brooklyn Collection of the Brooklyn Public Library; Peggy Haile at the Norfolk Public Library; Brigitte Kueppers and Charlotte Brown at the University of California at Los Angeles; Pat Hanson at the American Film Institute; Deborah Rosen at Universal Studios; Mary Bowling at the Rare Books and Manuscripts Division of the New York Public Library; Judith Schiff, Christine Baird, and Lisa Hopkins at Yale University; Annamarie Sandecki at the Tiffany Archives; Maxine Ducey at the Center for Film and Theater Research at the University of Wisconsin; Rachel Howarth and Melissa Miller at the Harry Ransom Humanities Research Center at the University of Texas at Austin; Michael Stier at Condé Nast; Rosemarie Gawelko at Warner Bros.; and staff members at the *Los Angeles Times,* the *San Francisco Chronicle,* the New York *Daily News,* the *New Yorker,* the New-York Historical Society, the Bettmann Archives, Culver Pictures, and the Earl Carroll Foundation. I'd also like to thank the New York Society Library, where I did much of the reading for this project, taking advantage of the institution's wonderfully rich and idiosyncratic collection.

Matthew Solomon in Los Angeles, Amy Waters Yarsinske in Norfolk, and Wendy Adams in Washington did yeoman's work in meeting my research needs, as did genealogist Joseph Silinonte. Other research help was provided by Kristen Hatch, Matthew Rose, Nathalie Dandache, Clive Skelton, Laura

Pincus, Annette Williams, and Greg LaLonde, who also made available an un-published manuscript by Beatrice Morosco. Paula Phelps, who checked the manuscript for factual accuracy, saved me from more errors than I care to admit.

I am also grateful to the many people who took time to share their knowl-edge, memories, insights, and research suggestions, among them Ammon Adams, Billy Altman, Emilie Armstrong, Steven Bach, Robert Bader, Eric Bentley, Milton Berle, Louise Berliner, Gerald Bordman, Patricia Bosworth, Leo Braudy, Carol Brody, Gene Brown, Arthur Cantor, Ben Cheever, Vincent Curcio, Robert Deacon, Gioia Diliberto, Ann Douglas, Stephen Drucker, Martin Duberman, Abe Feder, Cy Feuer, Kathleen Flom, Shirley Gassman, James Gavin, Brendan Gill, Sylviane Gold, Vicki Goldberg, Bruce Goldstein, Lois Gould, John Griffin, Bob Grimes, Philip Hamburger, Nils Hanson, Joan Harding, Aljean Harmetz, Kitty Carlisle Hart, Carolyn Heilbrun, Mary Henderson, Michael Herr, Al Hirschfeld, Dorothy Hirshon, Celeste Holm, Jean Howard, Sol Jacobson, Eddie Jaffe, John Kenley, Robert Kimball, Herman Klurfeld, Wayne Koestenbaum, Eva Korner, Miles Kreuger, Thomas Kunkel, Robert Lantz, Bruce Lawton, Billy Livingstone, Grayce Lizauskas, Phillip Lopate, John Loring, Kenneth Lynn, and Sylvia and Walter Lyons.

Thanks also to William Mann, Diane MacIntyre, Bonnie McCourt, Francine McDougal, Brooks McNamara, Muriel Merrill, Jim Mitchell, Ernest Mitler, Ethan Mordden, David Nasaw, Benedict Nightingale, Eleanor Dana O'Connell, Mitchell Owens, Tim Page, Barry Paris, Greg Palmer, Arva Parks, Don Pendergraft, Mary Philpot, Larry Quirk, Jessica Rosner, Randall Rothenberg, Julie Salamon, Jane Sandulli, Elaine St. Johns, Richard Schickel, Anne Kaufman Schneider, Murray Schumach, Allen Sheinman, Richard Shepard, Bobby Short, Sally Bedell Smith, Anna Sosenko, Patricia Ziegfeld Stephenson, David Stenn, Gary Stevens, Isabelle Stevenson, Haila Stoddard, Mary Anita Loos von Saltza, Terry Teachout, John Tebbel, Harriet Van Horne, Marc Wanamaker, Steve Weissman, Miles White, Robert Whitehead, Eileen Whitfield, Ben Yagoda, and Paulette Ziegfeld. I apologize to those whose names I have inadvertently omitted.

If Joseph Lelyveld, executive editor of the *New York Times,* had not been kind enough to give me a leave of absence to complete this project, I'd still be writing; *Times* editors Gene Roberts and John Darnton were good enough to endorse my request. My colleagues at the paper were unfailingly generous with their thoughts, ideas, and suggestions: I'd like to thank Linda Amster, Andrew Bluth, Linda Brewer, Vincent Canby, Diane Ceribelli, Phyllis Collazo, Susan Dryfoos, Jennifer Dunning, Warren Hoge, Stephen Holden,

Margo Jefferson, Pam Kent, Michael Kimmelman, Linda Lee, Peter Marks, Janet Maslin, William McDonald, Lawrie Mifflin, Enid Nemy, Peter Nichols, Michael Porter, Frank Rich, Barbara Richer, Alan Riding, Marvin Siegel, Dinitia Smith, Roberta Smith, Andrea Stevens, Charles Strum, Keith Urban, Joseph Vecchione, Bernard Weinraub, and, especially, Suzanne O'Connor, who contributed to this book in countless ways and whose enthusiasm for this project matched my own.

On a personal level, I'd like to thank all the friends who listened to me so patiently during the time I was working on this book and never once complained that I was boring them, among them Jonnet Abeles, Peggy Anderson, Manette Berlinger, Sherryl Connelly, Cory Dean, Marcia Glicksman, Tom Hine, Susan Hodara, Carol Horner, Nora Kerr, Ann Kolson, Carol Rocamora, Anne Rorimer, Karen Rothmyer, Beverly Stephen, Beverly Solochek, and Barbara Strauch.

Mary Evans is every writer's dream of an agent, and I am deeply grateful for her faith in me; her assistant, Tanya McKinnon, was also extremely helpful. As for my editor, Sara Bershtel at Metropolitan Books, there is simply no way I can thank her enough for her support, her enthusiasm, and her editorial acumen. Riva Hocherman's contributions were also enormously valuable. In every way, this book was strengthened by her advice and suggestions. I'd also like to thank Roslyn Schloss, who copyedited the manuscript; Sarah Engel, who handled a myriad of details; Raquel Jaramillo, who designed the beautiful jacket; and everyone else at Metropolitan who helped along the way.

There would never have been a book in the first place if my mother, Beatrice Rosenblum, had not had the foresight to buy Peggy's papers nearly two decades ago. My beloved cousin Ethel Berl offered endless encouragement. Sarah Fullerton made my life and my family's run smoothly.

Most of all, I'm grateful to my husband, Andy Geller, and my daughter, Sarah, for their constant love and support. It's hard to thank them properly without resorting to clichés. Suffice it to say that they both displayed superhuman patience and understanding during the several years Peggy was a de facto member of our family.

INDEX